TANZANIA

TANZANIA

A PROFILE

John Hatch

PRAEGER PUBLISHERS
New York • Washington • London

96?.8
Hat
c1

PRAEGER PUBLISHERS
111 Fourth Avenue, New York, N.Y. 10003, U.S.A.
5, Cromwell Place, London SW7 2JL, England

Published in the United States of America in 1972
by Praeger Publishers, Inc.

© 1972 by John Hatch

Library of Congress Catalog Card Number: 70–118053

Printed in the United States of America

Contents

A SECTION OF PHOTOGRAPHS FOLLOWS PAGE 74.

Introduction

Tanzania has risen dramatically to the leadership of a substantial section of the peoples of Africa. To many of the younger generation of Africans, it represents the ideal for the future. Outside the African continent, too, there are those who regard Tanzania as a prophetic proving ground for fresh values, as charting a new social course away from the materialist egocentricity characteristic of Euro-American industrialism.

This East African state, one of a score to gain independence from European rule during the 1960's, would at first appear to be an unlikely object of international attention. Its citizens are among the poorest in Africa, much of the land is barely habitable, its material resources are not the kind to attract unusual interest. Even its independence from British rule in December, 1961, did not make the headlines; it was achieved with a minimum of agitation, in stark contrast to the violent birth throes of neighboring Kenya, of Algeria, and of the Congo.

Yet, since the overthrow of Ghana's Kwame Nkrumah in 1966, Tanzania has taken the leading role in African affairs. It has exerted a decisive influence on relations between African states and those of other continents. It has developed a unique relationship with China, the Soviet Union, and the West, and has spearheaded the attack on white racism in southern Africa. Above all, its experiment in social architecture has offered a new philosophy to the developing world. A great deal of this pathbreaking initiative has derived from the mind of one man, Julius Nyerere. President of Tanzania.

I first met Nyerere in Scotland in 1950. He was a student at Edinburgh University while I was teaching at the University of Glasgow. In those days, student agitation against colonialism was at a peak. The first wave of students from the colonies swept into British universities under the stimulus of postwar colonial development policies. Many students, British and colonial, were ex-servicemen, who showed a greater maturity and involvement with political issues than the traditional university population.

Nyerere could never be called a typical colonial student. He was interested in the discussions on colonialism but played no role as an agitator. Unlike some of his colonial contemporaries, many of whom have since become respected pillars of their various establishments, he was never strident or dogmatic. He always seemed more contemplative, even introverted.

Since those first meetings, over twenty years ago, I have had the privilege of observing the development of Nyerere's personality and ideas. We have met in a variety of circumstances. When I was in charge of Commonwealth affairs in the Labour Party, he used to visit me in its London headquarters, Transport House. There we would discuss the intricacies of British colonial policies, plan the tactics of the Labour Party Opposition to meet them, consider his own efforts to organize a national party in Tanganyika.

On one occasion, in the fall of 1956, I took Nyerere to Blackpool, Britain's "Coney Island" on the northwest coast, where the Labour Party was holding its annual conference. At that time, Nyerere had only a little more than two years' experience of organizing a political party. He spent the week at the conference studying its machinery, talking to delegates and organizers, listening to the debates. Among those whom he met were Hugh Gaitskell, then leader of the Labour Party, and James Griffiths, his deputy.

The next year I spent a day with Tanganyika's leader on another continent. On this occasion, he came to Idlewild (now Kennedy) Airport to meet my plane from England, and we spent the rest of that day talking in the backyard of a house in Brooklyn. He was appearing at the United Nations to put his people's case to the Trusteeship Council. Since then I have encountered Nyerere in a peculiar variety of locations—in one of Farouk's palaces in Cairo, at a trade-union hall in Singapore, in the Hilton in London, in his presidential home in Dar es Salaam. To my observation, he has never deviated from the personality I first knew as a student; his single-minded but humble concern has been for the welfare of his fellow countrymen and for their place in the world.

Two other personal experiences are relevant here. The first took place in 1955 while I was on a tour of Africa on behalf of the Labour Party. Nyerere had asked me to speak to his party workers in Dar es Salaam. I anticipated addressing a score or so of faithful officials in a dingy school—having just had many such experiences in the British election of that year. Instead, I was taken to a vast unpaved square known as Mnazi Moja (One Coconut Tree). On a wooden platform I was invited to speak into a microphone to a squatting white-robed crowd stretching to the palm-fringed horizon. The audience I faced was estimated at between twenty and forty thousand, some of whom had been traveling for several days and nights to hear what the British Labour Party had to say about their country. A short time later, the colonial government banned all meetings on Mnazi Moja!

Nyerere's organization, the Tanganyika African National Union (TANU), was at that time less than a year old. The fact that it could already mobilize such massive interest indicated to me that something unique was happening in this comparatively remote corner of Africa, that the young student from Edinburgh University had struck a common chord in the hearts of thousands of his countrymen.

Six and a half years later, I was one of the spectators in the Dar es Salaam stadium when the British Union Jack was lowered and, after a moment's silence in the dark, a spotlight picked out the new green, yellow, and black national flag. Tanganyika at that moment ceased to be a dependent of the British Empire and became an independent state. My mind turned back to my first visit to the country, ten years earlier, when Nyerere, now being acclaimed by the packed crowds, was still in Edinburgh, when there were no deep-water docks and I had to go ashore from my ship in a rowboat, when Africans were not admitted to hotels and played no part in the government of their own country, when Dar es Salaam was a little-known outpost of the empire.

A day or two later, I had a long talk with Nyerere, now Prime Minister of the new state, on the veranda of his official residence. He was unchanged by the momentous events of the preceding few days. In fact, during the twenty years I have known him, I have observed no basic change in Nyerere's personality. He has had to teach himself administration, but he is still happiest when discussing ideas. He remains humble, antipathetic toward all forms of ostentation or charisma, firm in his belief that every individual is responsible for making a contribution to the community of which he is a member—village or world society. Although he is usually serious, Nyerere is never solemn, and he has a warm sense of humor. I remember his self-mocking submission when his security men forbade him to open his presidential gates to the populace watching outside on the occasion of a visit by a dance troup; his cryptic response to Marxist criticism of his liberalism was to declare that he did not intend to run his country like the Roman Catholic Church—and he is a devout Catholic!

During the independence celebration, it was clear from our conversation that he had reached the second stage of pragmatic meditation. All his energy had so far been concentrated on working out the means of securing freedom from colonial rule. On the morrow of having achieved this first goal, he exclaimed to me, "What am I going to do with this country now?" Already he realized that his devotion to the welfare of his people demanded a new approach with new assumptions, the formulation of fresh objectives. It took him over five years of concentrated effort and often bitter experience to forge a nation-building strategy out of the legacy left him by the British. From these endeavors and experiences emerged the Arusha Declaration of 1967, a set of guidelines for the construction of a unique kind of nation. Nyerere, however, is the first to insist that the work of nation-building will take much longer than the effort of decolonization.

It would be difficult to overemphasize the importance of Nyerere's role in the two sagas of anticolonialism and national construction. Yet it would be wrong to assume that this has been the work of one man. Nyerere is no dictator, and he could never become one. He is and has always been the inspired leader of a team. He has been most fortunate in attracting the cooperation of a notable selection of men and women drawn from various elements in his country. A few refused to follow his lead. The army mutineers of 1964, those convicted of treason in 1970 for conspiring to overthrow the regime, and Oscar Kambona, who defected, are notable examples. But these were exceptions. It is remarkable that the vast majority of the elite, those with training and education, all of whom have been brought up in the Western tradition of seeking personal advancement and the material rewards that are expected to accompany it, have been prepared to endorse and practice the self-restraint that is a cornerstone of Nyerere's austere philosophy.

One of the strengths of Nyerere's leadership is that he has always been able to count on the support of all racial groups in his country. Not only has he retained non-Africans in his government—appointing Amir Jamal, an Asian, and Derek Bryceson, a European, as top-level ministers—but both Asians and Europeans are to be found in key positions throughout state and parastate institutions. Although the Asian community includes a large proportion of Tanzania's small wealthy class, some of whom strongly resent Nyerere's anticapitalist measures, this discontent has never developed into the quasi-racial hostility seen in other parts of East Africa.

There are two outstanding features of the achievement realized by Nyerere and his team over the past decade. First, they are making a unique contribution to the concepts of social architecture, to the values, relationships, and practices of community life. Second, they are forging new communications internationally, especially in their relations with the Chinese, which are significantly affecting relations in the third world and which may influence the attitudes of the great powers and the Communist bloc.

Nyerere's adherence to socialist philosophy took several years to develop. It stemmed from his belief that, once colonial rule had been removed, the construction of a new society in Tanzania must provide for a better form of life for all his fellow countrymen. Experience taught him that the only way he could ensure this objective's being achieved was to adopt the first premise of socialism—the virtue of egalitarianism. He had then to meet the greater challenge of devising means to adapt socialist philosophy, which had been largely conceived within industrial Europe, to the particular circumstances of his own country.

Nyerere began his task of nation-building with the legacy of a colonial superstructure constructed first by the Germans and then by the British over a period of three-quarters of a century. The 10 million or so inhabitants of mainland Tanzania—that is of the area called Tanganyika until it merged with Zanzibar to form Tanzania in 1964—were scattered across enormous spaces. In the few fertile districts, habitation was reasonably concentrated and some degree of social organization had developed. But, over much of the country, family homesteads, or shambas, dotted the land, each eking out a bare subsistence. The British had governed this territory very lightly, in contrast to the more concentrated administration of neighboring Kenya.

Nyerere was thus left with both advantages and problems. While he did not have to contend with the deep-seated British traditions that perplexed some of his contemporaries, neither were his people accustomed to the strength of organization or discipline that British colonial rule bequeathed elsewhere. At the same time, although British influence might have been less pronounced than elsewhere, it had still colored every aspect of colonial rule, so that the institutions inherited by Tanzanians, their economic structure, their social and cultural patterns, and their political system had all been veneered by British attitudes. Apart from the argument among administrators throughout the British colonies concerning the education of Africans to Western ideas, it is doubtful whether the British ever examined their concepts in the light of the local environment. In the colonial service, it was assumed that British institutions and cultural attitudes were the finest created by man; the test of development was therefore the degree to which others could adopt them.

In particular, British society was based on the supposition that personal ambition should be encouraged for the benefit of society. This inevitably led to elitism in colonial social, economic, and educational concepts, as it did in Britain itself. Those among the governed who were accorded privileges belonged to traditional hierarchies, were wealthy, or had educational qualifications; others were urged to imitate them. It could not be expected that this elitist attitude would disappear after the end of British rule. Indeed, both economic expansion and Africanization augmented the numbers of Africans needed in government, business, and the professions, thus enlarging the privileged clan and intensifying competition within it.

At the same time, conventional economic expansion, capitalist or Marxist, laid its emphasis on industrial growth, which, in its turn, led to an increase in the number of wage earners. As wages in industry and the services needed for urban society greatly exceeded the incomes of peasant farmers—who remained the vast majority of the population—another privileged group arose from the mass of Tanzanians. It was paralleled by those farmers able to profit from the new markets in cash crops and land.

Nyerere was convinced that traditional African society was based on classless concepts of egalitarianism. He firmly believed that this feature of African tradition must be preserved if the nation he was building was to be founded on social unity and to offer a chance for an improved life to all the people. He thus realized that, if his major objective was to be achieved, he had to try to reverse the trends inherited from colonial rule.

Two other factors related to the colonial legacy also demanded decisions. As in virtually every other colony, economic development under imperial rule had been directed toward using the resources of the country to serve the economic interest of the colonial power. Those materials found within the territory that were useful to Britain were exported, while the modern needs of expatriate administrators and the small indigenous elite were imported, usually from Britain. Because Tanganyika was a poor country, this two-way process was not as prominent as in some other African colonies, but it dominated the little economic life that had developed. It therefore provided the only existing structure within which economic growth could be quickly achieved.

In addition, two distinct sets of institutions existed within Tanganyika at the time of independence. The colonial institutions—civil service, local government, judiciary, executive, and legislature—were all conceived as imitations of British experience. Those institutions created as agencies of the anticolonial struggle—TANU, the trade unions, the cooperatives, and various other bodies—although partially influenced by British tutelage, had been set up by the people. In the process of nation-building, the incipient conflicts between the two groups would have to be resolved. Each institution would have to be allotted its role in the task of unified national construction.

From his broad political experience, Nyerere saw that he had two alternatives: Either he could follow the example of the Ivory Coast, where economic growth has been given priority, even though this has entailed the entrenchment of an elite and even greater dependence on the French than during its period of colonial rule; or he could retain his conviction that social justice provided the only legitimate foundation for nation-building. Nyerere chose the latter alternative. In doing so, he was forced to fly in the face of accepted policies for developing an economically backward state.

The major tasks then confronting Nyerere and his colleagues were to merge the two sets of institutions, creating a unified governmental-party machine that could organize the people and direct them toward defined goals; to decrease the country's dependence on foreign capital and break up its colonial export-import pattern; to discover a strategy that would restrain personal materialistic ambition, while convincing the white-collar and laboring elites that rural development must take priority over urban growth; and to create a national vision of a unique society loosely described as rural socialism. To achieve this, after the European colonial powers had for so long educated Africans to antithetical values, would require trail-blazing of the most audacious kind. The attempt ensured the hostility of orthodox Marxists and capitalists alike.

This is the background of the complex of measures that culminated in the Arusha Declaration of 1967. The experiment is far too young for an assessment of its over-all success. It has had failures, notably the collapse of the Rovumu Development Association, which, though based on the principle of local initiative and self-reliance, was torn apart by a party bureaucracy that had absorbed little of the Arusha spirit. Zanzibar also continues to embarrass the humanistic character of Tanzanian philosophy. Nyerere can complain justifiably that, since he grasped this nettle in the interests of East Africa, he has had many critics but few helpers in his attempt to integrate the island into African society. On the other hand, one can actually see *Ujamaa* villages organized by their inhabitants on a cooperative basis, assisted by local and central government agencies; the influence of personal wealth has been almost totally removed; ostentation is despised; and the electorate in the 1970 elections gave Nyerere's government a massive vote of confidence.

The transformation within twenty years of what had been a sleepy backwater of the British Empire into a pioneering social experiment makes for a fascinating and meaningful human drama. To visit Dar es Salaam today is to experience the excitement of a genuinely cosmopolitan society. There are few other cities in the world where in hotels, bars, and restaurants it is common to meet Russians, Germans, Indians, Israelis, Egyptians, Yugoslavs, Chinese, Americans, Frenchmen, Italians, British, and a great variety of Africans. The Tanzanian experiment has already caught the imagination of those young people of all nationalities who have heard of it, but too few members of the younger generation have done so. If, as many of them assert, a considerable proportion of young people throughout the world are reacting against the values and practices of European and American industrial materialism (including the kind that is visible in the Soviet Union and Eastern Europe), and if, as they also assert, they feel a genuine compassion for developing peoples, Tanzania should be regarded as their mecca. It is one country where idealism, joined to capacities for understanding human beings and for devotion to hard work, is making a significant contribution to a society where privilege, wealth, and pomposity are being outlawed.

At present, the Chinese are making the greatest progress in recognizing the kind of contribution from the outside world most acceptable to Tanzanians. Which brings me to the second factor inherited from the colonial period on which Nyerere had to make a decision. Under the British, Tanganyika and Zanzibar had been entirely oriented toward the West. Their institutions, their recruitment for every sector of public life, and their international relations followed British policies. Like the rest of the Empire, they were treated as an extension of Britain.

After independence, therefore, Nyerere and his colleagues had to decide whether to follow the same pattern or diversify their relations. They chose to do the latter, knowing well that this would open them to accusations of becoming Communist; for, if they were to remove themselves from the ambit of the cold war, they would have to concentrate more on opening communications with the Communists than on extending those with the West. To reach a balance from a position of complete identification with the West, they would inevitably have to move some degrees eastward.

The policy of nonalignment adopted by Nyerere has frequently been misunderstood in both West and East. Some in the West have accused him of being a Communist, and some in the East have alleged that he is a liberal, which is an invidious term among Marxists. The fact is that Nyerere is above all a humanitarian. He believes in human beings, irrespective of their political or religious convictions. He is therefore willing to receive help from any country, provided that the aid is not part of an effort to intervene in the domestic affairs of Tanzania. The Canadians and Swedes have probably satisfied this condition more consistently than any other foreigners.

The association with China has caused greater misunderstanding and prejudice than any other. It has always seemed fantastic to Nyerere that he should be expected to ignore the existence of 800 million people, whatever their form of society. At first, however, the Chinese made gross mistakes in Africa. They believed in the early 1960's that the continent was "ripe for revolution," and Chou En-lai, during his African safari of 1963–64, antagonized many of his hosts by suggesting imminent revolution.

The Chinese, however, learned quickly. They had been told in a friendly but firm manner by Nyerere that, although he welcomed their help, his country was not for sale. They recognized that subversion, whether induced or supported by them, would yield few dividends in Africa. They soon realized that African friendship would be won by assistance in the economic development Africans themselves were planning, and by help to those Africans engaged in the battle against the minority white regimes of the south. In these efforts, they possessed two enormous advantages. Theirs was a developing nation itself still using techniques long forgotten by industrialized Europe; and they had never been part of the imperialist world and therefore had neither guilt to assuage nor suspicions of neocolonialism to allay.

The Chinese, therefore, brought to Tanzania middle-range techniques, as well as machines that were easily operated, repaired, and replaced. After a number of Western states, the Soviet Union, and the World Bank had rejected the project of building a railway from Dar es Salaam to the Zambian copper belt, the Chinese agreed not only to build it but also to provide the largest loan they had offered anywhere—interest-free. Most importantly they sent technicians and workers who trained Tanzanians, set an example of hard work, and lived by the same standards as the local people. In short, the Chinese demonstrated that they believe themselves to be part of the third world and act accordingly.

This relationship may become very important for both Tanzania and the world. There is every reason to suppose that China's bid to be accepted as a member of the third world will succeed. This would drastically alter the whole character of international relations. The accession of such a huge and potentially powerful nation as China to the third world would compel the United States, the Soviet Union, Europe, and Asia to reconsider their relations with one another. But it could also influence the relations of the developed world with China itself. Already, while the Chinese are building the Tan-Zam railway, the Americans are improving the main highway linking Tanzania and Zambia. It could be—and would be of obvious advantage to all concerned—that Tanzania might become the first area where deliberate cooperation can be practiced between capitalist and Communist countries in the organization of economic aid to a developing people.

Such an ideal, though rational, method of maximizing the aid effort may seem unworkable, given the long-standing prejudices and suspicions on both sides. It will depend on the courage of those prepared to break through the stereotyped images that have been forged in the West, in Russia, and in China. However, one complex issue could further exacerbate tensions between China and the West in the near future. The Chinese have no inhibitions about providing aid to the freedom fighters being trained, or actually engaged, in combat against South Africa, Rhodesia, and the Portuguese. Moreover, Tanzania, like the rest of the East African coast, is rapidly returning to its former position as an important part of Indian Ocean society. Dar es Salaam is the main port and base through which the freedom fighters are supplied, often by the Chinese. It is almost certain that incidents will occur along that coast, probably involving South African and Portuguese interference with shipping they suspect is supplying their enemies. The West will then be placed on trial: Who are the allies of southern Africa's whites, and which nations support the fight for majority rule in those countries? In such a confrontation, no one can be neutral.

This issue may well become of major importance as the center of international relations moves from the Atlantic to the Indian and Pacific oceans. With the Indian subcontinent destined to play a greater role in world affairs; the entrance of Indonesia, Malaysia, and Japan into the international arena; and Australasia, Canada, and the United States increasingly aware of their interests in the Pacific—the stage is set for the enactment of a significant drama in this sphere. The part played by China will obviously be crucial; China's relations with East Africa, also among the dramatis personae, will thus become both internationally and locally portentous.

While the story of Tanganyika and Zanzibar as entities dates from less than a century ago, a true understanding of it requires some knowledge of the people and their historical experience. President Nyerere has always claimed that he is trying to build his new nation on the foundations of African traditions, preserving those that are valuable and discarding only those that obstruct the development of a better life. To understand his policies, appreciate the difficulties, and assess the degree of success, one must first look at these traditions. In this book, I have tried to set the modern Tanzanian scene in its full historical context, providing the evidence from which readers can understand current and future events in this exciting nation. Where pounds sterling have translated into dollars, a rate of £1=$2.40 has been used.

TANZANIA

1 Geographical Background

East Africa, composed of Tanzania, Kenya, and Uganda, forms a geographical unit, extending from latitude 11° 45′ S. to 4° 30′ N., and from longitude 29° 28′ W. to 41° 55′ E., bounded by the Indian Ocean and the western Rift Valley. It consists of about 636,707 square miles of land surface and roughly 42,207 square miles of water or swamp. Tanzania forms the largest area within this region, with a total, including Zanzibar and Pemba, of 342,170 square miles of land and 20,650 square miles of water or swamp.

The major geographical feature marking off East Africa from the center and west of the continent is a remarkable series of faults that have made a specific contribution to Africa's physical uniqueness. They are known as the Rift Valley system; argument about their origins still continues. In fact, the Rift Valley extends outside the continent to the Dead Sea and the Jordan Valley. The Red Sea is part of the system, from which it can be traced through Ethiopia, eastern Africa, into Malawi and eventually to Natal and Swaziland. In East Africa the rift has two branches, the Western and Eastern rifts, and a stem extends into Malawi so that on a map the configuration resembles a wishbone. Here, huge fractures in the surface have caused the plateau to subside between parallel mountainous walls. Large lakes have collected in the troughs, between 20 and 60 miles long, though the depth of the floors vary from well below sea level to several thousand feet above it. Volcanoes have erupted in the mountainous walls, and the plateau has been considerably tilted, thus drastically altering the original drainage pattern. Earthquakes still occur in the Rift Valley and it seems virtually certain that the movements of the earth that created the rift are still in progress. Certainly, it is apparent that at one time the lakes in the valley were much larger than today.

The highlands in both the Eastern and Western rifts are comparatively fertile, for they are covered by volcanic soils. They are therefore capable of sustaining some of the highest population densities on the continent. Unfortunately for the East African economy, the rock formation does not seem to contain many valuable minerals. In the Shinyanga and Mwandui areas of Tanzania they yield useful diamonds, and small amounts of gold and copper are found in western Kenya. Large copper deposits have been found at Kilembe in Uganda; coal is known to exist in Tanzania, but in areas difficult for mining or transport; and crushed rock for cement manufacture is available in Uganda and near both Mombasa and Dar es Salaam. The volcanic rocks are also associated with soda deposits in Kenya and Uganda, producing both soda ash and common salt.

Between the two arms of the rift, the plateau is dominated by the huge expanse of Lake Victoria (or Nyanza as it is now called). The lake was caused by subsidence and is very shallow, the depression in which it is situated being fertile and well watered, thus also capable of supporting a sizable population. Much of the rest of the plateau between the two rift systems, however, consists of arid bush, heavily infested by the tsetse fly.

Much of the coastal hinterland to the east of the Eastern Rift is also too dry for farming, although there are exceptions, for example, the area inland from Tanga. But, in general, it was this wide tsetse-infested semidesert beginning between 10 and 40 miles from the coast that historically made communication between the cosmopolitan commercial peoples of the coastal belt and the large internal centers of population almost impossible.

The coastal belt itself is well watered, low-lying, and covered by tropical vegetation. Its equatorial climate encourages plant growth, although even here there are areas where the tsetse scourge comes right down to the shores. The belt is narrow, widening substantially only in the Tana River delta, north of Mombasa, and around the delta of the Rufiji, south of Dar es Salaam. The islands of Pemba, Zanzibar, and Mafia form part of the low shelf, although Pemba is more clearly separated from the mainland by a fault running north and south.

The hinterland of the region consists of a series of plateaus varying from 1,200 to 10,000 feet above sea level. West of the coastal fringe, from northern Kenya to southeastern Tanzania, an extensive plateau rises gradually to 3,000 feet. The central area of Tanzania, with Tabora as its hub, consists of an even larger plateau, of which the Serengeti Plains and the Masai Steppe are typical. It rises generally to 4,500 feet, though there are certain districts as high as 6,000 feet. In the north and south of Tanzania, the plateau is broken by highlands, which reach 19,340 feet at their highest peak—Kibo Cone on Mount Kilimanjaro. In the north, in addition to Kilimanjaro, Ngorongoro Crater, at 10,165 feet, Jaeger Summit, at 10,565 feet, and Loolmalasin, at 11,969 feet, are also worthy of mention. Mighty Kilimanjaro, snowcapped throughout the year, is actually composed of three separate volcanic peaks—Shira Cone, Mawenzi Cone, and Kibo Cone. They erupted during different periods, and, accordingly, they show varying degrees of erosion. In the south, the Rungwe Mountains between Mbeya and Lake Nyasa are of volcanic origin, while the Kipengere Range, the Livingstone Mountains, the Udzungwa Range, and the Fipa Plateau are ancient blocks whose surfaces provide some of the oldest examples of erosion on the continent.

These variations in altitude, together with the distribution of ocean, landmass, and lakes, produce a complex climatic pattern. From November to March, the prevailing winds are from the northeast. These create the tradewinds, or monsoons, which have been so important to the coast in bringing Arab and Indian traders across the Indian Ocean. In the east of the region, this maritime influence may bring some rain. In the west, though, the winds have blown across the Sahara, bringing a dry air current. From

April on, the wind veers round to the southeast and, because it has again crossed the Indian Ocean, it brings the main rainy season. As the winds cross the equator, they veer again to become a southwest monsoon approaching Arabia and India. These prevailing winds enabled Arab and Indian traders to return home.

Rainfall is also affected by the position of the sun, which produces a varied seasonal pattern. In the equatorial region, at least inland, short rains are usual between mid-October and December, the long rains falling from March to May. North and south of the equatorial belt, which includes most of mainland Tanzania, the year is usually divided between a December-April rainy season and the remaining months, which are the dry period. This is also the case on the coast south of Dar es Salaam, though to the north the peak rainy season is usually about May.

The extent of rainfall is conditioned by land relief and the position of the lakes. Two per cent of the region receives 2 inches of rain per month. In mainland Tanzania, 16 per cent of the country must expect less than 20 inches of rain in four years out of five, while only 4 per cent can depend on over 50 inches in the same period. But the highlands are better watered; there are glaciers on the chief mountains, and the lakes provide localized well-watered areas. In addition to the widespread aridity, however, it should be noted that most of East Africa suffers from irregular rainfall in terms of both time and quantity, and the heavy rains frequently result in considerable runoff, with consequent loss of top soil, but high temperatures cause early evaporation.

Temperatures in the region generally depend on altitude. The coastal belt is usually hot and steamy. The mean temperature at Dar es Salaam is 25.7°C., with humidity ranging between 79 and 82 per cent. Farther inland, as the plateau become higher, both humidity and temperatures fall, with the range between upper and lower becoming wider. It is this factor that has attracted most Europeans to settle in the interior highlands.

The Swahili term describing much of East Africa is Nyika, roughly translated as "wilderness." It is inspired by the appearance of vast areas covered with thorn bushes. This thorn-bush belt, with its aridity and heat, provided another of the main obstacles to frequent communication between hinterland and coast until recent times. Leeching and weathering, common to the tropics, have left much of the soil lacking in nutrient salts, and thus poor and fragile. The soil is usually red, which indicates a preponderance of oxides, often iron-induced laterites, and it sustains little vegetation and no crops. This soil poverty is aggravated by rain torrents and the traditional practice of firing to clear the bush.

East Africa is, in short, largely a harsh environment for man. It is world-famous for its wild animals—lion, elephant, zebra, gazelle, giraffe, and the like—but the creature that has most profoundly affected man's life in the region is the tsetse fly. Two-thirds of mainland Tanzania is infested by various species of this scourge, which makes life unbearable for man and beast by infecting with trypanosomiasis, or sleeping sickness. The central and southern areas of the country are plagued by the woodland variety of the insect; the lake and northern provinces suffer particularly from the bovine type; on the coast and around the lake again, another species endangers both men and cattle. As no method has yet been devised for destroying this pest, the tsetse remains one of the greatest menaces to man's prosperity throughout East Africa.

The lakes and mountains of the Western Rift Valley demarcate East Africa from the Congo Basin and Zambia. Lake Nyasa may be said to separate the region from Malawi and the Rovuma River marks its southern frontier with Mozambique. It could be argued that the Ethiopian masses and the Nile Sudd indicate the northern limits of East Africa. In geographical terms, East Africa forms a unitary region in which the internal political boundaries have no meaning. They were, in fact, drawn and imposed by the European imperial states at the end of the nineteenth century after having no previous existence in history. Thus, Tanzania's geographical, economical, or ethnic separation from the rest of East Africa is artificial and is justified only by political events since the last part of the nineteenth century. It has therefore been necessary to set the backdrop of East African geography before spotlighting Tanzania in its principal role of our drama.

Like the rest of East Africa, Tanzania is a land of infinite variety, of sharp contrasts in landscape, habitations, and peoples. Next to a broad plain, there suddenly appears a spectacular snowcapped mountain, silhouetted against a deep azure sky. The clear, cool air of the highlands is quickly replaced by the hot dust of the Rift Valley or the shores of a sparkling lake, fringed with luxuriant tropical foliage. Shining off-white sands lining the gently curving coastal bays of the Indian Ocean give way within a few yards to dark groves of broad-leaved palm trees.

This variety of landscape and climate is matched by the diversity of the peoples who have made their homes in Tanzania, their varying architecture, and their differing occupations. According to the 1965 census, mainland Tanzania had a population of 10,179,000 (1967 estimate: 12,231,342), of whom 17,300 were Europeans, 85,900 Indo-Pakistanis, and 25,600 Arabs; Zanzibar's inhabitants numbered 319,410, including 650 Europeans, and 19,700 Indo-Pakistanis. As we shall see in detail later, the contrasts in soil composition, climate, altitude, and drainage have long affected the areas of settlement of the various communities that make up the population. For many centuries, the coastal belt has attracted peoples from beyond the continent. Here came Arabs from Oman, Muscat, and other parts of the Arabian peninsula; Persians from near the Gulf; Hindus, Sikhs, and Muslims from India; even at one time Indonesians, most of whom eventually emigrated to Madagascar. These early visitors were followed from the beginning of the sixteenth century by Portuguese and then from the nineteenth century by British and Germans. Settlement has therefore been common for several thousand years. Along this ancient commercial coastline and on its immediate hinterland the Arabs, mixing their blood and culture with the Bantu Africans of the area, have made the strongest impact. The consequent formation of a distinctive Swahili people, accustomed to contact with peoples from other continents, is directly attributable to the attractive advantages of the coastline.

In the interior, the principal single influence has been the broad belt of dry, inhospitable territory that for centuries separated the coastal peoples from the interior settlements. Most of the hinterland communities came from Bantu-speaking stock, though one large section extending right across the Kenya border was formed by the Nilotic-tongued Masai. An important characteristic of the interior peoples was their dependence on land sufficiently well watered and free from the tsetse to enable food to be grown and cattle to be grazed. These communities were not static. Shifting cultivation was almost universal, requiring agriculturalists to move their farms every few years, and the pastoralists were constantly seeking new grazing lands. Another feature of these interior communities was the growth of societies along the lake shores, where they could supplement their diet by fishing.

The main concentrations of population are to be found around Lake Victoria, along the coastal belt, and in well-watered highland cases like those in the Kilimanjaro district, the Mbeya area, and the far west along the frontiers with Rwanda and Burundi. Town populations have grown rapidly since the last war, Dar es Salaam having 272,515 inhabitants at the last census (compared with 128,742 in 1957), Tanga 60,935, Mwanza 34,855, Moshi 26,969, and Arusha 32,348. Despite this rapid urbanization, however, the vast majority of Tanzanian peoples continue to live in rural areas. On the mainland, country folk still make up well over 90 per cent of the population; in Zanzibar, over 70 per cent, with the city of Zanzibar playing a more dominant role than mainland towns. The towns themselves may be divided into the old coastal ports, those that have grown around the lake harbors, the administrative-market towns of the interior, and the mining centers.

This mosaic of peoples drawn to Tanzania for a variety of reasons has brought diversified contributions to architecture and language. The mosque vies with a German Lutheran church; the British ex-administrator's brick bungalow stands beside thatched, mud-walled huts; the single-room glassless-windowed village school contrasts with the exotic architecture of the new university. In Dar es Salaam harbor, timeless Arab *dhows* sail alongside modern liners. Many major African languages are to be heard somewhere in the East Africa region, though Tanzania itself has gained great benefits from the widespread use of Swahili among its peoples.

Employment differs between town and country, but within each there are great variations. European farmers in Arusha, Chagga coffee-growers in Moshi, African merchants in Ujiji, diamond-miners in Mwadui, and sisal plantation workers around Tanga represent no more than a selection from the diversified character of Tanzanian towns. Dar es Salaam, the capital, of course, brings together the greatest variety of occupation and employment. In the countryside, too, many differences are apparent. Sisal-, cotton-, and coffee-growing, diamond- and gold-mining, fishing and cattle-grazing can all be seen in many parts of the country. Yet the vast majority of the people are still engaged in some form of agriculture, many of them growing only what is needed for consumption in the immediate vicinity. As is the case throughout Africa, land still plays a vital part in the economic and social life of the community. In Tanzania and throughout East Africa, possession of land remains the crucial social factor. Because of variations in climate, soil value, irrigation, and pest incidence, cultivation is only possible in certain areas. The East Africa Royal Commission of 1955 succinctly described the situation in these terms:

If a panorama picture could be taken slowly, and over a period, of the way people are living in East Africa, the most striking feature of it would be a restless anxiety to obtain and hold on to the land. Land is still, for the vast majority, a basic necessity from which each family derives its own food by its own physical effort. Where this can be done with the least effort for the greatest result, people have tended to collect and tend to want to stay. This tendency has been accentuated by the difficulty of penetrating the unknown where tsetse and lack of water have proved insurmountable obstacles, and by the hazards of uncertain rainfall over such a large part of the region. Thus the places where good rainfall, good soil, water and grazing are most easily obtained, the risks of human and animal disease most easily avoided, are in the greatest demand. As the population has increased—and this has generally been greatest in these most favourable localities—so has pressure increased in two directions, outwards, so as to get more land if possible and to obtain as fertile land as possible, and inwards, towards a more devastating use of the land itself. The inward pressure, under contemporary systems of land usage, is affecting production from the soil adversely. This is the most serious aspect of the land problem. The outward pressure results in conflict wherever fertile land is short.

As previously noted, Tanzania is still inhabited by many wild animals. In recent times, game parks have been established in order to both preserve animals from the depredations of hunters and attract tourists. The park in the Serengeti Plains just south of the Kenya border and to the east of Lake Victoria is among the most famous in the world.

Climate, water supply, and soil quality determine where people can live and what they can produce, in East Africa generally and in Tanzania in particular, to a much greater extent than in most other parts of the world. Many communities in Tanzania are accustomed to periods of near starvation. The pastoralists lose thousands of their cattle when the water supplies dry up and feeding stuffs are exhausted. The agriculturalists are dependent on effective rains during the wet season. Failure of any of these factors produces widespread hunger. Unfortunately, too, the high temperatures of the tropical zone, together with the rainstorm torrents, tend to produce soils lacking in lime, potash, magnesia, and phosphorous, which, combined with an absence of organic material and loss of nitrates, produces a leeching effect that results in low-fertility soils. It is this feature of much of African land that had induced many communities to adopt a policy of shifting cultivation. This was a necessary and intelligent adaptation to the local environment; but, as the population has grown while often confined under colonial rule to a defined area and as cash crops have become more important, human and bovine pressures on the land have increased, with consequent exhaustion and erosion.

About one-third of Tanzania has a water supply adequate for cultivation. The coastal belt, the mountainous slopes of Kilimanjaro and Meru, the area around Lake Victoria, the region west of Tabora, and the territory from the Southern Highlands to Morogoro are the best areas in this respect. The country has no large rivers, but the Rovumu provides a frontier with Mozambique, the Rufiji enters the Indian Ocean south of Dar es Salaam in a wide delta, the Ruvu, or Pangani, also flows into the Indian Ocean, while the Malagarasi drains into Lake Tanganyika and the Kagera into Lake Victoria. But many streams only flow during the rainy seasons, drying up for the rest of the year, thus often forcing local communities to go long distances for water.

There is still another difficulty: The cultivated areas of Tanzania are widely scattered, which requires transport over great distances. The country is about one thousand miles long from northwest to southwest and over six hundred miles wide. Although Tanga provides the port facilities for the cultivated area of its hinterland, stretching to the Usambara Mountains, Dar es Salaam similarly for its agricultural hinterland, and Mtwara for a third region, which specializes in the growing of peanuts, the other producing areas lie several hundred miles away from the main markets. The railways from Tanga to Arusha, from Dar es Salaam straight across the country to the lakes, and from Masan and Nachingwea to Mtwara provide a partial solution to this problem. Yet many of the productive areas lie on the periphery of the state and road transport must be used either to the nearest railway depot or to the capital. Because only a few of the major roads are paved over any distance and so can be used in all weathers, distance creates a further handicap and high distribution cost. In short, throughout history Tanzania's environment has presented formidable difficulties to its inhabitants; modern techniques only marginally mitigate them.

2 The Peoples

I have already briefly touched on the great diversities of East Africa. Yet the differences in climate and landscape are as nothing compared with the rich variety of peoples composing the nation of Tanzania. Sitting under the palms beside the deep blue lagoon harbor of Dar es Salaam in the early evening at promenade time, one sees an endless kaleidoscope of colors, dress, features, and racial types. Here the Indian families—men in smart white ducks, women in brilliantly colored saris or long silk trousers—take their evening stroll along the coastal road. They are interspersed with white-robed Arabs; turbaned, heavily bearded Sikhs; Muslim women entirely covered in the long black *biu-biu,* an all-covering gown. The Swahili or coastal people, descended from a mixture of Arabs and Africans, their skin color varying from golden to jet black, their facial features often clearly portraying Arab descent in fine aquiline noses, may be dressed in fashionable European suits if they are teachers or civil servants or in brightly colored shirts and shorts if they are laborers from the town. The Europeans may come from any of a dozen countries, East and West Europe now being represented, and occasionally a small group of Chinese may be seen. Then there are the Africans from the interior. Their home districts are difficult to identify, for, whereas some of the men in business or government service will be wearing European clothes, others may be dressed in shirts and khaki shorts, or in the long white *kanzu* with exotically embroidered styles; the women wear cotton *kangas* (gowns) patterned in every color of the rainbow, with a riot of designs and mottoes in Swahili or Arabic. Most easily distinguishable, though rarely seen today, are members of the Masai tribe, their hair in ringlets plastered with red ochre mud, pierced earlobes hanging like hoop earrings, their bodies wound in russet-colored blankets. The scene is vivacious, colorful, fascinating. Half a dozen different tongues are being spoken, and as many cultures and creeds are manifest. This is not merely East Africa's cosmopolitan heart; it is a microcosm of world society.

It is not only in the city or town that human variety is shown in the society of Tanzania. The population of the countryside is generally divided into a number of concentrated habitable areas, often separated by large expanses of scarcely populated semiwastelands. The contrasts among these settled communities are often as sharp as those among the different peoples living in the city. At the two extremes are to be found the Hadzapi or Watindega, living beside Lake Eyasi in the north, and the Chagga who inhabit the slopes of Mount Kilimanjaro not far away to the east. Although they are comparatively close together, the contrast between these two communities could hardly be wider. The Hadzapi, now only a few hundred strong, are a type of bushmen who live by hunting and collecting food from the vegetation, neither practicing agriculture nor owning cattle. They represent the survival of one of the simplest forms of society known to man. On the other hand, the Chagga are among the most adaptable of East African peoples. They have perceived the opportunities of Western commercial life, tailored them to fit their local environment, and, by growing excellent coffee, which they market through their own cooperative society, have developed into one of the wealthiest communities of Tanzania.

Between these two extremes are to be found wide variations of peoples and life. On the west bank of Lake Victoria, the Bahaya dwell on some of the richest land in the country. Their coffee and banana trees grow without tending. The coffee is sold for cash; the bananas are the staple of their diet. Their dark, soft-featured women are particularly proud of their hairdressing and their long veils of brightly colored material. They are also excellent craftswomen, weaving patterned grass coverings for their kitchenware and making fine drums. The Bahaya's thatched beehive-shaped huts also display their artistry, the rich grasses from the rolling countryside providing not only their structural material but also soft carpets for the floors.

A steamer crosses the lake from the little port of Bukoba to Mwanza in Sukumaland. The Sukuma constitute the largest tribal community of Tanzania, with a population of over a million. While the Bahaya are mostly Roman Catholic, with connections to the powerful Baganda across the borders of Uganda, the Sukuma are principally Muslim. Mwanza is a port town with a mixed population of Africans, Indians, Arabs, and Europeans. It used to be largely Arab-dominated and was a center for dhow-building, a few of the huge wooden ships still lying beached on the shore. More recently, however, Mwanza secured a new lease on life from the growing commercial activities of the Sukuma in the hinterland. During the past twenty years, cotton-growing has increased very rapidly, the little *shambas* ("small-holdings") near the lakeside now being almost entirely devoted to this crop. Most of the people also keep a few cattle, but farther south there are large ranches, which have from two thousand to three thousand head. Again the cooperative movement has been vital to economic development. The cotton cooperative collects the crop, uses its own gin, and then sells the product. Also the scene of gold-mining at Geita and diamond-mining in Shinyanga, Sukumaland has become the greatest wealth-producing area of the country.

Throughout a large part of the African continent, cattle have traditionally been regarded as wealth. They have been used as currency, savings, and a measure of social status. Thus the wealthy, respected, influential man has been not the one with a large bank balance from the sale of his produce, but he who possesses many cattle. Under these circumstances, cattle are infrequently sold or used as food. Even among poorer sections of society, it has been important to have cattle available to cement certain social contracts, such as marriage. This emphasis on the importance of owning cattle is nowhere stronger than in the Masai community, which covers a large area in the north of Tanzania, spreading across the frontier well into Kenya. The traditional Masai—tall, proud, aquiline-featured, very reserved, dressed in a single piece of calico, with long plaited hair, bodies covered with ochre mud—have been widely publicized as romantic survivors from a simpler past. They were interested only in cattle-tending across the great open spaces of their arid plains, which are broken only by thorn bushes and a few dead trees. The Masai and their cattle formed part of a natural relationship to this environment, moving from waterhole to waterhole according to the season, along with the elephant, lion, giraffe, buffalo, and antelope. They were reluctant to labor and contemptuous of efforts to introduce education, which would take their sons away from herding. They required practically no money for clothing, their cloth lasting many years and never being washed. The simplest corn mush was the staple of their diet, supplemented by beer they brewed and spirits they distilled themselves. Recently, however, the Masai began to realize the importance of having new water sources and they agreed to finance themselves by taxation. It was hoped that more settled communities would develop around the wells they dug, which could then be supplemented by dams to provide the irrigation for communal ranching. This would then make possible the establishment of educational facilities and the promotion of a greater degree of social cohesion. But it takes many years, if not generations, to transform a nomadic, semipastoral community into a settled agricultural society. Most Masai continue to live their traditional life among their cattle, wandering across the arid plains of the plateau.

West of the Masai, in the Mbulu district, live the Iraqw and a number of smaller, related tribes. These people have the distinction of displaying more obvious signs of Cushitic origins than any other Tanzanian community, and they speak Cushitic languages. Indeed, in this single district are found examples of each of the three main strains within Tanzania—Bantu, Nilotic, and Cushitic. The Iraqw live around Kainam, the green, hollowed core of the central highlands of Mbulu, a high, undulating plateau over the rift wall from the

Masai. They are a proud, reserved people, noted for a statuesque, immobile posture and sharply defined features. They tend to be withdrawn, growing their own food, tending their cattle, and only selling crops or beasts when essential to purchase their few needs. Yet, despite their lack of interest in modernization, the Iraqw have shown one example of reform important to the rest of the country. Their land-rehabilitation and destocking program was carried out, with the assistance of local leadership, without any of the resentment caused in other areas. Because they are traditionally wedded to the cattle cult, it is remarkable that individual cattle-owners could be compelled to sell as many as 17 per cent of their beasts every year. Moreover, the clearing of the bush for land expansion halted the advance of the tsetse from the west. Even before independence, the Iraqw provided an excellent example of successful agrarian reform conducted through an alliance between administrator and local leadership.

South of the lands of the Bahaya, on the stretch between Lake Victoria and Lake Tanganyika, lives the Ha tribe. This is remote territory, much of it woodland or bush where the tsetse breeds. Its lofty highlands, valleys, and grasslands extend along the frontier with Rwanda and Burundi. The Ha live mostly in scattered solitude—their often naked children tending their long-horned cattle, the adults frequently clad in garments of hide or, on special occasions, of fibers made from the bark of trees. Their beehive-shaped, grass-covered huts tend to be scattered around the countryside rather than grouped in settlements, although sometimes a collection of huts denotes that members of a clan or family group are living together. The Ha retain a deep sense of the magical. Outside each hut a collection of sticks serves as a shrine to the family's ancestors, where food and drink is left for the ancestral spirits. Superstition and actual instances of poisoning from a substance composed of herbs and honey have become indistinguishably interlaced in the community. Attempts to persuade the Ha to leave their tsetse-infested bushland and live in organized settlements where land is fertile and well watered have usually failed, for they generally shun communication with other people. It may be that one of the reasons for this lack of cohesion and progressive development has been the effects of conquest, for the Ha seem to have been conquered early in the nineteenth century by the powerful Watutsi from across their western borders. Nevertheless, despite, or perhaps because of, their remoteness, the Ha certainly have their own artistic expression. They have become famous for their dances, the celebration of which can often continue without pause for several days and nights; the music is made by drum-beating and gourd-blowing. Multicolored beads and curved cattle horns are features of the ceremonial dress, and the leader sits in the center, clad in a leopard skin. The dance is based on complicated rhythms, beaten out by the bare feet of the dancers.

On the fertile shores of Lake Tanganyika, around Kigoma and Ujiji, lives a mixture of peoples. This was the great collecting place for the slave trade of the eighteenth and nineteenth centuries, and inevitably that left heritages from peoples brought from various parts of the continent. Here are also to be found descendants of the Arab slave-traders, and a few Indians and Arabs still carry on small-scale commercial activities, though these are now of a more humane nature. The people spend their time in a mixture of peasant farming and fishing. The fishermen in their wooden canoes provide catches, which, after drying under the sun, supply a valuable source of protein to many districts throughout the country. The inhabitants have shown unusual skill in organizing farmers, fishermen, and tailors in craft societies.

One of the strangest and saddest stories in Tanzania is that of the Nyamwezi people of the western region, centered on the town of Tabora. Historically, the Nyamwezi were the great traders of the interior regions; they were sufficiently organized to challenge the commercial power of the Arabs under the Sultan of Zanzibar, who used Tabora as their base. Indeed, in 1880, under their famous Chief Mirambo, the Nyamwezi successfully attacked the Arab base in Tabora. Their commercial trading skill was such that they gained the reputation among nineteenth-century explorers of being the most powerful tribe of central Tanganyika.

Nevertheless, despite this reputation of erstwhile power, the

Nyamwezi have in recent times declined to a minor tribe. Much of their land is arid, beset by tsetse and consequently remains uninhabited. Tabora itself has suffered greatly from an inadequate water supply; the absence of irrigation inhibited land development and the introduction of cash crops which have increased local wealth elsewhere. So the bush was left largely undisturbed, providing a constant breeding ground for the tsetse pest. Meanwhile, trade stagnated, and many Arabs and Indians engaged alongside the Nyamwezi in trade and commerce left Tabora for more attractive centers.

Yet the decline of the Nyamwezi seems to date from an administrative crisis rather than simply to result from the natural harshness of the area. In 1917, Chief Saidi bin Fundikira established himself as one of the leading figures of Tanganyika. During the governorship of Sir Donald Cameron, Fundikira became a shining example in terms of the governor's policy of ruling through established local authorities. His palace outside Tabora illustrated the importance given to a powerful ruler supported by the British administration. Even today the size of the white building, with two knarled trees silhouetted against its frontage, is impressive.

In 1929, however, Fundikira was accused of embezzlement; he was sentenced to imprisonment, but the sentence was quashed by the court of appeal. It was widely charged at the time that the British administrators had handled the affair tactlessly. Apparent misuse of public funds was common at the time, not simply through dishonesty but because in African tradition public wealth can be dispensed at the discretion of the chief. The Fundikira affair was certainly badly managed and resulted in a serious reversal for the policy of rule through local help.

The affair also seems to have destroyed the self-confidence of the Nyamwezi. Although his sentence was quashed, Fundikira was sent away from his people, who were being concentrated by the administration into new settlements. The tribe very quickly felt the effects of its new insecurity; in three years, from 1928 to 1931, the population of the Tabora district declined from 173,000 to 120,000, in Fundikira's own chiefdom, from 120,000 to 59,000. This traumatic experience, together with the infertility of the land, lack of water, and consequent difficulties in participating in a market economy, led to widespread migration from the area. It was to affect the Nyamwezi for a generation; even with the natural increase, the Tabora area never again reached its 1928 population until just before independence. Tabora itself remained something of a ghost town, its straight, well-kept roads all leading to the German-built government center; its famous school still attracting a proportion of the most intelligent boys, but its streets largely empty.

To the west of the Nyamwezi lies Dodoma, dominated by a tall, yellow, Ismaili mosque. It is a small town, a group of white buildings surrounded by brown mud huts; it is also the center of the Gogo tribe. Here again, lack of water has seriously inhibited development, although the dam built outside Dodoma in 1955 provides a water supply for the town itself. But the Gogo have been accustomed throughout their history to periodic famine, largely caused by the absence of irrigation. Between 1953 and 1955, they suffered from one of the most severe famines in their history. Every activity had to be subordinated to desperate attempts to avoid death by starvation; but the colonial government expected the people themselves to pay the costs of this massive rescue campaign. When, a year after the famine, a pilot scheme was proposed to introduce an irrigation system, the Gogo were again expected to pay for it themselves. It is hardly surprising that development in Dodoma and surrounding Gogo areas has been seriously stunted. The effects are to be seen in the emaciated faces of the people and the protruding ribs of their cattle.

Perhaps the most interesting tribe of the south is the Hehe, located in the Iringa district of the highland grasslands which are between 5,000 and 6,000 feet high. It was organized into a unified community in the mid-nineteenth century by Chief Mujugumba after a series of successful tribal wars. His son, Mkwawa, who succeeded to the chiefdom after defeating his brother, became famous as a result of his part in a great Hehe achievement toward the end of the century. In 1891, Hehe warriors under the leadership of Mkwawa ambushed and defeated a German expedition composed of African and European soldiers, which had been sent to discipline the tribe. Three years later a second German expedition took its revenge against the Hehe, occupied their fort at Kalenga, near Iringa, and forced Mkwawa to spend the next five years as a fugitive until he finally committed suicide rather than surrender. The Germans beheaded him and sent his head to Germany. Yet the defeat of the first German force has remained an epic story in the history not only of the Hehe but of East Africa as a whole. After its defeat, the tribe was broken up into clans, and only in 1926 under Sir Donald Cameron's policy of indirect rule was the chiefdom of a united Hehe tribe revived, with first Mkwawa's son and later his grandson, Chief Adam Sapi, as chief. The Hehe have sustained their military traditions by continuing to supply a large proportion of recruits to the national army.

The Arabs have been a strong influence on this part of the country for many years, maintaining a trading post at Iringa. Their example was followed by many of the Hehe merchants who themselves traveled as far as the coast. It also led to widespread acceptance of Islam. Mkwawa's son was converted to the faith during his residence on the coast and brought the Muslim religion back with him and his court on their return to his tribe. One of the consequences has been that much of the law of the region is a mixture of the Muslim legal system with African customs.

The plateau that supports the Hehe is but thinly populated. They grow corn and beans and keep some cattle, their crop production being sufficient to be sold for cash. Since World War II, the Hehe have become enthusiastic about education—their chiefs being the first to set an example. Government and mission schools have proliferated, with Catholic missions predominating. Memories of their two great nineteenth-century chiefs have contributed to the respect accorded the present-day Hehe by other Africans and provided a foundation of cohesion and tribal consciousness that remains an outstanding characteristic of the Hehe community.

These have been some examples of the tribal communities in Tanzania, taken from the different regions of the country and illustrating the contrasting aspects of life. They are not, of course, by any means exhaustive, for in mainland Tanzania alone more than a hundred tribes can be found. Only a book of encyclopedic dimensions could attempt to describe them all. I have tried merely to give a picture of some of the larger tribes and those that illustrate a particular aspect of Tanzanian life. Even so, space has necessitated scores of significant omissions. I have not, for example, described the Nyakusa of Rungwe in the southern highlands, a people living a prosperous life with some similarities to that of the Chagga, from whom, indeed, the latter learned their cooperative methods. Nor has there been space to describe the remarkable though small Matengo tribe, which, through many centuries, cultivated its southern hills by means of a unique hole system of planting that prevents erosion and enriches the land—a remarkable example of inventiveness. We should also note the Yao in the south, who immigrated from Mozambique, dominated the slave trade in the nineteenth century and proved formidable opponents of the Germans. Nevertheless, the general picture given in this chapter should provide the imaginative reader with a backdrop for the lives of many different kinds of Tanzanians.

3 Ancient and Medieval History

It is ironic, considering the minimal attention paid to African history until recently, that the African continent is now established as a scene of crucial events in the emergence of mankind. The full story of man's evolution cannot yet be scientifically confirmed and is likely to remain a subject of argument for many years. It is a living story, constantly taking new directions as fresh clues are discovered. All the continents have provided hiding places for these clues, but the discoveries of the past half-century have shown that Africa contains some of the oldest evidence of man's development from his original primate stock.

Many areas of the continent have yielded finds revealing much of this story. East Africa has offered a special contribution. In the Olduvai Gorge of northern Tanzania the whole process by which a group of homo sapiens emerged from humanoid form can be observed. It has been the life's work of Louis Leakey, the famous anthropologist, to discover, analyze, and explain the evidence from this and other African sites. Skulls, jaws, teeth and bones, cutting-edge bone and pebble tools, and hand axes are the clues from which the story is reconstructed. According to Leakey's theory, from these humanoid species there evolved a creature that he names *Homo habilis,* from which human man, or homo sapiens, directly descended.

Whether or not Leakey's views, which are still disputed, are eventually established, this is a story of from some 3 million years ago to the emergence of homo sapiens perhaps less than 50,000 years ago. More important to an understanding of East African and Tanzanian history are the migrations of various types of human beings and diffusion of their cultural traits and patterns, which have brought today's peoples into the areas they inhabit.

Because the current state boundaries in East Africa, like those of the whole continent, bear no relation to the history of their peoples before the colonial era of the past hundred years, we have to describe movements of communities over a much wider area than Tanzania alone; for their paths traversed the whole of East and parts of Central Africa.

A word should be said here about semantics, which tends to be complicated however used in this context. We must distinguish between racial stocks and the families within them that, by their constant intermingling, have produced the hybrids we all are. This intermingling has, in modern times, reduced the concept of "pure" race to nonsense. In order to understand the development of different cultures, their interaction with each other, and the resultant relations of various communities, it is necessary to find a means of identifying different ethnic groups at varying stages of their development. The modern tendency is to use language relationships for this purpose, although these must be checked against the evidence of archeology, physical traits, political forms, and social habits.

In this connection, we need to clarify our attitude to the most controversial of the terms used in East Africa, the words "Hamite" and "Hamitic." The peoples from northeastern Africa, some of whom migrated into eastern areas, have often been called "Hamites." In the course of recent spurious racialist arguments, however, this term has become debased. Because these people and their descendants often appear to be physically related to Europeans, those who adhere to the sophistry of European superiority have often attributed the higher achievements of African society to "Hamitic" influence. In order to avoid confusion with this political pseudo science, many modern anthropologists have substituted the words "Cushite" and

"Cushitic" for "Hamite" and "Hamitic." These new terms should not be confused with the name of the Kushite peoples who inhabited the ancient Kingdom of Meroe. For strict scientific accuracy, the word "Cushitic" should be employed to describe only a language family, but, for convenience, "Cushite" is used to denote the peoples using these languages. I shall use these modern terms.

It should be pointed out in this "political" context that Africans, like the peoples of every other continent, are products of migration and intermixing among various stocks. A few of these stocks originated outside of Africa even before the recent arrival of Europeans. Caucasoid and Mongoloid stocks have been mixed with Negroid and Bushmanoid, with the Negroid almost always dominant. Apart from the migration of communities on the continent, there is specific evidence of Arabs from western Asia and Malayo-Polynesian–speaking peoples of Mongoloid race visiting the eastern shores of the continent, settling there and being absorbed into the local populations.

It is necessary to trace the evolution of communities that have formed the populations of East Africa and to identify the factors that have influenced their social development. Because, unless one is suffering from the "racial virus," it is people's actions, beliefs, and social organization that are interesting, rather than the complex biological character of their origins.

Of the three original racial types present in Africa—the Bushmanoid, Negroid, and Caucasoid, the first two are indigenous only to that continent, but the Caucasoid is the basic stock of Europe, Western Asia, and India. In East Africa, the communities of northeastern Kenya show a considerable Caucasoid element, and other peoples of East Africa, including some from Tanzania, show signs of the addition of Caucasoid blood to predominantly Negroid strains. On the coast, too, the Arabs contributed a Caucasoid strain to the Swahili peoples.

It seems probable that it was a Bushmanoid type of people that first inhabited Africa and later racial types evolved from that stock. There are still survivals of these early kinds of people, though with much admixture of Negroid blood. The Hadzapi, who live beside Lake Eyasi, and their neighbors, the Sandawe, about seventy miles to the south, lived until very recently much as their ancestors did—hunting, collecting wild foods, fishing, but practicing neither agriculture nor cattle-herding. They developed only the faintest signs of social organization and were little influenced by their contact with other cultures. Only very recently have some of these peoples gradually been persuaded to experiment with planting crops and tending a few cattle.

Physical traits can tell us very little about the peoples of East Africa and certainly do not explain the divisions into tribes or describe the character of these communities. A more revealing approach is through study of the language groups that prevail among East Africa's people. There are three main language families—the Bantu, Nilotic, and Cushitic. Khoisan, a fourth group, is used only by the surviving Bushmanoids.

Languages, of course, evolve continuously. Language families in East Africa have always acted and reacted on each other. Not only have they divided and subdivided many times over the centuries; as peoples have mingled, combined, and assimilated each other, their languages have changed, sometimes one replacing another, at other times a language splitting as a group divided. Nor have these impacts been confined within a language group. There has often been interaction between peoples from two language families, the one being absorbed into the other. In short, language families have never been static, nor can they be seen as rigidly limited to particular groups of people. Nevertheless, they remain important aids in tracing the history of communities.

In East Africa, the Bantu languages predominate. There are also a large wedge of Nilotic-speakers and, especially in northeastern Kenya, a number of Cushitic tongues. In Tanzania, all three groups are present. Bantu is dominant, but, in the north-central section, Nilotic, Cushitic, and Khoisan are contiguous. There is a connection between the language families and physical characteristics. With some exceptions, the Bantu and Nilotic languages are spoken by predominantly Negroid peoples, the Cushitic group by those with strong Caucasoid traits, and Khoisan by the few remaining Bushmanoids. The majority of Tanzanians, mainly Negroid peoples, speak one of the Bantu languages, with the Masai and scattered groups known as Dorobo using tongues from the Nilotic group; the more Caucasoid Iraqw are the best example of Cushitic-speakers; the Bushmanoid Sandawe and probably the Hadzapi speak a Khoisan form.

One other generalization can be made, though also with exceptions. By and large, Bantu-speaking peoples have been more interested in agriculture; the Nilotic speakers, with cattle-herding. The prevalence of these relationships helps to explain the kind of lands each group tends to favor, and therefore provides a clue to past migrations.

Using these approaches to classification, we can begin to sketch the outlines of the East African story so as both to describe and give some explanation of the evolution of the communities now inhabiting the region. It must be emphasized that the sketch will be tentative, for many riddles remain to be solved and every year new discoveries are made that alter our conceptions.

It seems probable that the first true men to inhabit East Africa were of the Bushmanoid family. They seem to have been larger than modern Bushmen, though there may have been pygmies in the area too. These early men, from whom it seems that later Negroids and Bushmen descended, lived largely by hunting and by gathering wild plants and berries. Game animals, fowl, and fish were hunted with weapons manufactured from stone or bone. Many of the camp sites, usually under overhanging rocks, from which game could be observed, were decorated with paintings of animals and scenes of the chase. The use of fire enabled men to protect themselves from carnivorous beasts, keep themselves warm in the highlands, use tree gums as glue for making implements, and cook their food.

After about 10,000 B.C., Caucasoid people began to filter into East Africa. They were physically similar to the people of Arabia and North Africa. They brought with them new techniques of stone toolmaking, which were learned by the peoples they encountered. These techniques, together with the advances made over the next several thousand years, made it possible for them to hunt in a more specialized and better organized way.

By about 1000 B.C., in the same highland areas that had seen the advance in hunting methods, knowledge of agriculture and pastoralism had appeared. They seem to have been brought by Caucasoid Cushitic-speaking immigrants from the north. Food production and domestication of cattle were accompanied or preceded by a knowledge of pottery-making. Certainly earthenware pots and stone bowls were used as food-containers. It seems likely that some types of sorghum and millet were grown originally and that cattle, sheep, and goats were kept. These agricultural and pastoral innovations did not, of course, suddenly revolutionize society. They were introduced gradually, long being a mere supplement to hunting. From findings in burial sites, it seems that these people made baskets, fashioned gourds, carved wooden vessels, and strung bone, eggshell, nut, and precious-stone beads into necklaces. They had as yet no knowledge of metals, their implements and weapons being of stone, their hoes either stone or wood. So far as we know, this society lived only in the Rift Valley as far south as Lake Eyasi and perhaps in the highlands and plains of Kenya and the north of Tanzania. Most of the rest of East Africa remained peopled by the hunting-gathering communities. But it is clear that the agricultural-pastoral immigrants interbred with the peoples they encountered, and many cultural practices—such as circumcision—still bear witness in this region to the influence of these Cushites.

The next stage in cultural development began with the introduction of iron. It is not certain who brought the knowledge of ironworking to East African or from what direction it entered the region. It may have come from Meroe in the central Nile area, where a considerable iron-smelting industry was flourishing before the Christian era. It has been suggested that it was brought across the Indian Ocean and, also, that it came from the Zambian region. None of these theories have yet been established. What is known is that the appearance of iron approximately coincided with the migration of two new family stocks into East Africa, though whether either or both of them brought metalworking techniques remains obscure. Again, it should be emphasized that ironworking did not appear as a sudden revolution. Its use spread slowly, even to the hunter-gatherers who began to use the metal for their arrow tips. But iron weapons provided increased military strength, so that those peoples still relying on hunting and gathering, as well as the earlier cultivators and pastoralists, were either absorbed by the newcomers or had to seek a more sheltered environment in the forests or other areas poorly suited to cultivation and herding.

The newcomers were both Negroid, Nilotic peoples from the north and Bantu-speaking communities from the south and west. Both began to migrate into East Africa during the first millennium A.D. This was a gradual process, the search for land providing the main stimulus. As suitable land was found and cleared, populations began to expand, necessitating still further searches. Generally, the Nilotes sought plains and grasslands on which to herd their cattle; the Bantu, areas suitable for cultivation. But there was a great deal of intermingling, absorption, and assimilation. Thus acculturation proceeded among the Cushites, Nilotes, and Bantu, with cultural traits from one or the other stock dominating almost haphazardly, though dominance was often associated with the ecology of the territory occupied.

The best example of an early iron-using community is the one that lived on the Engaruka site in northern Tanzania. There, several hundred people seem to have lived in a concentrated agricultural settlement that probably lasted for over a thousand years. It depended on an extensive system of irrigation from a river, for it is situated in an area of low rainfall. The houses and some of the cultivated fields were on steep hillsides from which platforms were cut. But the most significant point about this community is that the inhabitants used iron tools.

Another factor, which roughly coincided with the iron age, providing East Africans with the means to expand into the most fertile areas of the region, was the growth of bananas. Forests and high-rainfall areas proved suitable for the cultivation of this new food, which came to Africa from Asia about two thousand years ago. With the use of iron implements, the wetter areas, such as the lake regions, could be cleared and planted with the fruit, which provided sustenance for large concentrations of population. This indicates a growing ability to specialize in agriculture—bananas providing the staple crop in the well-watered districts, millet in the open country, cattle supplementing both.

So far I have been describing the evolution of East African society as a whole. This should not be confused with the smaller communities that composed it, which are usually termed "tribes." As I have said, racial stocks and language families continually intermixed. Cushites, Nilotes, and Bantu absorbed each other, and within each group there was constant fission and fusion, with cultural traits sometimes surviving, at other times disappearing. Within this welter of interaction, therefore, the communities people formed were essentially mixed. When we refer to a tribe by an ethnic term, we are almost always generalizing, for convenience categorizing the community according to its dominant traits. The search for new land, conquest, pressure from neighbors, and population increase have all caused communal migrations in the course of which tribes have divided, absorbed others or been absorbed, moved their location, altered their mores. The history of tribal communities is a story of constant evolution.

During the Iron Age, East Africa was very sparsely populated. Over large areas of the northeast and across the northern Tanzanian plains, the shortage of rainfall created semidesert conditions. Although certain pastoralists learned how to graze their cattle in these barren lands, the growth of substantial populations was impossible. Much of the soil has always been of poor quality, preventing the growing of much food, and the widespread incidence of the tsetse fly and mosquito brought the ravages of sleeping sickness and malaria to man and beast. Naturally, therefore, communities tended to settle in fertile areas, for instance, in the rich highlands of Kenya and Uganda and along the hillsides of the western Rift Valley.

It seems that only with the addition of the new foods from abroad could the native sorghum and millet of Africa be sufficiently supplemented to allow population expansion. Bananas, yams, sugar cane, fruits, and rice—all from Asia—appeared in East Africa during the first millennium A.D. Traders and sailors from across the Indian Ocean, very probably from Indonesia in particular, must have introduced them to the coastal societies of East Africa, whence they spread into the interior. Later, after Europeans had begun to trade between West Africa and the Americas during the sixteenth and seventeenth centuries, these foods were to be further supplemented by crops from the Americas and Caribbean. Corn, cassava, sweet potatoes, pineapples, and papaw gradually found their way from the west coast to East Africa, greatly increasing the ability of East African societies to expand and allowing a proportion of their people to concentrate on trade, simple manufacture, and crafts.

Yet, even to the present, the ecological factors of East Africa have left that region with pockets of concentrated populations scattered across large areas of almost deserted country. The other significant factor that has continued to determine the character of East African life is the separation of coastal communities from the peoples of the interior. This separation has never been complete, and in modern times it has been more strongly bridged by the development of some modern communications. But it has remained a feature of East African life, and it was crucial to the development of the whole area in medieval times.

From early times, small communities on the coast participated in Indian Ocean trade. Two classical texts testify to this. *Periplus of the Erythrean Sea,* probably written by a Greek sailor in the early second century A.D., describes the ports along the Somali coast, various islands, harbors, and settlements along the coasts of Kenya and, possibly, Zanzibar, completing the picture with mention of a trading center named Rhapta that was probably somewhere on what is now the Tanzanian coast. (The name "Rhapta," derived from the word for "sewn," referred to the sewn boats that were common in the area.) We are told how ships sailed among the Red Sea ports before rounding Cape Guardafui and swinging down the East African coast. A short distance south of the Cape, Opone, now Ras Hafun, was sighted. To this "emporium" ships brought cloth, grain, oil, and sugar from western India; cloaks and tunics, copper, tin, silverware, wine, and drinking cups from the Red Sea ports. They exchanged their cargoes for frankincense, spices, gum, tortoise shell, ivory, and increasing numbers of slaves, who were sent to Egypt.

It took some weeks to reach Rhapta, and several names of places passed en route are mentioned. Rhapta itself seems to have been much more primitive than Opone. It was a center for the export of ivory, which was exchanged for imports of manufactured iron implements and weapons. It was subject to a southern Arabian King under whom the people were ruled by local chiefs. Arab merchants who settled there intermarried with the inhabitants and learned to speak local languages. *Periplus* describes the local inhabitants as very tall but provides few clues as to their racial origins.

The second work from which we can draw information about the East African coast of this time is Ptolemy's *Geography*. This was probably originally compiled in the second century, with additional sections added three hundred years later from knowledge acquired during the ensuing period by geographers. Since the observations of the author of *Periplus*, the east coast commerce had grown considerably. Rhapta had become much more important and seems to have been a state capital with large trading interests to the south and into the interior. Nor was there then any mention of Arab overlordship. Exploration had clearly been widely extended, for Mount Kilimanjaro was known, as were the inland lakes from which the Nile emerges. Ptolemy also knew of communities living along the coast, south of Rhapta.

It is fairly clear that, during the first few centuries of the Christian era, Greek and Roman ships had begun to trade for spices and ivory down the northern part of the East African coast. They had also learned to use the monsoon winds that blow southwestward during the northern winter and northeastward during the summer. These vital winds determined the trading pattern of East Africa, facilitating regular commercial linkages among Arabian, East African, and western-Indian ports. The character of the East African coastal communities is still obscure, but, although in Greek and Roman times there was no mention of Negroid characteristics, there is no doubt that, later, people of Negro stock lived along the coast from what became Portuguese East Africa to Somalia. They were visited by Arab and Indian traders who added their genes to what came to be known as the Swahili peoples.

By the end of the first millennium A.D., a variety of communities had found land where they could support themselves in East Africa. In what is now Tanzania they were largely composed of predominantly Bantu peoples. They built villages, cultivated land, raised cattle, and smelted iron to make it into implements. As their population grew or their land lost its fertility, groups of them sought new habitats. Growing populations also brought about the need for more definite rules of behavior. Land had to be divided, cattle allocated, labor tasks determined, quarrels adjudicated, offenders punished, trading conditions regulated, enemies repelled. As yet we know little detail of the political system each community developed, except that some adopted the practice of appointing chiefs to rule with tribal elders, whereas others used forms of government that did not require the centralized rule of a chief. The latter usually based their government on the authority of linked sets of villages or of even smaller units of family clans.

On the coast, settlements of various sizes were to be found from the Horn to Mozambique, and also on some of the offshore islands. They were visited by Arab and Indian traders, perhaps also by Indonesians. The character of their populations began to diverge from those of the interior as foreign strains entered them. Ivory, gold, iron, rhinocerous horn, tortoiseshell, slaves, and coconut oil were sought here by foreign traders; African slaves were already visible in Arabia, India, and China. Cloth, metalware, glass vessels, beads, and shells were brought in exchange for them. The East African coast had become part of the Indian Ocean trading area, and its future was essentially linked to it.

The next five hundred years, until the appearance of the Portuguese in East Africa, saw the rise and fall of wealthy trading cities, the expansion of their trade and accumulation of wealth, their periodic jealousies of each other and consequent conflicts, and their varying relations with Asia. Most of these lively events took place on the coast, but the interior, although it changed much more slowly, was not entirely unaffected by them. For it was from the interior that the trading ports had to obtain their supplies of goods for exchange, so that the growth or diminution of Indian Ocean trade inevitably affected the production and exchange of some hinterland societies.

The medieval years from about 1000 A.D. to some time during the sixteenth century saw the rise of a prosperous and, in places, splendid coastal culture. In the fifteenth century, there were as many as thirty-seven towns established between Kilwa in southern Tanzania and Mogadishu in Somalia. Most of them seem to have developed from the twelfth century on, growing as their inhabitants discovered the possibilities of collecting commodities demanded by the merchants who came to the coast. Ivory and slaves served this purpose for the majority, but supplies of iron were found in Malindi in Kenya, while Rhodesian gold and Katangan copper provided Kilwa with its substantial wealth, whether exported directly from the port or through its control of trade out of southern Sofala. Each of these towns had its own ruler and form of government. They never formed an empire, voluntarily or through conquest, though at various times some of them would join together against others, when one or another of them had a period of supremacy.

The effects of various Arab cultures and of Islam were certainly felt before and throughout this period, though only along the coastline and on the islands. There is some dispute as to how early Islam became influential on the coast. It was certainly firmly established by the early fourteenth century, when the Moroccan traveler Ibn Battuta visited Mogadishu and Kilwa. Some local traditions place strong Islamic influences as early as the seventh century, but these are probably exaggerated local myths. There is no evidence that during this period Islam deliberately colonized the coastal towns. What seems most likely is that gradually increasing numbers of Islamic merchants sailed to the coast from Arabia, Persia, and India; some of them settled in the towns, mixed with the local African peoples, and were absorbed by them; and they and more transient visitors contributed their knowledge of architecture, building techniques, government, and trading practices, some of which were adopted by the local inhabitants. In certain towns there are many signs of the influence of Islamic architecture—influence that shows some connections with Islamic India as well as with Arabia. The citadel of Kilwa, for instance, was definitely built by Arab crafts-men; near Kilwa's great mosque, however, was excavated an elabo-rate stone carving that bears a distinct relation to the works of Indian Muslims.

There have been two theories on the original settlement of the important Shirazi peoples in the East African coastal cities. (Shiraz was the capital of Fars, the province that controlled the east of the Persian Gulf.) The earlier view was that the Shirazi came directly from their homeland to Kilwa toward the end of the tenth century and established a ruling dynasty there, which survived for over six hundred years. The more recent theory, propounded by Neville Chittick, an archaeologist who specialized in East Africa, is that the Shirazi migrated down the coast from the north. The suggestion is that most of the Shirazi settled in the Shungwaya area—the district from which the main northeastern Bantu tribes dispersed as the *Galla* drove them south—that they began to migrate from this area in the late twelfth century, settling in the coastal towns and islands as far south as Kilwa. In Kilwa itself, they established a dynasty of sultans under whom the city rose to a power second only to that of Mogadishu by gaining a monopoly of the Sofala gold trade. There were various dynastic struggles and new immigrations probably from South Arabia. Yet, by the time of the Portuguese appearance, most of the rulers on the coast were known as Shirazi, though they did not necessarily have the same origins. One of the principal ex-ceptions was in Pate, where the Nabahani clan from Oman ruled.

Yet, despite the power and wealth of Kilwa, the city never estab-lished anything resembling an empire. Indeed, each of the city-states developed a tradition of independence, even though at times some of them might have payed tribute to more powerful ones. This independence limited their vision to local interests and rivalries, in contrast to the wider view of Indian Ocean power held by the Portuguese.

Islamic influence along the coast was important to the prosperity of its towns. Beginning about the thirteenth century, Muslim culture began to dominate the western half of the Indian Ocean, on which East Africa depended for its commercial progress. The Egyptians on the Red Sea and around the Horn, the Muslim empire based in Delhi and spreading down the Indian west coast, Islamic Mongols in Iran and Iraq, even Muslim influence in Indonesia—all demonstrated the expanding trading power of Islam. So the adhesion of the East African coastal peoples to that faith brought them more than architectural knowledge. It ensured them a place within a universalist culture that could supply them with knowledge from other lands, unified general rules of conduct in life and trade, visitors like Ibn Battuta from a world in which scholarship was common, a language with which to converse and, on occasion, record events, and trading contacts whose markets were linked throughout the Muslim world. The prosperity of the coastal towns and the achievements made in building, the comforts of life, city government, and expanding trade—all bear witness to the advantages they received from membership in the medieval Islamic world. These benefits, of course, were mainly enjoyed by the wealthy classes, for Islam also introduced a class structure into African society. Many of the ordinary Africans, no doubt, had to work very hard to produce, transport (by human porterage), and market the goods that brought such prosperity to the rich, and many others found themselves shipped across the Indian Ocean as slaves to Muslim masters in alien lands. But, speaking generally, the acceptance of Islam brought economic progress, increased knowledge, and stronger, if not more just, social structures.

It would seem that the period between the late twelfth and early sixteenth centuries was that of the greatest prosperity for the east coast. Medieval Europe was seeking ever larger supplies of ivory and gold for the carved treasures of its wealthy classes and the newly minted coins of its expanding money economies. The Indians were constantly anxious to obtain supplies of iron, some of which eventually found its way as steel to Damascus for manufacture into sword blades. The Arab states jockeyed with each other for dominance in every type of trade. Even the Chinese continually demanded ivory for their palanquins. Supremacy over the trade routes of the Indian Ocean alternated among Arab, Indian, and Chinese, but all sought to expand the commerce, and this brought steadily increasing demand for African products.

Thus, life on the coast grew more sophisticated. Huts were replaced by stone houses; palaces with windows were built for the wealthy and within them could be found Ming porcelain, Indian cloth, and ceramics, vases, beads, and plates from Persia. Fortifications and mosques were built, and in the thirteenth century coins began to be minted. This growth in comfort and organization depended on constant supplies of ivory from the interior, gold from the Zimbabwe area, copper from Katanga, iron from the mines of the East African hinterland, and quantities of slaves. The most important trade routes were those from Rhodesia and Katanga to Sofala and Kilwa, which brought gold and copper to the coast. At times, Kilwa was able to secure control of the gold trade northward from Sofala, and it grew rich because of its strategic position. Other city-states on the coast sometimes emulated its example. Prosperity rose and fell according to local dominance, and conflicts were frequent. But throughout this period a string of coastal states, from Sofala through Kilwa, Kisimani, Mafia, Zanzibar, Pemba, Malindi, and Pate to Mogadishu in the north, had a flourishing culture because of their importance in the trading patterns of the Indian Ocean.

The aforementioned archaeologist Chittick composed a vivid description of the inhabitants in the coastal towns of the fourteenth century by combining the evidence of his excavations with contemporary eyewitness accounts. He writes:

The inhabitants can be considered as falling into three classes in most of the important settlements. The ruling class (except where a recently arrived immigrant group had succeeded in making itself dominant) was of mixed Arab and African ancestry, brown in colour, well read in the faith of Islam. Such would probably be also the landowners, the skilled artisans, and most of the religious functionaries and merchants. Inferior to them (in many cases in a state of slavery) were the pure-blooded Africans, some of them recently arrived, who performed the menial tasks, and tilled the fields. Apart from both were the transient or recently settled Arabs, still incompletely assimilated into the society.

Of occupations, that of merchant was the most prominent; also many were engaged in crewing the ships in which the merchants sailed. Apart from agriculture (including, no doubt, the growing of cotton), the weaving of cloth seems to have been the biggest industry. Other crafts include the striking of coins and other work in copper, the carving of bone and ivory, and the working of semi-precious stones. Many must have been employed as stonemasons and carvers, the standard achieved [by] the latter (especially in some inscriptions) being very high.*

Chittick continues by painting a picture of the homes in the towns. It is necessarily an effort of imagination, but one drawn from evidence. As it has never been bettered and comes from the mind of an expert, it is worth reproducing in full.

The houses were built very close to one another, often sharing a party wall and sometimes linked together, suggesting a family relationship between the occupiers. The blocks of buildings were separated by very narrow lanes, though often there were gardens behind. They were of one storey, except in the largest towns, up to three being found at Kilwa. Roofs were flat, built of stone laid on mangrove poles which were usually squared; the weight of these massive roofs and the strength of the timbers restricted the width of the rooms, which is eight feet or a little less. The houses followed a fairly uniform plan. They were entered by a doorway leading to a sunken courtyard. Facing on to this was usually a reception room or verandah, with the main living room behind, and bedrooms to the rear of this; such a basic arrangement was often much elaborated by the addition of other rooms. The main entrances into the courtyard of the larger houses were impressive, and in the Kilwa area ornamented with borders of recessed cut stone, sometimes with herringbone ornament, the commonest decorative motif at this period. At least one latrine, well constructed in cut stone was included in each house, with an adjoining "bidet" for ablutions. . . .

There were usually no windows, except in the facade facing the courtyard, so the inner rooms must have been dark, but their ceilings and thick walls would have been cool. The walls were plastered and

* Neville Chittick, "The Coast Before the Arrival of the Portuguese," in *Zamani*, edited by B. A. Ogot and J. A. Kieran (London: Longmans, 1968), pp. 113–14.

never painted. Decoration of any sort was sparing. Ornamental niches in cut stone were sometimes set in walls or on either side of doorways, which were often beautifully assembled of cut coral. Some of the main rooms were decorated with hangings, probably carpets, and carved wooden friezes, as is attested by rows of holes for suspension pegs. In the fourteenth century decorative motifs in cut stone are found; in the succeeding century their place, in the Kilwa region, was to some extent taken by glazed bowls of Persian and Chinese wares, which were inset in vaulted roofs of buildings.

Cooking was commonly done over a portable earthenware stove, with three horns on which the cooking vessel was placed, with charcoal beneath. A sort of bread was baked of rice or millet flour in an oven set on the floor. . . .

The upper classes ate off imported glazed Islamic ware, or Chinese porcelain; by the fifteenth century even the poorer people seem to have had their food served in an eating bowl rather than straight from the cooking-pot. At Kilwa, at least, those who could not afford glazed imported bowls had individual bowls to eat from.*

This description can be substantiated and extended by reference to the account given by Ibn Battuta, after his visit in the early fourteenth century; he refers to a meal sent to him by the Mogadishu sheikh, consisting of rice cooked in ghee (a sauce of meat and vegetables), dishes of bananas with milk and ginger, peppers, and mangoes in milk. He also describes the opulent courts of the sheikhs and of the Sultan in Kilwa, the raiding expeditions into the interior, and the flourishing trade in the cities. Two centuries later, the Portuguese were equally impressed by the luxury of the rich; by the fruits and vegetables grown; the cattle, fowl, and fish eaten; the rice cultivated so extensively it could be exported to Aden. But again it must be emphasized that this description applied only to the coastal culture; a short five miles inland stone buildings were unknown.

* *Ibid.,* pp. 114–15.

4 Arabs and Europeans

In the final years of the fifteenth century, new arrivals appeared on the Indian Ocean stage. Conflict between Christianity and Islam on the Iberian Peninsula, across the Mediterranean, and into the Near East had led the Portuguese throughout the century to seek means of breaking the Arab stranglehold on trade between Asia and Europe. Their sailors gradually extended their routes down the African west coast. In 1483, one expedition reached as far as the mouth of the Congo, where it encountered the Kongo Kingdom. Five years later, Bartolomew Diaz was blown round the Cape of Good Hope. In 1498, Vasco da Gama sailed the first European ships round the Cape, along the South African coast, and into the Indian Ocean. He was eventually to make his way to India, guided by a pilot from Malindi, but before he crossed the ocean he visited some of the East African ports and noted the flourishing trade carried on there, as well as the wealth that they had accumulated.

When da Gama returned to Portugal the following year, he took with him not only the vital knowledge of how to outflank Islam by sailing to India round Africa, thus bypassing the markets of the Near and Middle East, but also news of the riches to be found in East Africa. Because these markets also appeared to be controlled by the Muslim world, they were open to "justified" attack in the new mercantile competition between the Christian and the Islamic rulers and merchants. The Portuguese King quickly put da Gama's knowledge to use. During the years following the explorer's return, a continuous succession of maritime expeditions was sent in his wake. Their object was to take booty from the established entrepôts, set up a system of taxation that would produce an income for the Portuguese crown from the trading activities, and eventually gain control of all commerce throughout the Indian Ocean.

The Portuguese never achieved their central aim of dominating this lucrative Indian Ocean trade, perhaps because their country was too small and poor in resources, its social system never sufficiently geared to the needs of maritime paramountcy. In any case, by 1580 Portugal was absorbed by the Spanish monarchy, which never possessed the commercial vision to pursue the initial gains made by Portuguese merchants and sailors. But the appearance of the Portuguese in the Indian Ocean brought to an end a period of comparative calm for the African coast. Henceforth, invasion, sackings, rapine, looting, arson, and even reported cannibalism were to become the lot of the East African inhabitants. It was not solely the Portuguese who brought these disasters; Arabs, Turks, and certain African tribes also participated. Nor was the commerce of East Africa ever totally destroyed; certain ports virtually disappeared during this period, but others maintained some trade, though reduced in quantity and in importance to the Indian Ocean circuit.

The fact was that the Portuguese had nothing to offer East Africa, but the trading pattern was not strong enough to survive unscathed the entrance of a new power with crusading, mercantile zeal and superior military techniques. Indeed, the rulers of the African city ports had every reason to look with suspicion on the arrival of newcomers displaying an obvious desire to seize riches they had not earned. According to the *Kilwa Chronicle*, written some twenty years after the first appearance of the Portuguese, and not always reliable, they were considered "corrupt and dishonest men, who had come to spy out the land in order to seize it."

The reactions of the African rulers varied according to what they saw as their immediate interests. But they constantly ignored the one crucial tactic for their protection. Each of them insisted on acting independently, refusing to cooperate in an alliance that would have provided their only chance of repelling the invader. So, when Kilwa, which was in decline when the Portuguese arrived, after negotiating to pay tribute to da Gama on his second voyage in 1502, tried to resist attacks in 1505, it was sacked, and its neighbors did not come to its aid. Mombasa suffered the same fate in the same year and again in 1529. Ports up the coast were threatened in the following year. Of these, Lamu and Pate surrendered without resistance but Oja and Brava tried to repel the attackers and were both sacked, their buildings burned to the ground. The divided face proferred to the invader was visible most clearly in the case of Mombasa and Malindi. The King of Mombasa suggested an alliance to his fellow monarch in 1502, but the latter, regarding Mombasa as his chief enemy, preferred to come to terms with the Portuguese. He had made an arrangement with da Gama during the latter's 1498 voyage, and he remained Portugal's main ally throughout its period of aggression.

Eventually Portugal succeeded in imposing its authority over the coastal cities and in destroying those that resisted. Sofala, the seat of the gold trade, was seized in 1505, but rebellion against the new rulers quickly broke out. The gold trade declined, and the Portuguese found it almost impossible to make a profit out of it. The local people quietly refused to cooperate with the new masters, finding many means of smuggling gold out of the country and thereby circumventing Portuguese designs. The occupation of Kilwa led to further local resistance and many people left. The break in Kilwa's control of the Sofala gold trade ruined its economy. Meanwhile, Portugal's attempt to tax and control Indian Ocean trade through its occupation of the East African coast proved self-defeating. Commerce across the ocean rapidly declined in the face of such interference. With insufficient naval power, too few settlers or officials, and an inability to cooperate with the Arabs, Africans, and Indians on whom trade depended, the Portuguese soon proved incapable of accomplishing their grand design of turning the Indian Ocean into their own golden lake.

Nevertheless, despite the decline caused by their policies, the Portuguese held on to their tenuous power in East Africa until the end of the seventeenth century. Several attempts were made to dislodge them. The Turks began to raid down the coast in the second half of the sixteenth century. The Indian Ocean had become the new setting for a continuation of the Crusades, with Christian and Muslim each regarding the possessions of his rival as objects of looting and destruction. With the appearance of Ali Bey in 1585, the Turkish raids took on more significance. Not only did he plunder the cities he visited; he also urged the local inhabitants to revolt against the Portuguese. The first attempts at coastal revolt could be easily suppressed by Portuguese naval power based on Goa. But, in 1588, Ali Bey again visited the coast, the cities as far south as Pemba rose against Portugal, their inhabitants taking violent revenge for the massacres they had previously suffered at the hands of their alien rulers. This time the Portuguese were prepared. They quickly sent another fleet from Goa, defeated the Turks, and invested them together with their Arab and African followers within the walls of Mombasa's fort.

At this point, there came a dramatic intervention from another outside source. A group of Africans named Zimba by the Portuguese had begun to march northward from the lower valley of the Zambezi. A warrior band, they fought and killed as they went, but no explanation has been discovered as to why they left their homeland in the first place. In Mozambique, they slaughtered Portuguese and Arab settlers. Another of their expeditions moved up the coast. In 1587, it found its way across the mud flats at low tide into Kilwa, massacred its inhabitants, and sacked the city.

Immediately after the Portuguese had driven the Turks, Arabs, and Africans into the walled town of Mombasa, the Zimba arrived. Acknowledging the supremacy of the Portuguese on the sea but claiming dominance on land, the captain of the band proposed that it be left to complete the work of destruction begun by the Portuguese navy. So once more Mombasa was sacked, this time with horrible ferocity, the Zimba captain's ambition being, in the words of dos Santos, "to kill and eat every living thing in the land."

Then there appeared yet another force to add to the terrors of this destructive period of east-coast history. The Segeju tribe from the northeast, driven from their pastures by invasions from the Galla, began to move southward, also in a warlike mood. They encountered the Zimba as the latter were surrounding Malindi, whose King, still in alliance with the Portuguese, was defending the town with the aid of thirty European soldiers. The Segeju took the Zimba from the rear, killing all but a hundred, and thus spared Portugal's ally the fate of Kilwa and Mombasa.

This period of violence and destruction left much of the coastal belt depopulated and created a vacuum that was to be filled over the next century by further migrations from the interior. But it did not deter the Portuguese. In fact, it made them more determined to defend their overlordship. An Italian architect designed Fort Jesus for them in Mombasa, and Indian masons and laborers from Malindi built the fort, which was to protect Portuguese interests along the northern coastline. As a reward for his allegiance, the Portuguese made the King of Malindi Sultan of Mombasa, and Portuguese officials were stationed at key points down the coast. But Portugal was unable to restore prosperity to the trade of the Indian Ocean, while memories of feud and massacre kept the coast in continued agitation.

During the sixteenth century, the Portuguese had been content merely to receive tribute from the coastal towns. But, after the building of Fort Jesus, something resembling a Portuguese East African empire was created. It was based in Mombasa, where the Malindi ruler, Sheikh Ahmad, established himself as Sultan with a Portuguese garrison. Mombasa therefore became the military and commercial base for Portuguese power throughout the seventeenth century. Yet the government of Portugal never succeeded in building the kind of empire it wanted. It tried to persuade Portuguese to settle on the East African coast, but little interest was evinced. The most it was able to do was to attract a number of traders to move from Malindi and elsewhere to Mombasa, Zanzibar, and Pate and to increase the Portuguese share in trade, mainly with India. But this was bound to be on a small scale, for the Portuguese never established communications with the interior, from which came most of the products valued by the outside world.

Even in Mombasa itself, Portuguese power was never really secure. The Sultan, Sheikh Ahmad, who began to quarrel with the
Portuguese commandant, was not reassured by a visit to the Viceroy
of Goa, and he fled back to the mainland, where the Portuguese
bribed members of the Nyika tribe to murder him. This action
was disapproved of by Lisbon, which only wanted peace, trade, and
tribute from Mombasa. Ahmad's son Yusuf was therefore sent to
Goa to be educated as a Christian. He returned to Mombasa as
Sultan in 1627, not only converted but married to a Portuguese lady.
By 1631, Yusuf had reverted to Islam; on the Feast of the Assumption that year, he stabbed the commandant and called on his
people to revolt against their Portuguese masters. The Portuguese
were either slaughtered or sent as slaves to Mecca; Fort Jesus was
seized. An avenging fleet sent from Goa the next year failed to take
the fort. A second reprisal fleet arrived the year after, however, and
found the fort abandoned, the town in ruins, and the Sultan gone.
The Mombasa revolt had failed to secure serious support elsewhere
on the coast, though a few local rulers refused to pay tribute. It
did not take the Portuguese long to establish a new garrison in
Mombasa and regain their hold on the coast.

By the middle of the century, however, Portuguese power began
to show signs of decline. Across the Indian Ocean, they were increasingly being challenged by the Dutch and British. Their positions on the Persian Gulf and in Arabia were under attack by a revived Persia and by Oman, which was eventually to assist the
East African states in overthrowing Portuguese power in East
Africa.

The people of Mombasa and the Sheikh of Pate asked the Imam
of Oman to help them remove the "iron yoke and the injustices"
Portugal had imposed on them. In 1652, the Imam sent a fleet,
which wiped out the Portuguese of Zanzibar and Pate. Mombasa
was raided in 1660, and nine years later an expedition reached as far
south as Mozambique. The Portuguese took savage reprisals, be-
heading several rulers, including those of Pate and Lamu in 1678,
and, in 1686, they deported the King of Pate to Goa, where he and
twelve of his councilors were killed two years later.

But Omani intervention against the Portuguese was gathering momentum in alliance with the discontented local populations. The conflict between the Portuguese and their new enemies was approaching its dénouement. In 1696, an Omani fleet entered Kilindini harbor and laid siege to Mombasa for thirty-three months, until the defenders, exhausted and almost exterminated by hunger and disease, finally surrendered. With the fall of Mombasa, Portuguese power north of the Rovumu River was ended. They made a number of halfhearted attempts to recapture the fort on which their dominion had been based, but all except one failed. In 1728, Portugal did manage to take advantage of hostility between the Omani garrison and local inhabitants to recapture the fort and hold it for nearly two years. But, once again, the people of Mombasa became infuriated by the arrogance of their Portuguese overlords; with the assistance of neighboring Nyika warriors, they rose against them and drove them from fort and town for good. The period of Portuguese ascendancy on the coast north of the Rovumu had finally ended.

During the seventeenth century, there had been frequent movement among the peoples living in the immediate coastal hinterland. Indeed, the dislocation of life occasioned by this constant movement and the conflict it entailed had been one of the factors lowering resistance to the Portuguese. In general, the movement of peoples was from north to south. The Galla, from the north, pressed by the Somali and seeking new pastures, began a drive against the tribes of the Shungwaya area—an area that was, in any case, becoming more difficult to inhabit, because of increasing dessication. As a result, the peoples of this area, and particularly the Nyika, or Miji Kenda (Nine Tribes), as they now prefer to be called, began to seek safety in the hills. Pressure from the Galla also led to the abandonment of a number of Swahili settlements on the coast, the inhabitants usually moving southward to the better protected islands or to new settlements on the Tanganyikan coast further from their persecutors. It was during the latter part of the seventeenth century that most of today's Swahili communities of Mombasa, the Nyika tribes of the hinterland, and the small Swahili settlements of the Tanzanian coast first occupied their present homes.

If the seventeenth century was characterized by Portuguese dominance of the East African coast, the eighteenth brought its partial replacement by Omani influence. This was important culturally as well as politically. Under the dominance of the Portuguese and as a result of the dislocation caused by Galla raids, Arab influence in the coastal towns had seriously declined during the sixteenth and seventeenth centuries. With the appearance of Omani governors, garrisons, and merchants, the eighteenth century saw some revival of cultural influences from Arabia.

Yet the coastal towns were by no means inclined to lose the independence for which they had constantly fought against the Portuguese and each other. The return of the Portuguese to Mombasa in 1728 provided one sign of their unwillingness to accept Omani rule as an alternative to that of Portugal, for the return was the result of a treaty between the Sheikh of Pate and the Viceroy of Goa. The fact was that the rulers of East Africa were anxious to secure help from the outside against any alien rulers but were just as determined that their allies should not be allowed to assume power in their stead. They remained equally suspicious of each other, never approaching the joint East African alliance that might have kept all foreign aspirants at bay.

The Omanis' position in East Africa during the eighteenth century never attained the imperial power of their Portuguese predecessors. For one thing, they were continually at odds with each other in their homeland, where dynastic civil wars were frequent, and at the same time they often had to defend themselves against attacks from the Persians. Thus, few of their imams had sufficient time or resources to spare any for East Africa. Paradoxically, though, this internal situation in Oman actually strengthened one strand of power on the African coast, for it was as a result of civil strife in Oman during the year 1741 that the Mazrui family began its long and influential connection with Mombasa and other coastal towns. In that year, the Busaidi family, in the person of Ahmad ibn Said, seized power in Oman, whereupon the Mazrui governor of Mombasa renounced allegiance to Oman and declared Mombasa independent. Five years later, he was murdered by Busaidi agents for his defiance. His brother, Ali Mazrui was imprisoned, but he later escaped, defeated the newly appointed governor, and reasserted the independence of Mombasa. This was a struggle between two Omani families: The Mazruis increasingly identified themselves with Africa and the local inhabitants regarded them as a ruling family opposed to the power of Oman. Despite repeated attempts, the Busaidis could not drive the Mazruis from their African bases during the eighteenth century.

This Mazrui family now became involved in the domestic conflicts of East Africa. Rivalry continued between Mombasa and Pate, until they agreed to share the island of Pemba, which was important to Mombasa as a source of rice. Subsequently, the conflict reopened, with the Mazruis attempting to influence the succession to Pate's sultanate in their favor, eventually succeeding early in the nineteenth century, when Pate became virtually a Mombasan protectorate. Zanzibar, too, which had remained loyal to the Busaidis, was attacked by the Mombasans, though with only partial success. On the mainland, the settlements between Tanga and Malindi accepted some form of allegiance to Mombasa and its Mazrui rulers.

The success of the Mazruis during the eighteenth century in leading Mombasa back to dominance of the coast stemmed to a great extent from their constructive domestic policy. When they first became governors of the town, the Swahili inhabitants were divided between two federations that were often in conflict. The Mazrui achievement was to bridge the hostile gap between the two by securing the acceptance of both in recognizing them as heads of state. Once this was accomplished, it also proved possible to attract the support of the Nyika communities, which then provided Mombasa with valuable trade opportunities and supplies of soldiers. Yet, despite its renewed power and influence, Mombasa, like the rest of the coast, had seen most of its former Indian Ocean trade greatly diminished. Although the eighteenth century saw greater independence for the coastal settlements, the freedom was alloyed with comparative poverty.

Kilwa was the first state to discover a new source of wealth. It had been in decline since before the Portuguese arrived, and their treatment of it had hastened its slide from the proud position it had held in the fourteenth and fifteenth centuries. Yet Kilwa shared the desire of the other East African states for independence from alien control. The King even appealed to the Portuguese in Mozambique for aid in ridding himself and his people of Omani governors and garrisons, but in vain. However, the Omanis were often weakened by conflict at home, and during one of these periods, in 1771, the local people managed to force the Governor to leave. Kilwa was left alone for only nine years, but those were momentous years, during which trade revived so dramatically as to cause the Omanis to come hurrying back in 1780 in order to participate in the newly found wealth.

It was the slave trade that provided this new opportunity for the people of Kilwa. Slaves had been exported from East Africa for many centuries, being sent to markets in Arabia, Persia, India, and China. But the trade had never been large; according to the extant records, it had always been of less importance than trade in material goods such as ivory or gold. It was the French colonization of Mauritius, then called Île de France, and neighboring islands that caused the sudden boom in slave-trading from Kilwa and surrounding areas of the coast toward the end of the eighteenth century.

From the 1730's on, the French expanded the economies of their Indian Ocean islands. They increased sugar-planting, built textile and dyeing factories, constructed roads and bridges, and encouraged European settlement. Economic development created a demand for labor, which was first answered by seeking slaves in Madagascar. Local opinion on that island soon showed itself strongly hostile to slaving, however, while on the mainland the Portuguese tried to prevent other European countries from engaging in the trade.

A French sailor called Morice saw the opportunity in these circumstances for promoting a large-scale East African slave trade and succeeded in securing a monopoly of slave purchases in Zanzibar and Kilwa. From this time on the French and the Arabs followed the West African pattern of slave-trading. French ships took East African human cargoes not only to French islands in the Indian Ocean and to the East Indies but also around the Cape and across the Atlantic to their West Indian possessions and to the Spanish

West Indies. Arab dhows took them to Muscat, the Red Sea, and the markets of the Persian Gulf. Profits, both for the traders and for the rulers and merchants of East Africa, were enormous. Although figures regarding the slave trade are always speculative, it can be calculated from the report of a French captain in 1804 that over six thousand slaves were exported from Kilwa each year, and from another by an English captain in 1811 that six thousand to ten thousand slaves were being shipped annually from Zanzibar. At the same time, as had been seen in West Africa, though the slave trade provided riches for the few, the community as a whole suffered from this form of commerce. It encouraged warfare, inhibited genuine economic development, and inevitably brought great suffering to large numbers of people. Zanzibar showed some signs of prosperity as a result of the demand for slaves, though perhaps three out of every four inhabitants of the island were slaves; the rest of the coast, including Kilwa, experienced short booms, between periods of depression.

It was becoming apparent that, if the Omanis were to assert any serious authority along the East African coast, they would need to establish there a more united and better-organized presence. Yet, until the beginning of the nineteenth century, their dynastic conflicts at home made this impossible. With the death of the founder of the Busaidi dynasty, Ahmad ibn Said al Busaidi, in 1783, disputes over the succession erupted. The fresh importance accorded East Africa was evidenced by the involvement in these disputes of certain Swahili states. One of the rival contestants and his son sailed to Kilwa and Zanzibar in 1784, hoping to create a new domain for himself, but, though Kilwa accepted the new pretender, Zanzibar held out against him. The next year two more of the Busaidi clan arrived with a force that relieved Zanzibar and recaptured Kilwa, exiling the pretender to Lamu.

These dynastic struggles continued with several changes of fortune until 1806, when Sayyid Said finally established his paramount power by murdering his brother. It was to be under Sayyid Said's rule that Oman built its nineteenth-century East African empire based on Zanzibar, bringing a new and stronger ruling dynasty to the Swahili coast and initiating events that were to take East African peoples into the vortex of a newly developing international policy.

The dominance of Sayyid Said on the East African coast was not established without bitter struggles. When he first came to power, he had to consolidate his position in Muscat. At this time, Mombasa under the Mazruis was still the most powerful force on the coast— or *mrima,* as it is known in Swahili. In 1807, the Mazruis took advantage of a succession dispute in Pate and installed their own candidate. Then they overreached themselves. Pursuing their aggressive policy, they followed the success in Pate by attacking Lamu, where they met with a fateful defeat at the battle of Shela, the date of which is variously given as 1810 and 1812. This battle marked the beginning of Mombasa's decline, ended Pate's history of supremacy in the Bajun Islands, and opened the road for Sayyid Said to undermine Mazrui power. For Lamu immediately appealed to Muscat for protection; Said sent the island a governor and a garrison.

When the new ruler of Oman had sufficiently consolidated his position in Muscat to turn his attention to East Africa, he possessed two significant advantages over his Mazrui rivals. He had built a firm base in his homeland and he had established an alliance with Great Britain, the foremost European power, soon to become the strongest nation in the world. When Said had seized power he had been only fifteen years old; this fact, together with his firm control, allowed him to rule for half a century, a factor of great importance to East Africa in that it spared the people of the coast the dislocation of constant changes of dynasty and policy. Meanwhile, Said had to estimate the relative advantages of forming an alliance with either Britain or France, contenders for hegemony in Europe, in the Middle East, and across the Indian Ocean. He shrewdly chose to maintain treaties already made with Britain, though he retained a foot in the French camp until the decisive battle of Waterloo. By East African standards, Oman was a great power, but Said knew that in a world perspective his country had little importance. Thus, his alliance with Britain brought a two-tiered power structure to East Africa. Oman, infinitely stronger than any *mrima* state, was the immediate governing power, but behind it stood the much greater strength of nineteenth-century Britain, now beginning a period of world hegemony. That East Africa had begun to recognize the importance of such alliances was demonstrated by the fact that the Mazruis, too, sought Britain's aid, by sending delegations to Bombay, capital of British India. Britain rejected the Mazrui offers of overlordship, but it was now clear that the tradition of calling for foreign help to combat interference by other alien powers was to remain a significant political factor in the East African scene.

Sayyid Said awaited his opportunity to assert his authority on the Swahili coast. It was not until 1823 that the chance came to undermine Mazrui power directly. In that year, another succession dispute in Pate gave him the opportunity to take issue directly with the Mazruis. One faction appealed to Muscat for help against the Mazrui nominee. Said sent an Omani fleet, which quickly achieved Pate's submission. It then sailed to Pemba, where it was again victorious. Brava, on the north coast, and Lamu soon recognized Said's authority. Within a short time, therefore, Said had isolated the Mazruis in Mombasa. But it was not until 1837 that he managed to prize them out of their stronghold. He had hoped to do so immediately after his other conquests. He was prevented from achieving his objective by the intervention of an unusual British captain.

As the Omani fleet was in the process of bombarding Fort Jesus early in 1824, Captain William Fitzwilliam Wentworth Owen, commanding a survey ship, sailed into Mombasa harbor. Despite consistent refusals from London and Bombay of Mazrui requests for protection, Captain Owen, convinced that the Omanis were the worst slaving offenders, personally agreed to set up a British protectorate over Mombasa. Fearing to challenge the British, the Omani fleet withdrew. It was some time before the event was fully reported in London and Bombay. In any case, the British government, determined to stamp out the slave trade in East as in West Africa, was undecided as to how to handle Owen's *fait accompli*. For three years, British officers remained in Mombasa. Not until 1826 were they ordered to withdraw. Bereft of protection, the Mazruis could hardly hope to hold out against Said indefinitely.

For a time in the following year, they submitted to him and Omani troops occupied the fort, but in 1828 it was reoccupied by the Mazruis. Said made several subsequent attacks on it and conducted a series of negotiations, but he was still frequently preoccupied with revolts in Oman itself. It was not until the Mazruis resumed their traditional family quarrels over the succession in 1835–37 that Said finally achieved his goal. This time, his forces occupied Fort Jesus, the leading Mazruis were expelled from Mombasa, and the Arab appointed as governor divided domestic authority between the two Swahili federations. Said was now unchallenged master of the coast; he marked his achievement and demonstrated his personal interest by moving his capital from Muscat to Zanzibar, from where he presided over much of East African history for the next twenty years.

Sayyid Said's achievement in East Africa was much more than political. Under the conditions created by his government, trade once again flourished and caravans were encouraged to penetrate far into the hinterland. Early in the century, such trade had merely supplemented the commerce in grain up and down the coast and to southern Arabia; by the middle of the century, ivory and slaves had become a vital part of trading wealth. Said's rule and his encouragement of trade stimulated this increased commercial activity, as did financing by Indian capitalists.

Small Indian communities had lived in many of the larger *mrima* towns at least since the beginning of the nineteenth century, attracted there by the commercial opportunities provided by the reviving Indian Ocean trade. Indeed, Britain's first direct involvement with East Africa was occasioned by their presence. In 1811, a Captain Smee was sent by the Bombay government down the East African coast and found the Indian merchants excessively taxed by Said's government. He queried the right of Said to tax British subjects and left a brig behind to protect their interests. By the time caravan trade had expanded to significant proportions, Indians had sufficiently prospered to provide most of the capital for growth in agriculture, ivory, and slave-trading that, because of Said's initiative, made Zanzibar the base for renewed prosperity along the coast.

Yet the foundation of the *mrima* boom was just the form of trade that the British were attempting to extirpate. Although trade in ivory, grain, and various exotic goods continued to attract merchants from overseas, the sale of human labor to Arabia, the Caribbean, the French Indian Ocean islands, and then to Zanzibar itself and to nearby coastal settlements formed the staple of revived commercial wealth. For the last thirty years or so of his reign, Sayyid Said occupied the peculiar position of being Britain's chief ally on the East African coast, from which the British were trying to abolish the slave trade, and yet depending for his wealth and power on that same trade. For, although part of Said's achievement was the creation of a stable government under which commerce could be encouraged, he also led the way in active economic development, particularly by introducing into Zanzibar the clove plantations that were to provide the bulk of the island's economy for the next century. And plantations needed slave labor, whether they were growing sugar in Mauritius and the West Indies or cloves in Zanzibar. Moreover, the slave trade itself supplied Said's treasury with important contributions, for the vast market that developed in Zanzibar produced substantial taxes. At the same time, an attempt by Said to diminish or abolish the trade brought him into conflict with the very merchants on whom he depended for his economic and political power. This dilemma developed into the main factor in his reign; that it never caused his overthrow is a tribute to his diplomatic and political shrewdness.

The British assault on Indian Ocean slave trade was based on their administrations in Mauritius (which they had taken from the French) and Bombay. Their officials could not close their eyes to the obstacles, for slaves had become the main source of plantation labor, they were widely used in India, and the trade itself was extremely lucrative. Compromise therefore seemed inevitable, but the British in both Bombay and Mauritius recognized that, if the trade was to be even reduced, they would have to start at the source, which involved dealing with Sayyid Said.

During the Napoleonic wars, Oman was strategically vital to Britain's efforts to prevent the French from opening a way to India.

It was not until after the wars ended, therefore, that determined action could be taken to persuade Said that he must cooperate with the British in attacking the slave trade. The concessions required if Said was not to be overthrown by his own people were evidenced in the Moresby Treaty of 1822. Mauritius and Bombay pressed Said to cooperate in ending the slave trade, but with the proviso that, if he found this impossible, at least the trade between Omani subjects and Christian countries should be abolished. These provisions were embodied in the treaty Said signed. Of equal importance, however, was the recognition in the treaty that the slave trade among Muslims within Said's dominions could continue, and these dominions were recognized by Britain as including the whole East African coast north of Cape Delgado. Thus, even before the reduction of the Mazruis, Said had secured British support for his claims over the coast, a factor of infinite importance to him in asserting his authority over Mombasa and other recalcitrant settlements.

The slave trade therefore continued throughout Said's reign and, indeed, for most of the century. It was marked by the same horrors that had been witnessed in West Africa, though not, perhaps, by the same degree of warfare. Caravans combed the interior and marched their captives, often strung together in lines, to the coast, where they were kept in compounds until a sailing ship or a dhow arrived. Then they were loaded on to it, packed as tightly as possible, often on shelves with just sufficient room to lie flat. The ship or dhow would then make the long journey to Arabia, India, or, from the Portuguese area of the coast, to Brazil. The slaves suffered unimaginably, and, in many of the agricultural districts from which they had been seized, the reduction of manpower that resulted from their capture led to land deterioration and famine.

Despite the tragic effects of the slave trade, the measure of centralized control achieved by Said and his commercial interest brought new prosperity to the coast. Caravans to the interior substantially increased, seeking ivory as well as slaves. People from the interior appeared on the coast more often, bringing their own wares or those they had bartered for with their neighbors. The Nyika acted as middlemen between the Kamba and Swahili, Arab, and Indian merchants on the coast. The Kamba themselves began to bring their ivory to Mombasa. The Nyamwezi came down to the coast opposite Zanzibar; the Yao, to Kilwa. The conditions established by Said in Zanzibar encouraged the Indians to finance expeditions to the interior conducted by Arabs with African porters, he himself financing some of them. The first sizable two-way traffic between interior and coast began to develop. Cloth, wire, beads, and firearms purchased from foreign merchants were taken into the heart of East Africa and exchanged for the ivory that was in such demand in Europe and America during the mid-nineteenth century. Coastal commercial prosperity had always depended to varying degrees on the production of the interior peoples; now the relationship was beginning to change from dependence to partnership. East Africa began to emerge as a unit, still with two components, but with progressive interdependence.

Said's policy to raise revenues for his government services, the forces needed to maintain his power in Oman and on the coast, and his personal resources was simple and effective. He abolished the web of import-export taxes that had been the traditional means of raising revenue on the coast and substituted one import tax of 5 per cent on all goods entering his ports, retaining an export tax on the slave trade alone. Because he had only a small bureaucracy, he farmed out the tax collection to Indian firms, just as medieval English kings employed their feudal nobles. Thus, increased economic activity brought him greater revenues but no higher expense. Such activity was encouraged by the wealth it brought to the Indian community, which was consequently attracted by the rewards gained by financing it from their profits. The success of this economic policy was marked by the appointment of American, British, and French consuls and by the presence of four German commercial firms. East Africa, with its base in Zanzibar, was entering the international trading community.

This renewed prosperity made Zanzibar an attractive port of call for foreigners, an excellent source of livelihood for Said's followers, and a valuable locus of investment for the Indians;

yet it brought much misery to most of the island's inhabitants. We have already seen something of the agonies suffered by slaves. The local serfs, too, suffered from the activities that put wealth into their masters' pockets. On both Zanzibar and Pemba, the clearing of the land best suited to establishing clove plantations that were to make the islands the clove center of the world, pushed the local people on to less productive areas, where they were crowded together to scratch for a living. The Arab landowners, their local allies, and the Indian financiers might prosper; rapidly rising exports of ivory, cloves, gum copal, and slaves, together with correspondingly increased revenues, proved the point; but it was estimated in the middle of the century that only about one in five of the 450,000 inhabitants of the two islands was regarded as a free man—the other four were slaves from the mainland or local serfs.

The fates of other port towns on the coast varied. Kilwa had risen again in economic importance, owing to its attractions for French slavers. But it provided a tragic example of the dangers arising from concentrating solely on the slave trade. The greed induced by the trade prevented the wealth gained out of it from developing the economy of the town. It remained a dirty, mud-hut, slave-market town. As soon as the trade was reduced and then abolished, Kilwa rapidly declined. Two cholera epidemics in the second half of the century, feeding on the filth and poverty of the town, ended its social importance; what had been described as the most beautiful town on the coast sank into insignificance.

Tanga had a totally different experience. It is true that the town was used as a slave port, but not exclusively. It gained prominence through its favorable position as a base from which a growing number of caravans into the interior could start. It therefore enjoyed all the benefits of supplying these expeditions and reaping profits on their return. Consequently, by the middle of the century, its population had exceeded even that of Mombasa. Other neighboring coastal towns enjoyed the same fortune. Pangani, for instance, rivaled Tanga in size and reportedly exported up to 35,000 pounds of ivory annually, while Bagamoyo, opposite Zanzibar, became the base for many of the expeditions traveling to the lands of the Nyamwezi and to Lake Tanganyika.

Farther south, along the Mozambique coast, virtually the only commerce remaining was in slaves. In 1822, the Captain Owen who had become famous in Mombasa gave to the British authorities a report on one of the ports, which throws some light on conditions at the time:

> From eleven to fourteen slave ships come every year from Rio de Janeiro to this place, and go back with, on the average, four to five hundred slaves each. . . . They buy these slaves for blue dungaree, coloured cloths, arms, gunpowder, brass and pewter, red coloured beads in imitation of coral, cutlery. . . . To contain the slaves they have collected for sale, every Portuguese house has a big yard or enclosure, called a barracoon, usually surrounded by a high rock wall.

The captain noted that much of the country around was very poor, unable to supply itself with sufficient food, although in the past it had provided grain to other settlements along the coast.

The revival of commercial prosperity on the *mrima* affected not only the coastal peoples in their port towns but also many peoples of the interior. The growing demand for slaves inevitably brought violence, thuggery, and sorrow to many communities. But the trade in ivory, at least as important, constituted an exchange of goods on a scale never before experienced in this region. The Nyamwezi had traveled to the coast since the early eighteenth century. The Yao from northern Mozambique and southern Tanzania traded from Lake Nyasa to Kilwa. Some goods from abroad reached the Baganda by the end of the eighteenth century. A few Swahili from the coast had begun to venture inland along these various trade routes by the same period.

The coastal revival not only stimulated Arab and Swahili traders from the coast to become more venturesome in the interior; it also greatly encouraged those African communities with trading flair to increase their own activities. Thus a great part of the hinterland of East Africa saw a rapid growth in trading routes and exchange of goods, progressively widening communications throughout the nineteenth century.

The effect of this trade growth on the peoples of the interior varied according to their local strength and the character of the trade. In the south, the main sellers of slaves, the Yao, were far too strong to be challenged by Arab and Swahili traders. It was the Yao chiefs themselves who usually organized slave raids; they then sold their captives to visiting merchants for cloth, wire, beads, or firearms or took them to the coast themselves. In the central regions of Tanzania, however, the situation was different. Here slave trading was always secondary to the quest for ivory, which took the seekers to Ujiji, across Lake Tanganyika to the Congo, and north to Buganda. It was mainly the Arabs who conducted the slave trade, largely in order to secure porterage for their ivory cargoes en route to the coast. The Nyamwezi and Gogo were principally interested in the ivory trade, though certainly some of their merchants acquired large numbers of slaves. To the north, the situation again was different. Here, there was little slave raiding, for the routes were liable to be more strongly contested and the amiability of the Africans was therefore more important. The Kamba dominated trade in this region until they were supplanted by Arabs toward the latter part of the century. The Chagga around Mount Kilimanjaro provided a valuable market, and the search for ivory took traders to the shores of Lake Victoria or northward as far as Lake Rudolph.

As a result of this penetration, many small Arab commercial centers were established in various parts of East Africa where traders settled and came to terms with local Africans. One result was the valuable spread of the Swahili language throughout East Africa, but it was a small benefit in the face of the slave raiding and the wars, dislocation of life, and subsequent famine and disease that accompanied it. Some African communities were brought under Arab influence and thus prevented from uniting in a common front. Others deliberately allied themselves with the Arabs, either in procuring slaves or in finding ivory. Yet nowhere did Arab roots sink very deep, there was little cultural influence and few conversions to Islam. When the Europeans arrived, they found the Arabs but a slender barrier to the establishment of their power.

One of the important by-products of the increased trade in the interior and the slave trade was the introduction of new political systems and social structures. Trade naturally centered on towns, which consequently attracted many immigrants from the rural districts. This movement was accelerated by slave raiding, which made life in the villages increasingly hazardous. Thus, larger social units were being developed, necessitating stronger political structures to give them order. The *ntemi* system of chieftainship spread more widely than ever before, providing a central governmental direction essential for the lawful conditions needed for trade and for protection against the brigandage associated with the slave trade.

These developments were hastened by another external influence arriving at the same time—a wave of invasions by the Ngoni people from the south—which was to play a major role in the life and social structure of East Africa's future.

The Ngoni originated in South Africa, where they encountered the ruthless power of Shaka, the military chief of the Zulu. Led by their chief, Zwangendaba, the Ngoni fled from the might of Shaka's army about 1820, moved northward across the Zambezi into Malawi and Zambia, and eventually reached the Fipa area of Tanzania during the 1840's. On their travels, they had encountered, fought, and defeated many peoples. Their experience with Shaka had taught them the value of new military techniques: using short stabbing spears and shields in place of the old traditional throwing spear, keeping regiments organized by age groups as a standing army, and employing the tactic of outflanking and then encircling the enemy. They had also adopted the Zulu practice of assimilating their enemies after victory, using their warriors in their own army, integrating the women and children into their social structure.

Zwangendaba died in 1848, and his achievement in forging

a united nation was quickly dissipated. The Ngoni splintered into five groups; one, known as the Gwangara, marched eastward to Songea. Here it met another Ngoni group known as the Maseko which had traveled independently of Zwangendaba's followers. Eventually, the Maseko were driven out of Songea and they settled in Mozambique. This left the Gwangara to dominate the region between Lake Nyasa and the coast, constantly raiding other communities in their efforts to expand their dominion. In this they were often imitated by various robber bands who used Ngoni methods in order to take advantage of disturbed conditions and seize captives for sale to the slave merchants.

A second splinter from the Fipa region was called the Tuta. This group moved northward, only to be repelled by the Holoholo beside Lake Tanganyika. The Tuta therefore continued their northward march, cutting right across the trade routes between Tabora and Ujiji. They eventually established themselves north of Tabora, disrupting the central regions of Tanzania and constantly assaulting the Nyamwezi, many of whom became their prisoners.

Once again, however, some positive results accrued from the disasters of invasion and warfare. We have already seen that the Holoholo were strong enough to resist the Ngoni. This was because some of them, on encountering a section of the Ngoni on the west bank of Lake Tanganyika, had fled across the lake and then adopted Ngoni tactics. Similarly the Sangu, to the east of the Fipa Plateau, having suffered from Ngoni invasion, later recognized the value of unity and were forced together by the conquests of their strongest chief, Mwahawangu. Their neighbors, the Hehe, learned Ngoni lessons so well that they not only united but, under their powerful chief Mkwawa, challenged the Gwangara and dominated the southern regions of Tanzania alongside the Songea Ngoni. The Mbunga, a branch of the Maseko Ngoni, used Ngoni methods of reunification after their dispersal, eventually settling near Morogoro and mounting frequent raids against their neighbors. At the same time, as we have seen previously, Mirambo was building a strong Nyamwezi state; Isike created a parallel one from another section of the same tribe.

Thus, because of the twin influences of trade and invasion, political and military organization was becoming stronger in many parts of the country during the middle part of the century. Both slaving and warfare brought considerable devastation and gross dislocation of life; many smaller communities were weakened, absorbed, or wiped out; famine struck often and disease frequently accompanied it. Nevertheless, the stronger peoples, because they were forced to meet new challenges, sought new forms of organization for their protection; these were to strengthen social and political structures while creating new opportunities for local economic advance.

The newly-found strength of even the most powerful of these tribal states was, of course, quite insufficient to resist Europeans; for, during the nineteenth century, much of Western Europe had been developing techniques that gave its states a technological power hitherto unknown to man. It was not until the latter part of the century, however, that Europe displayed any deliberate design to intervene directly in the affairs of East Africa. Earlier, Europeans had been mainly interested in the prospects of trade, though both Britain and France gave sidelong glances at the strategic importance of Zanzibar to their rival communications with India.

It was, in fact, the Americans who first displayed a serious commercial interest in East Africa. Until they gained independence from Britain, Americans had been excluded from the Indian Ocean by the monopoly granted to the British East India Company. After independence, a number of American vessels, especially from Boston and Salem, sought cargoes in India and other Asian waters. They were joined in the Indian Ocean by whaling ships, which began to call on the East African coast for fresh water and supplies. By 1833, American trade with the coast was sufficient to justify the signing of a treaty of friendship by Sayyid Said and an American officer, together with various commercial arrangements. Americans were allowed to trade in any port within Said's dominions, import duty was lowered from 7 to 5 per cent, and the U.S. President was to be allowed to appoint consuls to all ports engaged in this trade. The trade itself was never very large, but it brought to East Africa the white cotton cloth of Massachusetts mills that not only replaced most British and Indian cloth but became a common form of exchange throughout the region. From the East African ports the Americans took ivory, cloves, skins, and gumcopal.

Yet, despite this special American interest and some similar trading by the Germans and French, Britain retained the strongest influence in Zanzibar and, through its Sultan, along the coast. Throughout Sayyid Said's long reign, he carefully preserved his friendship with Britain, even when it endangered his reputation among his own people. The British were not only anxious to use their relations with Said to stamp out the slave trade, but remained suspicious of French ambitions in India, to which both Said's East African and Omani dominions could be strategically important. Constant pressure was exerted on Said to reduce the slave-trading of his subjects. The Moresby Treaty was followed in 1845 by the Hammerton Treaty, which prohibited the export of slaves from the Sultan's African empire to his Asian dominions, though coastal slave-trading was still allowed so as not to interfere with the domestic slavery on which many societies still depended.

The special influence of Britain on Zanzibar was clearly demonstrated after the death of Said in 1856. The succession was to be divided, with one son inheriting Oman and another Zanzibar. When the two came into conflict over the arrangement, they were persuaded to submit the decision to Lord Canning, Governor-General of India, who confirmed the territorial division made by Said, though with an annual payment made by the richer Zanzibar to Oman.

Up to then, the Sultan's policies had been constructed under the strong influence of the British consul. This influence greatly increased after Said's death, for his son Majid was a much weaker character. Indeed, he found politics in Zanzibar so wearing that he built himself a new home on the mainland, which he christened Dar es Salaam ("Haven of Peace"). Under the consulship of John Kirk, British influence over Majid and his successor, Barghash, became stronger than ever. It was marked by a new treaty, which prohibited all slave exports and decreed the closure of all slave markets. By this time, the Sultan, having flouted the slaving interests of many of his subjects, was almost entirely dependent on British support for maintaining his position. He even took a British officer as his Prime Minister. Kirk, meanwhile, pursued his campaign against the slave trade while loyally sustaining Barghash in office, but by then other eyes were seeking the attractions of the east coast, and Britain's policy of indirect influence without responsibility or absolute control was to prove inadequate for diverting them.

Trade and strategic considerations were not the only ones that attracted Europeans to East Africa in the nineteenth century. One of the factors that brought the region to the notice of people in Europe was the information gathered by missionaries and explorers. Their discoveries and revelations stimulated the antislavery campaign, attracted traders, and eventually paved the way for direct imperial control. They had but slight impact on African society but were encouraged to pursue their activities so long as they did not actively interfere in local affairs. Even the Arab Muslim traders settled in the region did little to obstruct Christian missionaries, except when the latter tried to undermine the slave trade. But, as soon as Europeans tried to penetrate the interior for commercial ends, they were repulsed. The Frenchman Segère, who tried to break into the ivory trade in 1881, had to flee for his life. Later, German attempts to establish trading stations were so resented by Arabs and Africans that one German lost his life. The only exception was the remarkable Irishman Charles Stokes, who succeeded in reaching a commercial agreement with the Nyamwezi.

Missionary activities were generally regarded more kindly. At first, they were usually associated with exploration, and the mission stations proliferated only after the discoveries of the explorers had become known in Europe. Two Germans, Krapf and Rebmann, were sent to East Africa by the British Church Missionary Society in 1844, Krapf visiting the Kingdom of Shambalai, inland from Tanga, and Rebmann the Chagga, beside Kilimanjaro. Burton and Speke followed the caravan route from Bagamoyo to Lake Tanganyika in 1857, Speke continuing northward to Lake Victoria. Grant, Barth, Roscher, Decker, Stanley, Thomson, Cameron, and others added their efforts to the exploration that was gradually mapping the interior of East and Central Africa. But it was David Livingstone, of course, who attracted most notice. His dramatic journeys and the reports he made of them appealed to both the romantic and the evangelical strains of nineteenth century European society. The effect was to secure missionary resources and personnel devoted to Livingstone's aims of combining Christianity and commerce with an effort to exorcise slavery and raise the standard of civilization.

Something of the romantic picture of life in Africa transmitted to Europe at this time may be envisioned from a description by the explorer Richard Burton, who visited the East African great lakes in 1858.

The African rises with the dawn from his couch of cowhide. The hut is cool and comfortable during the day, but the barred door impeding ventilation at night causes it to be close and disagreeable. The hour before sunrise being the coldest time, he usually kindles a fire, and addresses himself to his constant companion, the pipe. When the sun becomes sufficiently powerful, he removes the reed screen from the entrance, and issues forth to bask in the morning beams. The villages are populous, and the houses touching one another enable the occupants when squatting outside and fronting the central square, to chat and chatter without moving. About 7 a.m., when the dew has partially disappeared from the grass, the elder boys drive the flocks and herds to pasture with loud shouts and sound applications of the quarter-staffs. They return only when the sun is sinking behind the western horizon. At 8 a.m. those who have provisions at home enter the hut for reflection with ugali or holusporridge; those who have not, join a friend. Pombe, (beer), when procurable, is drunk from the earliest dawn. After breaking his fast the African repairs, pipe in hand, to the iwanza, the village "public", previously described. Here, in the society of his own sex, he will spend the greater part of the day talking and laughing, smoking or torpid with sleep. Occasionally he sits down to play. . . . Towards sunset all issue forth to enjoy the coolness: the men sit outside the iwanza, whilst the women and girls, after fetching water for household wants from the well, collecting in a group upon their little stools, indulge in the pleasures of gossip and the pipe. This hour in the most favoured parts of the country is replete with enjoyment, which even the barbarian feels, though not yet indoctrinated into aesthetics. As the hours of darkness draw nigh, the village doors are carefully closed, and, after milking his cows, each peasant retires to his hut, or passes the time in the iwanza.

Here, of course, is a perfect example of the overromanticized portrait of the "noble savage" that titillated so many Europeans in the nineteenth century. There is no mention of hunger or disease, hard work in fields and village, warfare, and slave raiding. Another British traveler, Joseph Thomson, more than twenty years later, was still mesmerized by an imaginative Arcadia when he described the scene as he saw it in the land of the Nyakusa, in 1880:

Imagine a magnificent grove of bananas, laden with bunches of fruit, each of which would form a man's load, growing on a perfectly level plain from which all weeds, garbage, and ugly things are carefully cleared away. Dotted here and there are a number of immense shady sycamore trees, with branches each almost as large as a separate tree. At every few paces are charmingly neat circular huts, with conical roofs, and walls . . . with the clay worked prettily into rounded bricks, and daubed symmetrically with spots.

The same writer, in the same year, described the scene in Ujiji, with "bands of Swahili, strings of slaves laden with grain or ivory, flocks of sheep and goats, and small herds of cattle together with canoes on the waters of the Lake."

The Church Missionary Society sent an expedition to Buganda in 1876, and, to support it, stations were planned along the route inland. One was established in Mpwapwa, an Arab trading center, and neither the Arabs nor the African ruler objected, though, when the slave trade was attacked by the missionaries, the Arabs bypassed the settlement. The London Missionary Society set up a station at Ujiji, but here, without violence, the Arabs prevented the missionaries from gaining serious influence over the local Ha people, and after five years the station was abandoned. The Roman Catholics were also active, the White Fathers in particular setting up stations on the shores of Lake Tanganyika. In all cases, the missionaries found that they were dependent on the attitude of local African rulers, who normally tolerated and helped them if they did not interfere in their affairs. Not all of the missionaries were blind to the anomalies into which they were led by the necessity of relying on African help. One of them wrote:

> The first thing on arriving in camp is, for us, who have carried nothing heavier than an umbrella and a monstrous hat, to rest—for the men, who have carried a load of 50 lb to 60 lb (sometimes more), generally on their heads, to fetch firewood and water. . . . The contrast will have struck you already. The people, to whom we have come to preach, lie on the ground or in a reed or grass hut, eat rice and a bit of dried fish . . . carry a load under a burning sun for ten to twelve miles which I should be sorry to carry for a mile in England, walk barefoot on the scorching ground while we live in grand houses or tents (palaces to these people), sleep on beds as comfortable as any at home, eat chickens (carried in a box alive), preserved meat, green peas (preserved), tea, cocoa, biscuits, bread, butter, jam.

By the 1870's, East Africa was attracting men of several European nations. Belgians, French, and Germans followed the British initiative—some as missionaries, some as representatives of Leopold II's International African Association, others as merchants or concession-hunters, independently or as representatives of various commercial firms. Again, they were tolerated by Arabs and Africans so long as they did not interfere with trade or politics. But these few early European adventurers were to be the precursors of the rapidly approaching European powers; the stage had been set for the age of imperialism.

5 The German Era

Before the 1880's, very little of Africa and few of its peoples were ruled by any European states. Although Europe's first contact with sub-Saharan Africa dates from the fifteenth century, the next 400 years witnessed a relationship between the two continents that was almost solely commercial. The Europeans were certainly the stronger, for their science and technology had progressed much faster than had those of the Africans, making possible economic and military advances that opened a wide gap between the two cultures. Yet the chief attraction of Africa to Europeans was trade, and, in any case, most African communities inland from the coast were far too strong to permit the small European groups that visited the continent to interfere in their affairs. So almost all European contact with Africa until the middle of the nineteenth century was confined to the coast, and even there it was usually conducted at the will of local African rulers. As late as 1879, although British, French, Portuguese, Germans, and Belgians were all present on parts of the continent, the only substantial areas governed by any of them were Algeria and Senegal, by France; parts of South Africa, by Britain; Angola and Mozambique, by Portugal. Even if one adds the shadowy control of Egypt and sections of North Africa by the Ottoman Empire, the vast mass of Africa and Africans remained under indigenous rule.

During most of these four centuries, the major commodity sought by Europeans on the African continent had been human beings. The search for gold and later ivory, diamonds, and various substances such as palm oil and gumcopal had attracted some European merchants or adventurers, but by far the strongest magnet had been the trade in slaves, first from the west coast and later, to a much lesser extent, from East Africa. But the slave trade had never depended on political control. It was generally conducted by African rulers and merchants seizing captives in the interior and selling them to European merchants at the coast. When most of Europe outlawed the trade in the early nineteenth century, alternative commodities had to be sought. Where they were readily available, as were the palm oil of West Africa and the ivory from the East, some continuity in commercial relations was maintained. Where they were not, relations languished, though the efforts of the British Navy and certain humanitarians to destroy the remaining slave trade sometimes sustained interest in the region.

From the end of the Napoleonic wars to the last quarter of the century, Britain was supreme in naval and economic power. It was the first great state to experience the industrial and agrarian revolutions, and its lead in these vital fields was maintained until the last two decades of the century. Throughout this crucial period, successive British governments determinedly rejected proposals for any extension of the empire they had inherited—Canada, the Cape, Australia, some West Indian islands, various strategic outposts, and the supreme jewel, India—and took very little interest in Africa. When they were forced to adopt some active policy, it was usually only to overcome a temporary crisis.

This reluctance to conduct an imperialist policy was due to materialistic, rather than idealistic, motives. Britain was the paramount supplier of the goods the world sought. It had only to see that no restraints were placed on trade and its progressive prosperity would be ensured. Empire and imperial control were associated with national monopoly, which Britain itself had been wont to employ in its earlier, mercantilist days. So "free trade" became nineteenth-century Britain's Holy Grail—and free trade was seen as the antithesis of imperialism. Indeed, British policy during most of the century was devoted to transferring as much responsibility as possible to the local inhabitants of its existing empire—with the notable exception of India. Whatever annexation or "protection" of new territories was accomplished was almost always for the purpose of safeguarding Britain's naval strategy and designed to keep the sea lanes free from any interference with its vast commercial activities.

The attitude of other European powers and of America was entirely different. It was, indeed, a corollary to that of Britain. Because of Britain's economic lead and paramountcy in a free market, its competitors in Europe and America needed to acquire closed markets in order to protect their weaker industries. They could do this by building tariff walls around their domestic markets and by acquiring colonies in which they could grant trading monopolies to their own merchants. In both cases, they would be protecting their industries against Britain. The French recognized the value of this tactic consistently, though not completely continuously, throughout the nineteenth century. The Americans were mainly concerned with the development of their own enormous domestic market but took certain imperial opportunities when they were offered. The Germans had to be converted by the proimperial faction within their own polity.

All of Britain's rivals confused cause and effect in her success. They all assumed that her industrial power had been achieved because she possessed an empire; in fact, there was little connection between the two phenomena: The Empire had been created because of Britain's industrial strength, rather than vice versa. Britain's commercial empire was much more lucrative than her political version.

The leading French political economist declared "Colonization is for France a question of life and death; either France will become a great African power; or in a century or two it will be no more than a secondary European power"; Bismarck, after describing projects for German colonization in the 1870's as "just like the silken sables of Polish noble families who have no shirts," had been so far converted a decade or so later as to tell the Reichstag that

"Colonies would mean the winning of new markets for German industries, the expansion of trade, and a new field for German activity, civilization, and capital." It was a German publicist acting as adviser to a procolonialist association whose words were most prophetic regarding East Africa: "Make yourself a focus for the wishes and interests of our traders on unappropriated [African] coastlands," he told his readers, "and I am convinced that the day will come when suddenly and unawares a German warship will produce a *fait accompli* there, where the Association shall have prepared the ground."

Of course, many reasons were adduced for European imperial expansion into Africa—the "civilizing mission," Christian evangelism, vulgarized Darwinism, patriotic destiny, but the authorities quoted above were more honest and nearer to the truth. It was competition in pursuit of commercial profit that led the foremost nations of the Continent to Africa. Why, then, did Britain accompany them if it was satisfied with its world paramountcy and still wedded to the idea of free trade? There were prominent imperialists in Britain—scholars such as Charles Dilke and John Seely, politicians such as the same Dilke, Joseph Chamberlain, and Benjamin Disraeli. But they never succeeded in overthrowing the established doctrine of *laissez faire*. When Britain joined its rivals in the partition of Africa it was in reaction to the moves of other Europeans, rather than in pursuit of a deliberate expansionist policy of its own. Britain saw its trade routes menaced by the imperial policies of Germany, France, Belgium, and Italy. Above all, it feared again for its supremely important routes to India, where much of its commercial wealth originated. The protection of the Suez Canal, the Red Sea, the Cape, and the Indian Ocean was crucial to Britain's global strategy. At the same time, British investors and merchants, a powerful political lobby, were concerned with the German threat to their ambitions in the African interior north of South Africa and with dangers from French and German expansion in West Africa.

As it turned out, the acquisition of African territories proved of minor significance to European economies. South Africa became a valuable investment for the mining companies as, later, did Northern Rhodesia. The Congo produced a personal fortune for Leopold of Belgium and was also to become a major mining investment. Some merchants and companies profited from their activities in West Africa and Egypt, as did some individuals in East Africa and in the French territories along the Mediterranean. But Africa as a whole remained peripheral to European capital and commercial expansion, for the burgeoning industry of Europe found its major profits in the needs of industrializing countries that, except for South Africa, were not on the African continent.

Nevertheless, at the time, particularly during the 1880's and 1890's, the prospect looked different. Within a few years, from the Berlin Conference of 1884–85 to the end of the century, virtually the entire continent was partitioned among the major European powers. This was accomplished in terms of the interests and balance of power of the European states; the Africans were never consulted. Nor were their histories, communal areas or economic activities taken into account. The map was unrolled in Europe, and the lines were drawn on it according to European bargains.

As a result of this diplomatic-commercial horse-trading, the Germans became masters of what was to become Tanganyika. There had been some German commercial interest shown in the area for many years. Some firms had been established as early as 1844; fifteen years later the Sultan signed a commercial treaty with the Hanseatic League. A number of German missionaries established stations in the region, and, at one time in the 1870's, there was a proposal to place Zanzibar under the protection of Germany; it was Bismarck who rejected the idea.

It seems strange that, after exercising so great an authority over Zanzibar from the beginning of the century, the British should acquiesce quietly when the Germans declared a protectorate over the mainland opposite the island in 1885, for Britain had strongly influenced the Sultan's government, virtually controlling his policies after the death of Sayyid Said in 1856. A British agent had been installed as early as 1822, and later the British consuls had been able to use gunboats, marines, and soldiers to keep Zanzibar in line with their objectives. But the British were mainly concerned in

Zanzibar with abolishing the slave trade and ensuring that the French did not threaten their paramount position in the Indian Ocean. They did not at this time see much prospect of trade in East Africa. Indeed, when the Sultan offered a trading concession that would have enabled a British company to take over political and administrative responsibility for his mainland territories, the British Government was so cold toward the project that it was abandoned.

But, in any case, by the 1880's Britain was under such diplomatic pressure that it probably could not have withstood the pressure of German ambitions without war. The occupation of Egypt in 1882 had been a unilateral action. The other European nations responsible for handling Egyptian debts did not participate. Bismarck wished the action to alienate France from association with the British. Indeed, throughout this period, Bismarck hoped that, by setting France and Britain at each other's throats in Africa, he could assuage the French mood for *revanche* against his own country, which had followed the German victory of 1871. At the same time, he expected Britain to show gratitude for his support in its Egyptian policies by protecting the interests of German merchants in African territories. When the British Government showed no intention of doing so in Southwest Africa, he brusquely declared a protectorate over the territory in 1884. For a short time, an uneasy entente existed between Germany and France toward the British position in Africa. In the same year, Germany annexed the Cameroons, and, together with France, blocked British plans in Egypt, on the Niger, and in the Congo basin.

There were then proimperial groups in both Britain and Germany. Chamberlain and Dilke tried to persuade Britain's Liberal government to support Harry Johnston, then in East Africa under the aegis of the Royal Geographical Society, in his proposal that British settlers be sent to the Kilimanjaro area and that a British protectorate be declared over it. Only Gladstone's intervention prevented their acceptance, Gladstone scathingly referring to "a scheme such as that touching the mountain country behind Zanzibar with an unrememberable name."

But the German colonists were shrewder. In the same year, 1884, under the leadership of Carl Peters, they founded a commercial company named the Gesellschaft für Deutsche Kolonisation. Its object was to persuade the German Government to annex African territory before it was pre-empted by their rivals. Despite government coolness, Peters traveled to East Africa disguised as a mechanic. He quickly persuaded a number of African rulers to accept German "protection," though the terms were extremely vague. Returning to Berlin early in 1885 with a bundle of treaties in his pocket, he used them to persuade the government to support him. In March, 1885, immediately after the delegates to the Berlin Conference had left the city, a declaration of German "protection" for the territories claimed by Peters was published and their administration entrusted to Peters's company.

The declaration of the German protectorate brusquely ended the period of Britain's paramount influence on the east coast. The German claims were a direct affront to the authority of the Sultan, and Britain had depended on guiding the Sultan along lines favorable to its interests. To make use of Peters's inland territories, the Germans would have to establish their power on the coast, directly involving the British and the Sultan's positions. Britain was certainly capable of repulsing this threat, but it would have necessitated a show of force. Within a few weeks of the Gordon disaster at Khartoum, the British Government faced by Russian threats to Afghanistan and without allies in Europe, had no desire to antagonize the Germans for the sake of an area they did not regard as near the center of their interests. In any case, the Germans at this stage observed the principle of free trade in their colonies, so no major British interest was threatened, and few people in Europe believed that the East African interior was likely to prove of much commercial worth. In addition to the activities of Peters, Clemens Denhardt was allowed to make a treaty with Witu, part of Lamu in the north, and Dr. Karl Juhlke to take over the area Harry Johnston had hoped to colonize. Both actions were resented by the Sultan, but Britain was no longer concerned with his interests. Even when a German naval squadron sailed to Zanzibar in the summer of 1885 and forced Sultan Barghash to make concessions

On December 9, 1961, Tanganyika gained its independence and Julius Nyerere became the country's first Prime Minister. During Independence Day ceremonies in Dar es Salaam, Prime Minister Nyerere and British Governor Sir Richard Turnbull saluted the national flag as it was raised for the first time.

Tanzania
Information Services

The harbor of Dar es Salaam.   *Jenga Photo*

At the end of 1962,
when a new constitution
was approved,
Julius Nyerere was elected
the first President of
Tanganyika. At the
inauguration ceremony,
he was presented with
the traditional robe,
spear, and shield of
authority and anointed
by a chief.

*Tanzania
Information
Services*

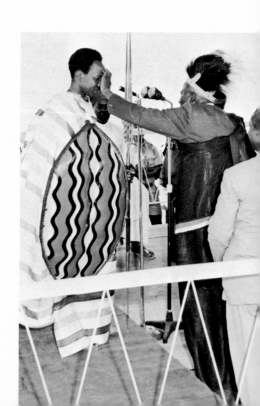

In 1964, President
Nyerere of Tanganyika
(left) and President
Karume of Zanzibar
formed the United
Republic of Tanzania.
Nyerere became its
President and
Karume became
First Vice-President.

Jenga Photo

Mwanza North Port, Lake Victoria.   *Tanzania Information Services*

Pugu Road in Dar es Salaam, which links the center of the city with the Chang'ombe industrial area.

Jenga Photo

This agricultural village is situated on an Usambara mountainside.

Tanzania Information Services

Crowds marching through the streets of Dar es Salaam in support of the 1967 Arusha Declaration, which set Tanzania on a course of self-reliance.   *Jenga Photo*

A large work crew builds a road in Zanzibar.   *Tanzania*
                                                  Information Services

Ambassadors from African countries visit the Isunga Ujamaa Village near Tabora, where seventy-six farmers have planted 81 acres of tobacco. *Tanzania Information Services*

The Tanzania Portland Cement factory is among the largest industrial plants established in Dar es Salaam since independence. *Jenga Photo*

Young athletes
performed
acrobatics during
the celebration
of the third
anniversary
of the Arusha
Declaration,
in 1970.

Tanzania
Information
Services

A truck loaded
with fertilizers
leaves a plant in
the Tanga region.

Jenga Photo

In the annual race with the Uhuru (freedom) torch, young men run through the eighteen regions of Tanzania, finishing on July 7, the anniversary of the founding of TANU at Dar es Salaam. The torch then remains at TANU headquarters until December, when it is planted on top of Kilimanjaro, Africa's highest mountain.

Tanzania Information Services Photos

A climbing party prepares to scale Mount Kilimanjaro with the Uhuru torch.

to the new German expansion, including allowing it virtually to take over Dar es Salaam, no protest arose from London.

British governments of this time, both Liberal and Conservative, appeared anxious not only to conciliate the Germans but also to avoid their own entanglement in the East African scene. A joint commission of Germany, France, and Britain—without the Sultan—defined the limits of the Sultan's domains. In 1886, Germany and Britain agreed to limiting them to a strip of the coastline 10 miles wide, the islands of Zanzibar, Pemba, Mafia, and Lamu, and some of the northern towns. They also mapped out their own spheres of influence on the mainland with a view to future development. At the end of 1886, Germany and Portugal agreed on the southern limit of the Sultan's authority, which was to be the Rovuma River. At this the Sultan protested, the Portuguese bombarded a number of villages, and the boundary was moved a little further south to Cape Delgado.

Having completed these negotiations over the head of the Sultan, the British Government virtually turned over its responsibility to commercial interests. William Mackinnon and his associates formed the British East African Association to exploit the ivory resources and seek further trading opportunities. Similarly, Bismarck, suspicious of being involved in the expenses of administration, allowed Peters to form a German East African Company. Mackinnon then persuaded the Sultan to concede his coastal belt in the north, and the Germans secured a similar concession on the southern coast. Rivalry between the two nations continued, with the British Government always nervous lest the Germans or any other power threaten its control of Uganda and the Nile Basin. But, in 1890, the two governments came to another agreement, by which the Germans consented to recognize Uganda as a British sphere of interest, abandon Witu on the northern coast, and accept a British protectorate over Zanzibar and Pemba. In return, Britain gave up its claim—made by Mackinnon with the connivance of King Leopold of Belgium—to the strip of territory between Lakes Albert and Tanganyika and ceded the strategic island of Heligoland in the North Sea. The period of scrambling for East African territory was concluded; the region called German East Africa consisted of areas later named Tanganyika, Burundi, and Rwanda.

These maneuvers were made without any reference to the several million people whose fate they determined. The only scene they played in this drama took place when some of their chiefs signed certain documents with various European adventurers, which, though vague in terminology, granted concessions over their land. Whether the chiefs had any right to pledge the land of their peoples was beside the point; it was the Europeans who decided such matters. But the people did not sit idly by and watch the Europeans take control of their territories without a murmur.

The first serious opposition to the imposition of German rule came on the coast and from its immediate hinterland. During the past nearly four hundred years, the coastal peoples had valued their independence. Under the leadership of Abushiri bin Salim, an Arab who had settled near Pangani, the peoples from Pangani throughout the length of the *mrima* rose against the German company. They were joined by the Zigua tribe from around Morogoro, led by Bwani Heri. One reason for the revolt was the fear of losing profits from the slave trade; but this was also a popular uprising. It forced the German Government to intervene despite its wish to avoid involvement. Troops were sent in 1889, and the revolt was suppressed within a year. Abushiri was hanged in Pangani, and Heri surrendered. Before his death, Abushiri plaintively told the Germans, "At the beginning of the rising we all swore on the Koran not to rest until we had driven the Germans out. All the others have broken their word. I am the only one who has remained true to that oath until today."

The resistance shown by the Arabs, Swahili, and Africans from the interior compelled the German Government to recognize that the company was unable to control the people over whom it had been given administrative power. As national reputation was at stake, the government could not afford to leave the company to its fate. It, therefore, was forced to take over administrative responsibility at the beginning of 1891.

The assumption of power by the German Government did not,

however, assuage the hostility of the Africans. Those kingdoms that had been forged during the midcentury and had adopted the military techniques of the Ngoni resisted the imposition of government rule as violently as they had that of the company. The story of Mkwawa of the Hehe has already been told. Another chief, Isike of Unyanyembe in Tabora, like Mkwawa, preferred to commit suicide rather than submit to the Germans when they broke into his fortress. Machemba, chief of the Yao—a notorious slaver—nevertheless raised a popular revolt and demonstrated his courage when the German military commander demanded his submission. Machemba sent his reply in Swahili:

> I have listened to your words, but can find no reason why I should obey you. I would rather die first. . . . If it should be friendship that you want, then I am ready for it, today and always. But I will not be your subject. . . . If it should be war that you desire, then I am also ready. . . . I do not fall at your feet, for you are God's creature just as I am. . . . I am Sultan here in my land. You are Sultan there in yours. . . . I do not say that you should obey me, for I know that you are a free man. . . . I will not come to you, and, if you are strong enough, then come and fetch me.

Machemba defeated several German expeditions sent to "fetch" him; it was nine years after he had written that letter in 1890 before he was finally overcome.

Although opposition to German rule was widespread, it was not universal. As on other parts of the continent where Europeans were bringing vast territories under their imperial authority, each African community had to decide what policy was most likely to preserve its own interests. The communities of East Africa were still not united: There had been long-standing rivalry and conflict between them, in addition to the divisive and debilitating effects of the slave trade. There were few Germans in the region; their occupation of the lands they had claimed on maps could only proceed gradually; and they were prepared to reward those peoples who were ready to offer them much needed help. After the early revolt on the coast, many of the defeated Arabs became agents for the Germans in the *mrima* towns. In the interior, chiefs like Merere of the Sangu, Marealle of Marangu, and Kahigi of Kianja made use of their understandings with the Germans to gain increased power and territorial aggrandizement at the expense of their rivals. In doing so, they preserved not only their own position but the safety of their communities as well. As a result of these varying reactions to German imperialism, the balance of power among African societies within East Africa was considerably altered.

From the start, the administration of the Germans in East Africa tended to be rigid and depersonalized. As was the case in other European colonies in Africa, there were always too few administrators and too meager revenues. Consequently, the administrative officers rarely mixed with the people but farmed out administrative authority to many unsuitable subordinates, while the program of economic development always emphasized the need to produce funds for the treasury. Both policies brought trouble.

A governor, often from the army, was placed in a *boma* commanding a small police or military force. When possible, the district officers used cooperative chiefs to collect taxes, try cases, and mete out punishment. Where no suitable chief existed, the Sultan of Zanzibar's method of appointing *akidas,* or government agents, was applied. The men selected were usually from another area, were frequently Muslims without sympathy for local tradition, and often used their authority for personal extortion. Under them, a number of village headmen were appointed as *jumbes,* with authority to represent the government, which often undermined their local reputation.

The insecurity felt by the German district officers because of their lack of numbers, added to the fact that many of them came from military backgrounds, together with their remoteness from the people themselves, often induced gross brutality. They were constantly apprehensive of African revolt, because of both their experience of resistance to the imposition of German rule and also the constant grumblings of discontent over the activities of *akidas.* Therefore, the first signs of resentment were instantly and harshly suppressed. Yet the discontent continued to show itself, not least as a result of German economic policies.

Like the British, French, and Belgians, the Germans had no intention of paying for their colonial administration out of their national revenues. They expected their colonial servants to raise their own revenues in the colonies they administered. The two accepted methods of achieving this were to attract European settlers to the colonies to produce exports that could be taxed and to encourage or coerce the local inhabitants to produce cash crops that could also provide resources for taxation. Both methods were applied in East Africa. Because all land in the colony had been declared Crown land, the colonial government could grant it at will to settlers. Settlements were started in the highlands of Usambara, Meru, and Kilimanjaro, most of the land being taken from the Masai. Coffee and rubber were planted, but the shortage of labor, caused by low wages and resistance to working for Europeans, proved a continual handicap. The sisal plantations, started from plants imported from Florida in 1892, proved the most productive form of investment. Yet the labor shortage itself and the methods used to force Africans to work on the Europeans' land continued to aggravate tension between the Europeans and the Africans.

These rumblings of discontent were amplified by attempts to coerce the Africans themselves to produce cash crops. It was one thing for the missionaries to bring coffee-growing to their followers around Kilimanjaro or for Buhaya's traditional coffee production to be extended to the export trade; it was quite another for the Governor to order cotton to be grown in every village in the south. Not only was this so badly organized that it was scarcely self-supporting; it also introduced into local economic activities governmental compulsion that was enforced with considerable brutality. Out of the hostility it created arose the revolt known as *Maji Maji,* the impact of which was to be felt in Tanganyika for half a century.

At the end of July, 1905, the uprising began in the Matumbi Hills south of the Rufiji River. The *akida* and other aliens were driven out of the villages, and the revolt quickly spread throughout the southern area—down to the Makonde plateau, westward to the southern highlands, and northward through Dar es Salaam to Bagamoyo, Morogoro, and Kilosa. The German reaction was one of apprehension, lest the disaffection should involve the strongly organized military societies of the Nyamwezi and Hehe that had caused them so much trouble earlier. So they met the revolt with a systematic military campaign from the start, and their organization and deadly machine-gun firepower quenched it after eighteen months of bitter and ruthless fighting.

The rebellion was significant to both Tanganyikans and Germans. Having learned earlier the lesson that tribal disunity brought defeat, the Africans this time tried to appeal to an interest above that of tribe. To achieve this they relied on religious mysticism. The term *Maji Maji* was taken from the potion sprinkled on every warrior; composed of water, corn, and sorghum seed, it was supposed to make the warrior immune to bullets while committing him to the fraternity of freedom fighters. The self-confidence it produced was demonstrated when 8,000 warriors, armed only with spears, attacked the German fort at Mahenge and tried to capture the defenders' machine guns with their bare hands—inevitably at a huge cost in casualties. The mythology of the movement also involved a belief in a kind of utopia governed by a new god who would banish all evil.

The attempt to organize a popular movement strong enough to repel the Germans and reassert traditional values failed. It needed much stronger organizational powers than the Africans yet possessed. Tribal loyalties still brought division. The Ngoni, for instance, probably the strongest military force, who resisted longest and hardest, still fought on their own. The failure and the terrible casualties from the warfare and the devastating famine that succeeded it cost at least 75,000 African lives and taught the Africans that they were not strong enough to challenge the Germans directly; they would have to seek other means of dealing with imperial power in order to circumvent it.

The *Maji Maji* uprising shook the Germans out of their complacency. It was clearly not going to be in their national interest to leave the local Governor and his officials and settlers to handle the new colony as they thought best, with the ever present risk of further revolts, which would involve the imperial government in accepting responsibility for the consequences of their mismanagement. A commission was appointed to investigate charges of misgovernment; its exposure of cruelties aroused indignation in Germany, and offenders were sharply punished. The example was salutary for future German administration, which was placed under a separate colonial department. One of the most important reforms was the insistence that labor contracts be put in written from. Because commissioners were appointed to control labor recruiting and act as negotiators between employers and workers, some of the abuses in labor relations were removed. Indeed, many of the European planters were to complain that the government was favoring the Africans against themselves, discriminating against their interests in order to encourage African production.

The *Maji Maji* rebellion thus marks a turning point in the German administration of East Africa and in African reactions to it. The new relationship was not to have time to mature sufficiently for its effectiveness to be judged. But, before the Germans lost their colony in World War I, they had some constructive achievements to their credit. A government school had been opened as early as 1893, and the missionaries had steadily increased their educational work. It is estimated that, by the outbreak of war in 1914, 60,000 African children were being taught in 2,000 schools—99 run by the government, most at the primary level. This educational effort, as was the case in Germany itself, was geared to the economic development of the territory, producing junior clerks for the administration and minor craftsmen in carpentry and similar occupations. This particularly German concept of integrating education with economic need was best illustrated in cotton production. At the turn of the century, European cotton manufacturers were becoming increasingly apprehensive of American competition, especially because they depended on America for most of their supplies of raw cotton. In the search for alternative provisions, the British Cotton Growing Association and its German equivalent, the Kolonialwirtschaftliches Komitee, turned to Egypt, Uganda, and German East Africa. As mentioned above, efforts to coerce Africans into growing cotton became one of the causes of *Maji Maji*. But the German association was sufficiently involved to start a school in Mpanganya on the Rufiji. There Africans were taught the best methods of growing cotton, instruction books were published in local languages, and a minimum price was guaranteed to growers. The colonial government took over the cotton school in 1910 and opened two more. As a consequence, cotton exports, negligible at the beginning of the century, reached 1,882 tons by 1912.

The Germans also concentrated on developing the natural-rubber resource they had found on their arrival. Considerable progress was made in collecting wild rubber and cultivating plantations, but hopes were dashed when the market crashed in 1913. The export of skins and hides also proved valuable, and the Germans showed characteristic scientific concern by studying the problems of tropical agriculture in an institute established for this purpose. Because these productive ventures were accompanied by the building of railways from Tanga to Moshi and from Dar es Salaam to Kigoma on Lake Tanganyika, it can be see that a part, at least, of the economic expansion that characterized the Reich of Bismarck and Kaiser Wilhelm found its expression in German policies within its East African colony.

For over four years, from 1914 to 1918, East Africa was one of the fronts in World War I. During most of this period, the brilliant German general, Paul von Lettow-Vorbeck, kept a variety of British troops tied up in East Africa chasing him around the country. This was his main objective, though the British and Smuts, who was in command for much of the time, believed that the German's task was to defend his country's colony and perhaps to attack the British territories to the north.

What was particularly astonishing was the fact that the Africans fought with whichever side governed their country. The Germans drew troops from their colony, despite the hostility they had faced there, while Kenyans and Ugandans enlisted with the British. No attempt was made to use the war situation to embarrass either imperial government as, for example, some Afrikaners did in South Africa. Indeed, in the British forces, Africans from Kenya, Uganda, and Nigeria mixed with Indian, South African, and Rhodesian troops. It seemed as though the past conflicts against imperial rule by Germans and British were put aside and the Africans who had

previously fought against European governments now realized that
not until they had absorbed the education in modern methods offered by their imperial masters would it be wise to mount a new
campaign for independence.

War itself taught some new lessons. The Africans saw that the
mighty Europeans were capable of fighting not only against weak
African warriors but against each other as well. They saw European
soldiers behaving like common, rough human beings, instead of
with the manners of the administrators and officers to which they
were accustomed. They learned something of the new organization
and discipline of any army and its logistic support, some the trades
essential to military activity. They also found that they were needed
by the Europeans to serve at a higher level than that of unskilled
field laborers.

Inevitably, the economic system in the process of being built by
the Germans was destroyed by the war. Exports had to cease; many
of the plantations to be abandoned; stocks of rubber, sisal, cotton,
and coffee produced on them were seized by the British. As British
forces advanced, from 1916, hundreds of square miles of German
territory fell into their hands. In the following year, a Custodian of
Enemy Property was appointed, responsible for selling confiscated
goods and dealing with businesses and surrendered lands. It was at
this point that many Greeks were attracted by the opportunities
prevalent and took leases on land and businesses. Some economic
activities were thus maintained, but, with troops marching around
the country and Dar es Salaam occupied militarily, economic and
social activities were thrown back to local initiative and organization. And the effects of the war itself were, of course, disastrous to
the Africans. Devastation was followed by famine and an influenza
epidemic. Well over 100,000 Africans died as a result.

Before the war ended, the British appointed an Administrator of
the Occupied Territory, who, with the aid of a skeleton staff of administrative officers from the British territories, local settlers, and
friendly chiefs, began to sort out the administrative confusion.
Meanwhile, the Belgians, who had advanced into Rwanda, Burundi,
and Ufipa, set up their own administration in these territories,

clearly with the object of gaining some German lands from the peace settlement.

At the end of the war, various proposals for the future of German colonies were bruited about. Britain tried to persuade both the Italians and the Americans to accept administrative responsibility in East Africa, but both refused. The settlers in the British territories had developed quite a xenophobic attitude toward their German neighbors during the war and now saw an opportunity to link British territory in East, Central, and South Africa so as to facilitate white domination. The eventual settlement largely satisfied their ambitions. Britain and Belgium did not annex the territories they had occupied. The areas were, in fact, internationalized to the extent that they took on the new status of mandates under the Covenant of the League of Nations. German East Africa was given the new name of Tanganyika and became a "B" mandate, a territory in which it was necessary for some external authority to be responsible, under the League, for administration. Britain was assigned this mandatory authority, as was Belgium for the territory then known as Ruanda-Urundi, which was detached from the ex-German colony, later to become the two independent nations of Rwanda and Burundi. But, although a mandates commission was given the responsibility of hearing reports on Britain's administration, in all important respects Tanganyika was now part of British East Africa.

6 Forty Years Under British Rule

Officially, Britain was charged with administering the former German colony on behalf of the League and with preparing its inhabitants for self-government. In practice, Tanganyika became part of the British Empire, administered by the Colonial Office. Although periodic reports had to be made to the League's mandates commission, which could and did criticize British policies, the commission had no power to require the British Government to take or desist from any action. It was little more than an advisory agency, relying solely for its influence on international opinion.

During the first years under British rule, the impression gained currency that Tanganyika was to follow the model of Kenya and become part of white-settled East and Central Africa. Even the Kenyan conflict between European and Indian was repeated in the new territory. The deportation of German settlers at the end of the war provided economic opportunities for the 10,000 or so Indians who resided in Tanganyika. They soon replaced German traders in towns, before long controlling over 96 per cent of retail trade in Dar es Salaam. They also bought some of the formerly German sisal plantations. This began to alarm Europeans, especially the South African Afrikaner community that had settled around Moshi and Arusha from the early 1900's. In 1921, they protested against the sale of German plantations to Indians, declaring: "Socially the indians [*sic*] and the white settlers can and will never mix owing to their different civilization, morals and creed." Nevertheless, land was turned over to Indians and to the gradual flow of immigrants from Britain. The Germans had alienated over a million acres to immigrants; between the wars, Britain added another million; and, in the first decade of British administration, nearly 6,000 Europeans entered the country as settlers.

The settlers were not the only people concerned about the Indians' role in Tanganyika. One of the most revealing statements illustrating the attitude of many British officials of this time was made by the Director of Education when he commented on proposals to established mixed African-Indian schools:

> With the knowledge of political developments during the last few years in India, we cannot afford to ignore the possibility of an unfortunate African political repercussion in future years as a result of the development of a closer liaison between the two races which might be the result of co-education. At present we have a healthy rivalry and a growing race-consciousness amongst the Africans and a certain feeling of resentment that the Asiatics get so many of the "plums." In my opinion co-education might conceivably weaken this healthy and natural rivalry and eventually lead to making common cause for political ends.

The British colonial principle of "divide and rule" had arrived in Tanganyika, reinforced by apprehension among conservative colonial servants about the risk of Africa's becoming infected with the nationalist virus that was attacking the British establishment in India. Furthermore, the presence of Indian inhabitants in East and South Africa constantly served to aggravate this fear.

Moreover, the white settlers and the officials sympathetic to them had reason to fear that the British colonial government did not see the future of their country as they did. In 1923, the Devonshire Declaration, made by the Colonial Secretary in London, declared that, where any controversial policy issue arose, the interests of the Africans were to be considered paramount. This declaration applied to East Africa as a whole. So far as Tanganyika was concerned, it did no more than reaffirm the terms of the mandate. Outrage was expressed more forcibly in Kenya, where the white settlers were far more numerous and powerful, but many Europeans in both territories expected that Tanganyika would be associated with the rest of British East Africa under white rule similar to that established in Southern Rhodesia. The following year, the Europeans in Tanganyika reacted by demanding the creation of a legislative council to be consulted by the Governor before legislation was promulgated. They anticipated that such a council would be dominated by Europeans, as it was in Kenya. In fact, their wish was granted two years later. The first legislative council was set up, consisting of thirteen officials, with a maximum of ten unofficial members nominated by the governor. Only seven nonofficials were nominated initially—five Europeans and two Asians. Constitutionally, there was no restriction on racial grounds (though the provision that membership should be confined to British subjects excluded the German settlers who were readmitted in 1925,) but it was considered that too few Africans could speak sufficient English to warrant African representation at this stage.

By that time, however, British policy was becoming more clearly defined. A new outlook was brought by Sir Donald Cameron, who became Governor in 1925. Cameron had served under Lord Lugard, whose influence on British colonial policy between the wars was unrivaled. Lugard's "Dual Mandate," a belief that the colonies should be developed in the interest of the world at large as well as for the benefit of their indigenous inhabitants, gave British policy a moral justification. His colonial method, termed "indirect rule," provided both a tactic to meet the problems posed by a shortage of administrators and a strategy for restraining the ambitions of *évolué* colonial politicians. Cameron proved a perfect pupil. He expressed his master's philosophy succinctly when, in an address in 1925, he declared, "Everyone, whatever his opinion may be in regard to direct or indirect administration, will agree, I think, that it is our duty to do everything in our power to develop the native on lines which will not Westernize him and turn him into a bad imitation of a European—our whole education policy is directed to that end." To his own administrative officers he was even more blunt: "If we set up merely a European form of administration," he told them in a circular in the same year, "the day will come when the people of the Territory will demand that that British form of administration shall be passed into their hands—we have India at our door as an object lesson." So much for the spirit of the mandate! And note the repeated neurosis shown by British officials toward the incipient growth of nationalism in Gandhi's India.

The policy of indirect rule was constitutionally confirmed by a native-authority ordinance proclaimed in 1926. Under it, African leaders were identified in each area and granted executive, judicial, and financial powers within their tribal boundaries, backed by the authority of the British colonial government and its officers. These chiefs were made responsible for maintaining law and order, collecting taxes, maintaining local roads, and keeping a census of people and livestock in their area. A part of the taxes was retained to pay the administrative costs of these functions and to go to a Common Purpose Fund, which financed the provision of schools, hospitals, and other social services. To facilitate the administration of this system, Cameron reduced the twenty-two German districts to eleven administrative provinces, later further reduced to eight.

The principles and practices of indirect rule were of immense importance to many parts of Africa between the wars. They were to leave a legacy that is still with us—for instance, in the recent tragic case of Nigeria's civil war and in the conflicts within Uganda. In one respect, the policy was inevitable. With the few administrators available, it would have been impossible to govern a huge territory such as Tanganyika without help from some local people. It was therefore essential that local leaders or rulers be identified. Yet investing them with the authority of imperial power often distorted their function. Either they became suspect because of their association with alien rule or they were given powers they had never previously possessed; in both cases the emphasis placed by the imperial administration on the paramount necessity for order tended to lead to it giving its support to conservative individuals. The constant supervision of the European administrative officer and, according to his personality, his frequent intervention, almost inevitably weighted the scales against the young, educated Africans who usually sought more radical policies. Those whom Lugard contemptuously termed the "trousered blacks" were the constant bane of British administrators between the wars, again with the frightening example of India before them. In Tanganyika, this was often demonstrated by refusal to send boys to the college at Makerere in Uganda—that is, to the only institution of higher education in East Africa—lest they return as political agitators.

In short, the policy of indirect rule always tended to strengthen traditional authority, because it was more likely to preserve order, and hindered the political innovations that might have speeded modernization. It is true that one objective of the policy was to preserve African traditions and customs in so far as they did not offend European concepts of humanity and ethics, and some emphasis was placed on local economic growth; but the administrator's ideas of African tradition usually included only the authoritarian-conservative elements and ignored the factor of popular decision-making, as well as modernization and national planning. Where reform was encouraged by the colonial administration, it was usually in a localized economic field—as in agriculture and animal husbandry—but there was even there a frequent reluctance to consult with and involve the young, progressive sections of the community. Often, too, agricultural education or craft training was considered solely as an alternative to dangerous book learning, as part of the effort to preserve Africa as a rural environment where the "noble savage" would be insulated from the evils of the modern industrial world, rather than as a stimulant to an agrarian revolution. Thus, much of the agricultural training given to African children in schools was conducted by teachers with scant knowledge of tropical agriculture, and consisted of little more than practicing on school plots what they learned at home about planting, weeding, and picking.

Firsthand examples of the principles and practice of "indirect rule" are given by Sir Charles Dundas, one of the administrators under that system, in his book *African Crossroads*. Because he was the first Secretary for Native Affairs in Tanganyika, his recollections can be quoted with confidence. He describes how the local leaders were selected:

> Indirect rule was in actuality no entirely new device, it was rather the systemisation of a long-standing British colonial practice. For we never ruled directly. Always we controlled subject races—unholy word in these days—through their indigenous authorities. So indispensable had they seemed to us that where we did not find such authorities we created them. In tribal areas in which there were no conspicuous leaders, almost any man who brought himself to notice or made himself useful might become a chief. The so-called Paramount Chief of the Kikuyu in my time had been donkey-boy to an early administrator; another "paramount" of Nyeri had come to that dignity by scrounging food supplies for the station. I knew one whose patent of chiefship was a chit given him by an early elephant-hunter recommending him as a "good tracker."

Dundas then explains the current justification for the application of this policy:

> In the nineteen-twenties one was given to understand that Indirect Rule was to be regarded in a measure as a *quid pro quo* for political rights from which the African was then excluded. Having no part in the central government of the territorial State, he was to be accorded a degree of autonomy in the ordering of his domestic affairs. This point was repeatedly made in those years to cut the ground from under the feet of any potential agitator.

Despite his enthusiastic promotion of this policy, Donald Cameron took one action that was to have far-reaching effects, although he certainly did not foresee them. In 1929, he participated in the formation of the Tanganyika African Association (TAA), which was ultimately to conceive the organization that brought the colony to independence. Cameron, who in many ways was a liberal man for his time, believed that it would be beneficial to have an organization where discussions could take place among people with ideas in the urban areas. It was with this in mind that he approved the formation of the TAA.

The Tanganyika African Association was not the first organization with a national character to appear in the territory. In 1922, a Tanganyika Territory African Civil Service Association had been formed in Tanga. It was the brainchild of an African who probably played a larger role in the interwar years than any other individual. His name was Martin Kayamba, and he had been educated at the mission school, Kiungani, in Zanzibar, where his father was a schoolmaster. After spending some years as a clerk and trader, traveling throughout East Africa and being imprisoned by the Germans, he was appointed chief clerk to the Tanga Provincial Office. He was encouraged by the government to set up his organization, which was really a social club for the tiny educated elite of teachers and civil servants, providing them with newspapers and a soccer team. Most of the elite at this stage assumed that the way to progress was through education, which would bring them the privileged status they witnessed among the better-educated Europeans. They dwelt on self-improvement rather than political ideology, though their discussions inevitably became concerned with the political development of the country. Their main significance was that they represented, albeit in a very minor role, the supratribal concept, which could only lead toward a national consciousness. It was from members of this association that the TAA was constituted, and they took their detribalized outlook with them into the new organization.

Meanwhile, though Cameron believed in preserving the African character of the country, which involved starting from a tribal base, he had no intention of allowing his policy to stunt African progress or provide Europeans with the opportunity to entrench their political dominance. He was a consistent opponent of moves to unite the whole of East Africa in some form of closer union, which would have meant placing its future under the kind of white domination developing in Kenya. When tribal communities showed initiative, therefore, they found encouragement from the Governor.

One example was seen in the Shinyanga area south of Lake Victoria, where the Sukuma realized that they could gain strength by pooling their resources; so their nine chiefs organized a confederation that enabled them to operate a common treasury. Something similar happened in the neighborhood of Tabora, among the Nyamwezi.

The most impressive example of this was the strong initiative taken by the Bahaya in the fertile lands around Bukoba west of Lake Victoria. They went further than simply forming an association between chiefs; they established the first tribal organization, called the Bukoba Bahaya Union. The proximity of the Bahaya to Uganda gave them an early chance to associate with Christianity, form their own church, and gain literacy. Consequently, there grew among them an educated sector whose members resented the powers given to the chiefs under the policy of indirect rule. In 1924, the Bukoba Bahaya Union was founded by Klemens Kiiza, himself an educated, experienced man who had worked for the government and missionaries under the Germans and had been a trader under the British. His union criticized the Council of Chiefs, resenting the privileges its mostly illiterate members assumed, and demanding that an educated man replace them. When Kiiza went into the coffee business, he tried to widen the appeal of his union by persuading farmers to join the association. His opportunity came in the mid-1930's, when the chiefs, under government direction and some pressure from European farmers, tried to control the methods used for coffee-growing in order to reduce the incidence of disease. The orders were resented and resisted by the farmers, provoking considerable discontent. For a time, Kiiza commanded popular support. His opposition to the chiefs and championing of local grievances opened one path along which the people were able to involve themselves in political issues.

Such community movements tended to be the exception rather than the rule. Many of Tanganyika's peoples and chiefs resisted any attempt to establish this tidy form of administrative authority over them. The Gogo in the central plains refused to amalgamate their numerous chiefdoms; the Masai maintained their traditional system of elders' authority; around Mwanza, the institution of paramount chief was considered alien and never accepted; the Chagga on the slopes of Kilimanjaro retained their allegiance to their twenty or so chieftainships.

At the same time, the Chagga showed that, though they might not be prepared to alter their administrative and judicial traditions, they would cooperate in an economic venture. The same Charles Dundas quoted earlier became an administrative officer in the Kilimanjaro district after the war. He encouraged the Chagga to resume the coffee-growing they had abandoned under the Germans. In order to increase production, he persuaded the growers to form a Kilimanjaro Native Planters' Association, which pooled the crops and sold them to Indian merchants. Despite opposition by nearby European coffee farmers who feared that African coffee-growing might spread disease, Cameron encouraged this enterprise among the Chagga and allowed them to market their coffee themselves in order to circumvent the Indian monopoly. Although tension between European and African persisted in this area for some years, eventually coffee-growing on Kilimanjaro became one of the best examples of interracial cooperation.

Cameron left Tanganyika in 1931. But, the year before he did so, a significant conference had been held in London. For some years, the white settlers, particularly in Kenya, had been pressing for some form of association among the three British East African territories, with perhaps Nyasaland and Northern Rhodesia also included. Cameron, however, had shown himself just as strongly opposed to such a scheme, fearing lest his experiment in Tanganyika, which he hoped would eventually prepare the Africans for participation in government, would be sabotaged by white supremacists in Kenya.

In 1930, under a Labour Government, with Lord Passfield (Sidney Webb) in charge of the Colonial Office, it was decided that a Joint Select Committee of Parliament should hear evidence from all races on the subject. Several aspects of this event throw light on the outlook of the time. Africans were to be represented in London, though there was no method of securing representative men or providing for them to be mandated by their people. Three were selected by the government to represent Tanganyika: Martin Kayamba, who, as well as being the chief clerk in Tanga and founder of the African Association, was a member of the Advisory Committee on African Education; Chief Makwaia, a Sukuma who spoke no English; and Francis Lwamgira, a rival to Kiiza in Bukoba and secretary of the chiefs' council there. These African representatives were not invited to travel with the rest of the Tanganyika delegation, were not allowed to sail on a British ship, and were forbidden to accompany the Africans from Kenya on their journey. Thus the Africans were treated very much like children and carefully isolated from those rough types who were accustomed to agitate in neighboring Kenya, but were not regarded as sufficiently grown up to mix with their elders and betters in their own delegation.

In the event, the three men, despite their difficulties and varied backgrounds, presented a unanimous case to the committee. And, most significantly, they were cast in a role in which they represented Tanganyika as a national entity. They cogently expressed their opposition to any scheme that would allow the influence of Kenyan white settlers to penetrate Tanganyika, condemned the Kenyan system of African reserves, and raised the issue of differences in land-tenure policies. The outcome of the investigation brought little more than increased common services to East Africa—a joint postal service, for instance—so that Cameron and the Africans were satisfied. Even many Europeans in Tanganyika were now beginning to express serious doubts over the wisdom of providing an opportunity for Kenyan whites to spread their influence southward.

The years following Cameron's departure were cheerless for Tanganyikans. The country suffered, as did the rest of the world, from the economic depression that inevitably hit its development schemes. Thus, the efforts that had only just begun to lift some of the people from the slough of poverty were largely abandoned. It often seemed that, added to the poor harvests, droughts, locust plagues, and other natural disasters that were the heritage of Tanganyikans, European administration had done no more than raise hopes that were almost instantly shattered. Moreover, the 1930's saw the reassertion of German nationalism with the rise of Hitler. His demand for the return of German colonies, combined with his racist philosophy, brought new apprehension to Tanganyika. The British settlers formed a league to oppose any suggestion of returning the territory to Germany, but it was not until shortly before World War II broke out in 1939 that the British Government made it clear that it would not contemplate handing back the administration to the Germans.

Meanwhile, early in 1931, a Retrenchment Commission had been appointed by the British government to deal with the problems raised by the slump that was drastically reducing the revenues of the country. Sisal, the main export staple, was particularly affected by low world prices and the drastic limitation of international trade; its price remained low throughout the 1930's, thus seriously reducing revenue and the ability to import much needed goods from abroad. The government, with Stewart Symes as Governor, sought more effective means of collecting taxes from the Africans, a poll tax on non-Africans, the cultivation of more crops, and improved marketing. But it was difficult to persuade African farmers to increase their production when prices were falling so steeply. Between 1929–30 and 1931–32, revenue from the combined African hut and poll tax fell from $1,800,000 to $1,080,000 and as both government and native authorities largely depended on this tax for their income, the inevitable reaction was to curtail expenditure. The very modest program of social development that had been initiated under Cameron offered the most tempting target; its curtailment left the British administration with very little to show in the area of social improvement by the time the war broke out in 1939. And this failure was only partially caused by the world slump. By 1944, the Tanganyikan Government, largely through reduced expenditure on social services, had again balanced its budget, the Holy Grail of colonial administration. Thereafter, in the prevailing British preoccupation with Europe and with the emphasis on retrenchment in public spending, the Tanganyikan Government adopted a passive posture, content to balance its books. Moreover, the attitude toward public spending began to reveal another feature. It became clear during the 1930's that the European community was beginning to exert increasing pressure on the government. The effects of this pressure became visible in the racial composition of financial allocations.

All these factors were present—in perhaps the clearest, and certainly the most tragic, example—in education. It was Donald Cameron himself who pointed out in his recollections: "In the five years ending in 1936 the expenditure on African education from general revenue has declined by more than 30 per cent although over the same period the total revenue has increased over 40 per cent." Statistics substantiate Cameron's allegation. The cuts made in provision for African education at the time of the 1931 financial crisis were not restored when trade and revenues recovered.

Inevitably, this decline in educational provision for Africans retarded the development of the African community. But, within this framework, a number of especially significant factors can be perceived. The distaste for sending African students to the college at Makerere that had been evident during the 1920's was strengthened by financial stringency. Between 1930 and 1939, 390 Ugandan, 79 Kenyan, but only 33 Tanganyikan students entered the college. In 1938, eight Tanganyikan boys were being trained at Makerere to be English-language teachers and six to be medical assistants—for a population of 5 million. And, as would be expected, as a corollary to this conservative attitude, women's education was especially handicapped. Between 1930 and 1940, only a dozen female teachers were registered; the maximum grant-in-aid offered by the government to African teachers in girls' schools was $57.6, just half that given to African assistant teachers in schools for boys.

World War II did not affect Tanganyika as drastically as had World War I, for this time its territory was not a war theater. The war, nevertheless, had some effects on the people and their economy. Despite its meager resources, the Tanganyikan Government beggared its reserves to contribute $480,000 to Britain's war treasury. The 3,000 or so Germans in the territory were interned, thus eliminating the various Nazi groups that had been formed in the country. Nearly 100,000 Africans joined the armed forces, serving in Somaliland, Burma, and Madagascar—some losing their lives, others returning with a widened experience of the world and its inhabitants. In particular, they met other East Africans, Africans from Nigeria and the Gold Coast, whites from South Africa, Indians and Burmese. They saw the Emperor of Ethiopia returned to his throne; they witnessed the defeat of Italy, the successes of the Japanese against Europeans, and they participated in the overthrow of the Vichy French in Madagascar. In short, they were thrown into the vortex of a world where European power was being challenged and defeated, where many of their comrades were talking of ending colonial rule and seeking independence.

The economy of Tanganyika was considerably affected by the war, but the major effects were, in a sense, contradictory. On the one hand, it became increasingly difficult to export Tanganyikan products; on the other, there arose a greater demand for some of them than ever before. The Japanese successes in the Far East had the greatest impact. They greatly increased Britain's need for sisal, the price of which accordingly rose to new heights, and they brought a feverish search for rubber, which could be found in Tanganyika. The great increase in prices paid for such essential wartime materials produced a sense of financial prosperity, and the shortage of goods available for sale ensured that more money remained in the pockets of the producers. At the end of the war, however, they were to discover that the universal increase in prices also applied to the goods they wished to buy, greatly reducing the value of their savings. Indeed, before the war ended, Tanganyikans found that their ancient enemies could not be defeated by the extra flow of money. The Tanganyikans still depended heavily on their crop production, but in 1943 drought struck the country again, this time accompanied by a wave of locusts. Corn, the dietary staple, became so scarce that famine provision had to be made and corn had to be imported for the duration of the war.

During the war, a number of political developments occurred that were overshadowed by military events, and, perhaps for that reason, they have often been neglected in the recounting of Tanzania's history; but they are significant for an understanding of postwar events. In the first place, the removal of district officers or their preoccupation with military needs left the native authorities with much less supervision. As we have seen, some of them had begun even before the war to arrogate to themselves an authority the government had never intended them to have. Under wartime conditions, the tension that had already risen between them and their people, particularly with the younger educated section, was aggravated. This foreshadowed struggles that were to influence the political scene after the war.

Nor were the urban politicians idle during the war. In May, 1940, the president and officers of the African Association issued a memorandum calling for the betterment of the African races, demanding that the government appoint a special member to consider those matters particularly affecting Africans—condemning profiteering among Indian and Arab traders, criticizing the lack of education provisions for Africans, demanding that Tanganyika be granted equivalent status with West Africa, proposing that representatives be appointed to participate in municipal services—while at the same time offering to help the government and promising that the Association would confine itself to social concerns without entering into political activity. This last promise was perhaps a little naïve, for the memorandum was obviously steeped in political issues. What is more, it again demonstrated that there were Africans in Tanganyika who were considering the country as an entity, making demands and proposals that applied to Africans throughout the territory, irrespective of tribe or locality.

This wider vision was maintained by the African Association during the war years. In 1942, it held its first territorial conference, which, although poorly attended, testified to the fact that the Association now regarded itself as responsible for considering the interests of the whole country. This national outlook was not yet militant and grew only slowly, always within the framework of respect for Britain and the colonial government. Yet its continued growth was evident by 1945, when the third territorial conference of the Association was held in Dodoma. This conference, much better attended than earlier ones had been, brought together representatives from most parts of the country. Its communiqué presaged the kind of manifesto that was soon to become common to nationalist movements throughout Africa. It combined general principles with specific complaints and demands, though still within the context of accepted colonial rule.

The Dodoma conference first called for universal brotherhood, to take precedence over local, divisive loyalties based on tribal, religious, political, cultural, or territorial divergencies. It then took a stand against the concept of Tanganyika as an area of white settlement, especially rejecting white domination of political and economic power. Next, it complained that African educational opportunities were unsatisfactory, proposed that education for both sexes should be made compulsory, and suggested that Negroes from America and Africans from South Africa be recruited into the teaching profession. It called for the establishment and recognition of trade unions in an effort to develop a healthy system of labor relations. Yet the conference specifically did not attack the existing form of government; indeed, it asked that the mandate system be preserved, and it praised Britain's liberal and humane traditions, especially commending the declared principle of regarding indigenous interests in British dependencies as paramount.

Another subject considered and reported on by the Dodoma conference was education. Late in the war, a British Colonial Office committee had produced a report entitled "Mass Education in African Society," proposing that universal education and the elimination of illiteracy among adults should be achieved by all African dependencies within thirty years. Tanganyikan education officials reacted skeptically. In February, 1944, for the first time since November, 1934, the Advisory Committee on African education met to consider the report. Its findings reflect the conservatism, traditionalism, and patronizing attitude that had characterized many of Tanganyika's education policies during the two preceding decades. "To educate 5½ million people," they wrote, "and to take it for granted that a happy life was therefore ensured, would be a doubtful proposition in the view of some members." The committee went on to doubt the economic feasibility of the proposal, and, in the traditional manner of British educationalists, it insisted that quality must not be sacrificed for quantity.

The African Association conference, however, took the Colonial Office report as a challenge and addressed itself to methods of implementation. It demanded that the government take the lead and cited Russia as an example of how the task could be achieved with governmental initiative. It then suggested that evening classes for adult men and women be started, with employers, police authorities, and the Association itself responsible for organizing them. It proposed that illiterate civil servants and police be compelled to attend them and particularly stressed the importance of the classes in spreading a knowledge of Swahili. The slogan "Teach your illiterate neighbor" was coined, and educated young people were exhorted to give one hour to the teaching of illiterates on certain days each week. As in every other African country, those leaders who thought nationally set education as their first priority in the postwar period.

Thus, by the end of the war, two strands had appeared in the political skein of African Tanganyika: Tribal organization and agitation could be seen in unions and federations for both economic and political purposes, and broader, territory-wide considerations increasingly activated the minds of a small minority of professionals and intellectuals. But the two elements were never hostile to each other. At some points they coalesced, for instance, in the young educated people's dissatisfaction with the rule of illiterate privileged chiefs; this dissatisfaction was entirely in line with the gradually growing demands of the TAA for representation and modern institutions. Only when their agricultural interests were threatened did large numbers of people in any area become involved in the issues of the time, but the future was to depend on how the interests of the people were portrayed—whether they were considered as tribal responsibilities or of national concern, how the returning ex-servicemen reacted, and to what extent tribally minded and nationally minded leaders saw their responsibilities as conflicting or integrated. All these crucial issues were to be determined in the decade after the end of the war.

In the immediate postwar years, political interest and argument increased appreciably. Tanganyikans, though comparatively remote from world events, could not be entirely divorced from the ferment of ideas pouring out within the colonial scene. The educated youth, though still few in number, were gradually increasing—from 1940 to 1949, 85 Tanganyikans entered Makerere, compared with 33 in the previous decade. Nor was it only the intelligentsia who were involved. Changes were taking place in rural areas, bringing doubts, questioning, and sometimes resistance. It was Tanganyika's distinction that it had a national hub around which the localized spokes could revolve when discontent became rife. In Kenya and Uganda, dissatisfaction tended to become particularized within the tribes, among the Kikuyu or Baganda, for example; in Tanganyika, there were no dominant tribes—although there were large ones, as populous as the Kikuyu. A collective spirit of common responsibility overrode any intertribal jealousies, and the common use of the Swahili language provided a form of lingua franca. Moreover, Dar es Salaam never rivaled the focal economic and political position that Nairobi or Kampala held. The large tribal areas in Tanganyika were therefore much more remote from the administrative center than the Kikuyu or Baganda were, which diffused political activity and obviated the rivalries for influence and position in the capital. Nor had there ever been the degree of European economic activity seen in the rest of East, West, and Central Africa. Consequently, hardly any Tanganyikans had been absorbed into a capitalist stratum that gave them a stake in the retention of colonialism.

It was also important to the political situation of the postwar years that Tanganyika never knew the intense obsession with political dominance shown by Kenya's Europeans. In Tanganyika, the European community was only a third the size of Kenya's and much more mixed in composition, including Greeks and Germans along with the British and the small Afrikaner group. If it ever had any pretensions to dominate the future government, its intelligent members must have known that such ideas were vain.

In any case, Tanganyika, in contrast to the other territories, became a U.N. Trust Territory after the war, when the League of Nations officially ceased to exist. And the Trusteeship Council was a much more active body than the mandates commission, sending visiting missions to tour the territory triennially, hearing petitions, and making recommendations to the administering trustee. The United Nations was much more suspicious of European ambitions in dependent territories than the League had ever been. Not only could it be relied on to block any attempt to establish white domination in Tanganyika, but its own activities spurred the Africans on to new demands and encouraged them to develop political pretentions. Moreover, the trust agreement was now specific: It charged Britain with the responsibility of developing Tanganyika toward independence.

The new mood of political awareness grew in an atmosphere of increased economic opportunity. The British Government, at the moment of maximum national danger in 1940, had passed its first Development and Welfare Act, allocating money to both economic investment and social-welfare schemes. The sum was paltry—a mere $12 million a year—but it established the principle of metropolitan responsibility for subsidizing colonial development. In 1945, the money to be made available was considerably increased. In Tanganyika, a ten-year plan was published, with a budget of £18 million—£13 million to be provided in grants and loans from Britain. Rapidly rising costs and unforeseen obstacles were to bring disappointment to the ambitious schemes, but at the time the plan contributed to the general air of optimism. In any case, quite apart from external aid, the first five years after the war constituted a period in which the world, after its mass squandering of materials, was desperately seeking to rebuild and restock. East Africa's primary products were in great demand. The total value of Tanganyika's trade rose between 1946 and 1949 from about $42 million to $126 million. This sudden leap forward should have provided some of the resources needed for economic development.

Yet, the effects of rapid economic development also created the usual kinds of discontent. Vested and traditionalist interests were impinged upon; regional, group, and individual jealousies were provoked; weak or ignorant administration interfered with local production; new ambitions were often frustrated. Hopes were more often dashed than realized. The trust territory was never regarded by the British Colonial Office as worthy of the same attention as Kenya or Uganda, nor were foreign investors as attracted to it as to its two neighbors. Administration was usually desultory and weak, providing frequent opportunities for the expression of discontent and a tendency toward inefficient planning.

This situation can be illustrated by the fate of the major planning sectors in the immediate postwar years. In education, the aim was to provide for 36 per cent of school-age children to attend school at a cost of $11.4 million over ten years. Yet a census revealed that the population was so much greater than had been estimated that in 1950 the whole scheme had to be reassessed. Communications were to be the central feature of Tanganyika's economic development. Yet, after three railway extensions had been started, East Africa's railways were amalgamated under the High Commission and subjected to the interests of the other territories; and the road-building schemes, like those for education, had to be revised in 1950 because of rising costs.

But the greatest disappointment, of course, was the notorious "groundnut scheme." In an effort to overcome the world shortage of fats, the British Government devised a plan to supply its own needs while at the same time investing in the development of its trust territory. The plan cost $86.4 million, of which $60 million were lost. Bad planning, ignorance, and lack of thorough preparation caused the scheme to collapse. It was a classic example of good intentions by a government being ruined by the lack of trained, motivated officials to supervise the work of private contractors. A new port, roads, and a railway were left behind, some Africans were trained and housed and the cleared land was handed over to the Tanganyika Agricultural Corporation; but these facilities were situated out of the main productive areas and provided scant recompense for the hopes which were dashed.

Another effect of rapid economic development—or plans to achieve it—together with the impact of world shortages and inflation, was a steep rise in the cost of living. This particularly affected Africans living in the towns, but it was also felt in the rural areas. Inevitably, it increased the tensions beginning to pressure both the urban and the rural leadership into political action.

Events in the constitutional field were also stimulating political thought and activity. After the war, in line with Britain's general colonial policy of increasing local representation, the legislative council, which served as a kind of parliament with limited power, was significantly enlarged. It was to consist of the Governor as its president, fifteen government officials, and fourteen nonofficials who would be nominated by the government. What was most important was that, of the latter group, provision was made to appoint four Africans—the first time that Africans had been admitted to a political institution of the central government. In fact, only two Africans were actually appointed in 1945, both chiefs, but another was appointed in 1947 and the fourth in 1948. The other nonofficials consisted of three Asians and seven Europeans, one of the latter being appointed especially to represent African interests.

In 1948, the executive council, or advisory government to the Governor, was reorganized, again including nonofficial members, but this time no Africans. For the first time, certain members of the executive were to become responsible for specific governmental departments, a kind of "ministerial" system, although they were called "members" of their departments, not "ministers." Yet the revision of the executive, together with the form of the new legislature, clearly offered opportunities for Africans to exercise influence, and later power, once they had organized sufficient pressure to gain representation.

In this they were assisted by the first visit of the U.N. mission in 1948. This event provided an opportunity for the African Association to make representations to the U.N. body, a process that stimulated the association members' political ideas and stirred interest throughout the country. The association's claims for greater and better African representation were supported by the mission in its report. The report recommended that an electoral system be introduced so that African members of the legislature would be genuinely representative of their people, that the number of African members be increased to become a majority of unofficial members, that Africans be given seats on the executive council, and that measures be taken to accelerate development toward self-government.

Naturally, these proposals caused great controversy in both Tanganyika and Britain. The British Government argued that elections could not yet be introduced as they would lead to representation of sectional interests rather than those of the masses, and that its policy was to start with popular representation in local councils before introducing the system into national government.

Nevertheless, the argument had started, and, in the following year, leaders from all the races published a statement in the local papers calling for an electoral system to replace government nomination. So, when the new Governor, Edward Twining, set up a constitutional committee at the end of 1949, many interests were anxious to

give evidence before it. The existence of the committee itself stimulated political discussion still further. When its report came out in
1951, proposing that the legislature be enlarged and that expert advice be sought on the vexing issue of elections, it became obvious
that organized political groups were essential to meet the rapidly
approaching constitutional challenges.

The other noteworthy feature of the report was its recognition
that Tanganyika had enjoyed comparative racial harmony and that
this was worth preserving. To do so, it proposed that the enlarged
legislature consist of twenty-one unofficial members, seven to represent each of the three races, and that an official government majority
be maintained to act as a balancing factor. It also suggested that
multiracial county councils replace the existing provincial councils.
The proposals for this kind of representational parity, which was
revolutionary in comparison with previous political experience, were
not accepted without some opposition. The African Association and
the Chagga Cultural Association, both of which gave evidence before
the committee, were prepared to accept the scheme tentatively, but
only as an interim measure, and thought that Africans should be
given greater representation. Several groups of members of the European Council strongly criticized the proposals, taking the common
European line that what was most needed in colonial territories was
a period of stability in which economic activities could flourish, that
the Europeans had played a predominant role in development, and
that the non-Europeans were politically immature. But all Europeans
did not think alike, and the report of the committee had been signed
by the unofficial European members of the legislative council.

In the meantime, the Governor had appointed the first African
to his executive council (a young chief, Kidaha Makwaia) and the
British Government had appointed a special commissioner (W. J. M.
Mackenzie, a Manchester University professor) to investigate the
issue of elections. The 1951 U.N. mission to Tanganyika had also accepted the report of the constitutional committee, but only as an
interim measure, expressing the hope that communal representation would soon be abandoned and a qualified common-roll system
introduced.

By May, 1954, the Governor was ready to announce his decision on constitutional reform. The new legislature was to be composed of 55 members, 27 of whom would be unofficial, 9 from each race. (This was amended to 30 and 10, respectively, later that year.) The government would retain its official majority, with 28 official members (31 after amendment), and all unofficial members would be nominated by the Governor, not elected. The executive was reorganized later the same year, with officials becoming ministers in charge of departments and each race being allocated two unofficial members, who became assistant ministers.

In the same year, another U.N. mission visited the country. This time its report raised a furor, for it recommended a timetable that would give Tanganyika independence by 1975 or, at the latest, 1985. It also pressed for an electoral system to be introduced and for a rapid increase in African representation in the legislature. It was starkly obvious that Tanganyika had moved to the threshold of political climax. The maneuvers, battles, and tactics of the next few years would determine the future of the country for many generations. They would be conducted on the stage of the African continent, still under the direction of British, French, and Belgian governments. They would therefore be influenced by events in Kenya, now in the midst of its Mau Mau emergency; in Central Africa, where the federation of the Rhodesias and Nyasaland had created a ferment of controversy; in Uganda, where the Kabaka of Buganda had just been exiled; and in West Africa, where the Gold Coast had already achieved self-governing status in 1951 and was rapidly marching toward independence. In this maelstrom, final decisions on Tanganyika's future would still be made in Whitehall and they would assuredly be conditioned by their anticipated effects elsewhere on the continent; but the character of those decisions would also be crucially influenced by the pressures of all groups in Tanganyika itself, and these would depend on the organizational power mobilized behind each set of ideas.

7 The Trials and Triumphs of Nationalism

The Tanganyika African National Union (TANU) grew out of the Tanganyika African Association (TAA). Its membership was drawn from two elements: the intellectuals and the ex-servicemen. During the 1940's, a group of students in Makerere constantly discussing the future of Tanganyika and looking for a political home, tried to gain entrance into the TAA. They were repulsed by a leadership frightened by radicalism. Realizing that, as an established organization with many branches, the TAA would provide a better instrument for political action than any new body they could form themselves, they determined to circumvent the leaders' antagonism. Those who returned from their studies to Dar es Salaam, led by two doctors, Vedast Kyaruzi and Luciano Tsere, encountered a number of politically minded ex-servicemen there who, when abroad with the army, had been discussing the same subjects that preoccupied the students. An Action Group was formed to present a memorandum to Twining's constitutional committee, and plans were laid to take over the TAA. In 1950, they succeeded in this stratagem and Kyaruzi was elected president of the association.

One of the Makerere students who took a significant, though quietly modest, part in the political discussions was Julius Kambarage Nyerere. He was the son of one of the eight chiefs of the small Zanaki tribe living to the east of Lake Victoria, and of the chief's eighteenth wife. As a boy of eight, he tended the family goats all day, ate his one meal of corn, millet porridge, and occasionally meat or fish in the evening, and slept in his mother's grass hut. But the boy conceived an ambition to go to school, and he was allowed to leave home for the native-authority boarding school in Musoma. He lived there with the other boys in a large grass hut, cooking for himself and learning, among other things, the catechism. From there his abilities took him to the famous government school in Tabora, where political discussion flourished. He pursued his religious interests with the white fathers at the neighboring Tabora Mission, obtained his school-leaving certificate, and was baptized "Julius" on his return to Musoma. With the support of his headmaster, Nyerere was granted a scholarship and he proceeded to Makerere to be trained as a teacher. There he pursued both his political and his religious concerns, participating in the debating society, in the ferment of political thought among Tanganyikan students, and in founding Catholic Action. He had as yet revealed few indications of leadership to his contemporaries, but evidence of a reserved though friendly nature, a clear, profound mind, outstanding academic prowess, and the ability to make his companions think realistically was there.

At the time when Kyaruzi and Tsere were planning to take over the TAA, Nyerere was far away in Tabora, teaching history and biology at Saint Mary's College for $15 a month. He indulged his political interest there by participating in the Tabora activities of the local TAA, but he was mainly concerned with fitting himself for the future by studying for and passing London matriculation. This qualified him to accept a scholarship from the director of the college to go to Britain and continue his higher education. It was the same director, Father Walsh, who ensured that his scholarship also included grants to Nyerere's mother, brother, and fiancée, Maria Gabriel, to whom he had become engaged during the Christmas period of 1948. In April, 1949, Nyerere arrived in Britain; in October he enrolled at Edinburgh University to study as broadly as possible, read widely, think deeply, and obtain an arts degree.

In Edinburgh, Nyerere entered into many student political discussions but took no active part in politics. Rather, he thought out his own political philosophy and its relevance to his own country. While still in Edinburgh, he recorded his thoughts in a long essay entitled "The Race Problem in East Africa." In it he expressed views he later was able to try out in practice, particularly his belief in the intrinsic worth of every individual, irrespective of race, with the natural corollaries of repudiation of the domination of a white minority, hatred of privilege, and hope that an East African society could be created above tribe, based on social harmony. It was this opportunity to meditate and view the situation from the outside, free from the pressure of immediate events, that was probably Edinburgh's greatest gift to Nyerere. It provided him with a knowledge of himself and a personal philosophy that were to make him the most relaxed and contemplative of African leaders.

On his return to Tanganyika in 1952, Nyerere was given a teaching position at Saint Francis College, Pugu, about twelve miles outside Dar es Salaam. In January of the next year, he and Maria married and took up residence together at Pugu. He was soon in touch with the Dar es Salaam group that had captured the TAA. By then, there were new politically minded Africans in the capital. They began to look to the Arnoutoglu Community Centre as a base of operations where two Europeans—Fraser Murray, a lawyer, and Jimmy McGairl, a community development officer—formed an interracial group to discuss political issues. Among its members were a number of personalities who were to be prominent in the country's future history. Nyerere was introduced to the group, and it was not long before he began to be accepted as a leader. In April, 1953, he was persuaded to run for the presidency of the TAA and was elected by a narrow margin.

Nyerere soon realized, however, that he could not turn the TAA into a political party. This was made explicit when Governor Edward Twining prohibited civil servants from joining the organization. When Nyerere protested that this meant excluding most educated Africans, he did not even receive a reply from the Governor. He recognized that he would have to organize a political party that could, if need be, compel the government to heed African opinion.

So, in October, 1953, a group of the TAA's leading members decided to form a new party, which was to be named the Tanganyika African National Union. It was "to fight relentlessly until Tanganyika is self-governing and independent, to build a united nationalism," to fight against "tribalism . . . against racialism and racial discrimination," and to press for elections to all governmental institutions. Nyerere wanted to sound out opinion in the country and to be sure that his party could take over the many local branches of the TAA, which would be invaluable to him in building a national organization. So he visited Tabora, Dodoma, Iringa, and Bukoba. Pamphlets and leaflets were written, plans made to recruit members, the railway workers pressed into distributing literature on their journeys. On July 7, 1954, at the annual meeting of the TAA, it was announced that the association was to be transformed into the Tanganyika African National Union. The first specifically political party was born, and Nyerere, at the age of thirty-two, was unanimously elected as its president.

No one had any clear idea of what the character of the new party was to be. All that was clarified in the original constitution was that only Africans were to be allowed to join, that they must be at least eighteen years old, and that other organizations, such as tribal associations and trade unions, could affiliate on the payment of a levy proportionate to their membership. It was decided to confine membership to Africans because it was felt that the African community, unlike the other communities, had never had its own political organization and that Africans needed to acquire confidence in their ability to conduct their own affairs.

What determined the actual nature of TANU was not so much deliberate decisions on the part of the leadership as political moods throughout the country. These differed in detail in various regions, but they all saw a need for African organization and action. The postwar growth of the economy, for instance, had led to the establishment of an increasing number of cooperatives in certain areas. In the early 1950's, the Sukuma showed the greatest advance in this direction when they created the Victoria Federation of Cooperative Unions. These farmer cooperatives threw up new leaders who became of greater local significance than the traditional chiefs. Centered in Mwanza, the focus of radical political economics at the time that TANU was being created, men such as Paul Bomani and I. M. Bhoke Mananka were making their names in the cooperative movement, which led them to study and criticize the government's economic policies, especially those concerned with agricultural production and marketing. The cooperatives also brought many farmers into the political arena for the first time, in order to express the grievances they felt against the government's agricultural regulations.

The most famous and significant example of awakening militancy, revealing the connection between local issues and growing national consciousness, was the Meru Lands case, which began in 1951. The incident started when the government decided to move about 3,000 Meru from land they had bought between the two mountains Meru and Kilimanjaro to an alternative area so that European-held lands on the fertile slopes could be consolidated. The Meru were resentful, believing that European farmers had incited the government to evict them. They set up a local union to organize their resistance, and they lobbied the U.N. visiting mission. Eventually they approached the TAA, as their chief spokesman, Kirilo Japhet, was secretary of its Arusha branch. A safari was arranged on which money was collected to send Japhet to New York to petition the United Nations. Not only did it succeed in raising the money needed, but it brought the case to the attention of many people far from Meru territory. Alienation of land touched the deepest core of African sensitivity. This case, together with other resentments against government land policies, brought the farmers on to the national political stage, where they joined the intellectuals, the ex-servicemen, and the urban workers from Dar es Salaam, Tanga, Tabora, and Mwanza. By the time TANU was born, a good deal of discontent stretched across the country ready to be coordinated into opposition to the government. Thus TANU from the start was called on to become a popular national movement.

It should not be thought, however, that all Nyerere and his colleagues had to do was create a party bureaucracy that would weld these elements into a single centralized party. One feature of Tanzania that is often ignored is the disparity among its various regions. In the early days of TANU, a party that was the brainchild of a few visionaries with virtually no resources, it would have been quite impossible to establish an organized network of officials centered in Dar es Salaam. Nor was this the original objective. Tanganyika was, after all, a very large country with a scattered population and rudimentary communications. Many of its people did not even live in villages but, rather, in dispersed homesteads.

The group around Nyerere, therefore, had the task of creating a catalyst for all of these disparate discontents. The TAA provided model local branches, and it had also conditioned local groups with particular grievances to recognize that a national organization could mobilize greater pressure than any single locality could. It was Nyerere's genius to identify a single national issue that would appeal to all sections without risking the divisive effects of representing particularist issues. He recognized that every local complaint could increase the demand for *Uhuru,* or freedom from colonial rule, provided he kept the call simple and avoided causing confusion by identifying his party with the local issues themselves, many of which involved contradictory viewpoints.

So TANU, with its simple demand for self-government, became the focus for the ruling family of the Fipa under pressure from a young, educated group of Catholics; for the educated radicals of the Kilimanjaro areas; for an underprivileged Muslim minority in Bukoba; for the cash-crop cooperatives of Sukumaland, where the elite was using popular resentment against agricultural regulations to campaign against traditionalist chiefs. Yet it was often felt to represent the interests of those who had experienced little development, as opposed to the wealthier cash crop farmers. Under Nyerere's shrewd leadership, the variety of political and social systems, the different resentments, and the various local leaders could all merge into a single national movement, based on the simple principle of *Uhuru,* in the conviction that the principle was relevant to their special problems.

The founders of TANU were fortunate in that the year of its creation, 1954, also saw another U.N. mission in the country. This enabled the new party to take a national initiative on the international stage within a few weeks of its birth. There were no full-time party officials then; Nyerere himself was still teaching at Pugu, often walking the twelve miles into Dar es Salaam at the end of the school day to attend a party meeting and returning on its completion. Yet the national executive of the party was able to meet a month after its formation and draft a memorandum to submit to the mission. In it, demands were made for immediate democratic elections, at least in the capital; for greater economic and educational aid; and for the freezing of all wages and salaries, the funds saved to be allocated to raising the living standards of the mass of ordinary people. This last proposal is particularly interesting in that it reveals Nyerere's attitude to an issue that was to be embodied in the Arusha Declaration thirteen years later: On both occasions, it raised some criticism from Africans who had absorbed the outside world's ethic that ambition should be rewarded by a higher income.

The 1954 mission developed into a somewhat confused group, with its members at odds. Nevertheless, under the influence of the American delegate, Mason Sears, it gave virtually uncritical support to the African case and was particularly sympathetic to TANU. The most important recommendation was that Britain should draw up a timetable for progress toward independence, which was to be achieved, as proposed by TANU, within twenty-five years. This immediately became an issue in British and Tanganyikan politics, with the British and colonial governments entirely rejecting the concept.

Encouraged by the support they had received from the mission, early in 1955 TANU decided to send Nyerere to New York to put its case before the Trusteeship Council. Money was collected for his fare, and at the end of February he left for America. There he was supported by Mason Sears and the Soviet delegate but opposed by the Tanganyikan Government's representatives—the Attorney-General, a European, an Asian, and an African. He made his case temperately and modestly, claiming that TANU was not opposed to the colonial administration but simply wanted assurance that the future would see a predominantly African government in power, the elective principle established, and practical progress made in preparing the people for self-government. He assured the Council that guarantees would be made for safeguarding the Asian and European inhabitants.

Nyerere had impressed both the U.N. members and the public who had heard his reasoned statement. But his moderation and reason did not secure him or his party acceptance by Governor Twining and his government. They still regarded such African politicians as agitators. They preferred to believe that the African members they nominated to the legislative council, most of whom supported government policies, were representative of African opinion. Nyerere himself had been an alternate member of the council in 1954, deputy to David Makwaia, the young chief who could always be relied on to follow the Governor's line. But Twining had very quickly dropped Nyerere from this position, realizing that he would never become a colonial-government man. So nervous had the government become about Nyerere's activities that when he went to New York it persuaded the Americans to limit his movements and get him out of the country immediately after addressing the Trusteeship Council.

It had become clear that the political struggle in Tanganyika had developed into a combat between Nyerere and Twining. In March, 1955, the new constitution was introduced, providing equal representation for each of the three racial communities. This was Twining's ideal and was known as "multiracialism." The Governor expected the model to last many years, as a preparation for self-government. Nyerere, on the other hand, enunciated a policy of "nonracialism:" representation for people irrespective of their racial origins. To Nyerere, democracy meant the participation of each person in the determination of his society's affairs through the representatives elected to speak for him. This could not be equated with dividing people into racial groups, and certainly not with giving 20,000 Europeans and 80,000 Asians equal representation with 8 million Africans.

On his return from New York, Nyerere had to make a difficult decision. He realized that, despite the sympathy he had received from the fathers in his school, he could not continue indefinitely to combine teaching and national politics. What finally decided him was his recognition that it would not be fair to his pupils to give them only half his attention. He therefore resigned and for some months found it difficult to support his wife and children. After a spell at home in Musoma, where he soon abandoned an attempt to farm and another working for a mission, he returned to the capital, where his wife opened a small store. By then, however, Oscar Kambona had begun to have some success in his organizational efforts, which included collecting subscriptions for the party. Nyerere himself made several visits to various regions, successfully attracting new membership for TANU with his persuasive speeches. One special feature of these early days of the party was the sudden and large recruitment of women, almost unknown in African political history, except for the market women of West Africa. This was largely due to the efforts of a remarkable, almost illiterate Muslim, Bibi Titi, who formed a women's section of TANU so effectively that by the end of 1955 there were more female than male party members.

In 1955, a new issue arose that could have become either a strength or a weakness of the party. The government began to offer scholarships to some of its leading members to study abroad, and foreign organizations interested in the new party did the same. This could have weakened the organization by removing key personalities at a time when its fate was still in the balance. But Nyerere had such self-confidence that he never hesitated. He had personal experience of the advantages to be gained by living in another society and urged his lieutenants to take advantage of their opportunity. Nyerere himself was so confident that, on his second visit to the United States in 1956, he sought scholarships for his people to study in that country. He was determined that his movement should be led by men and women with maximum education and experience.

In 1955, TANU also acquired the support of an important group of people, albeit some of them were to prove troublesome in later years. In that year, a national trade-union center, the Tanganyika Federation of Labor, was formed after a visit from Tom Mboya, whose union work in Kenya had gained the support of the International Confederation of Free Trade Unions (ICFTU). Rashidi Kawawa, who, though interested in TANU, had been unable to join because he was a civil servant, became TFL's first secretary-general. He resigned from the service, joined TANU, and devoted himself to organizing the trade-union movement. A series of strikes during 1956 revealed its growing strength and added another organized section of discontented Tanganyikans to the forces behind TANU.

Toward the end of 1956, Nyerere paid his second visit to America, where he not only spoke to the Fourth Committee of the United Nations but also lectured in New York, Washington, Boston, and Chicago and appeared on television. And on this visit his demands increased. He now asked that all unofficial members of the legislature be elected and that half of the seats of that body and of the executive be allocated to Africans. When asked when he thought independence should come, he hesitatingly suggested that it be granted in about ten years. On his return, it became obvious that the Governor was becoming more frightened of his opponent, even though Nyerere had reiterated in New York that his quarrel was not with the Europeans but with British policy. The government published a pamphlet that angrily, and at times scurrilously, refuted Nyerere's arguments and banned him from speaking at open-air meetings.

Yet these actions rebounded on the government. Nyerere had already gained widespread respect for his challenge to colonial power at the United Nations. It now seemed that the Governor considered him so important that he was throwing governmental power against him. If the Governor thought he warranted so much attention, Nyerere must be a powerful man. Whatever the Governor did seemed doomed to increase his opponent's prestige.

Twining's political action only increased Nyerere's party's solidarity. At the end of 1955, a new organization, the United Tanganyika Party (UTP), was formed. It was well-known that it had the support of the government, including the Governor, who had inspired its formation. It even secured the services of a British Conservative Party ex-organizer. There was never any possibility of its undermining TANU among the Africans, but it might have denied to Nyerere the support and advice of Asian and European supporters, which were invaluable to him, particularly in sustaining his nonracial image; for the UTP boasted that its membership was multiracial, and it did manage to recruit members from all races. Its most prominent African was Kidaha Makwaia, who never had any mass support. The UTP attempted to tar TANU with the brush of racialism because the latter group only allowed Africans to join; yet the UTP essentially represented the multiracial approach, with checks and balances among racial blocs. It was easy for Nyerere to point out that multiracialism would leave white domination unchecked for many years and to pour scorn on its pretension to remove color bars by degrees. Much the same attitude was taken to it as that shown by American blacks to white liberals who promise gradual integration as whites are converted from racism—it is the whites who are left to decide who shall be integrated and when. In Tanganyika, the blacks comprised over 99 per cent of the population, and the inequity of such a policy there would be more than obvious.

The most important function performed by the UTP was to present some challenge to TANU. This stimulated the efforts of TANU officers to increase the party's size and strength, to insist on discipline —which was often lax away from Dar es Salaam—and to mobilize all available resources. A rival party was just what Nyerere needed to sharpen his party's weapons; it marked TANU's coming of age.

The year 1957 was crucial to the battle between Governor and nationalist. It began with further harassment of TANU: A member of the party was convicted of sedition; the Korogwe branch was deregistered; several others refused registration; Nyerere was banned from Tanga province. But in March Kwame Nkrumah achieved independence for Ghana; his policy of cooperation with his governor had succeeded. The only argument that could now be deployed against Nyerere's claims was that similar progress toward self-government in Tanganyika would undermine the British Government's policy of multiracialism under white domination in Kenya and the Central African Federation—and the British Government did not wish to be exposed in that posture. In any case, Tanganyika was moving toward an elective system, partially as a result of Nyerere's constant pressure at the United Nations, in Britain, and through his party. Although the government had included five UTP members to one TANU representative on its Franchise Committee, the election act passed in May, 1957, provided for a common electoral roll, with educational, property, office, or income qualifications. Each voter was to have three votes, one for a candidate of each race, and all three votes had to be cast. It was obvious that, even though only a fraction of Africans would qualify to vote under these restrictions, their total number would far exceed those of other races. The only hope for the UTP was that TANU would be incapable of providing European and Asian candidates sufficiently attractive to compete with those from its own multiracial ranks. There was also the possibility that TANU would follow the tactics of some other African parties and refuse to contest elections held on the basis of a restricted roll.

When Nyerere appeared again before the Trusteeship Council, surprisingly supported this time by Tom Marealle, the Chagga chief who had been expected to support the government, and announced that TANU wanted to contest the elections, this doubt appeared settled. On his return from New York, his popularity was so clearly demonstrated that the Governor now considered it expedient to remove the prohibitions on Nyerere and his party and appoint him to the legislative council. Nyerere did not retain that office for long. He found himself isolated among government supporters, including Africans such as David Makwaia. At the end of the year he resigned, pointing out that every proposal he had made had been rejected. For Nyerere, the battle was still in the countryside, though it was still useful for the other TANU members to retain their seats and thus preserve a national platform.

This was a critical moment for Tanganyika; only Nyerere and his most intimate friends held the bridge against disaster. In October, the British Colonial Secretary, Alan Lennox-Boyd, in the course of a visit to the territory, had brusquely supported the Governor's policy and rebuked the nationalists.

In the context of this British repudiation of Nyerere and TANU, of the barely concealed threat of drastic repression, and of Nyerere's resignation from the council, the party had to decide its policy toward the elections to be held in 1958 and 1959. It was not generally known that Nyerere had told the United Nations that TANU wished to contest the elections. When the annual conference of the party met in Tabora at the beginning of 1958, therefore, the decision on whether to contest or boycott the elections was the principal item on the agenda. The hundred delegates, who came from all over the country, argued heatedly for four days, most of them opposed to contesting the "fraudulent" elections, and calling for a general strike. But Nyerere knew that this would mean the end of constitutional progress toward self-government and a relapse into violence. If that course had been taken, he might well have felt constrained to resign; certainly the whole history of Tanganyika, and of East and Central Africa, would have been radically different.

This was the supreme test of his nerve and of his ability to persuade his passionate followers to choose reason rather than emotion. It was perhaps his closing speech, facing a crowd that had already made up its mind against his policy, which won the bitter battle. Characteristically, he related his argument by metaphor to a commonplace of African life:

> Imagine that you have a shamba and that in front of it there is a pond, with a lot of mud around it. If you want to harvest your crops and carry them out of the shamba you must step into the mud and dirty your feet. What would you prefer? To lose your crops and keep your feet clean? Or to harvest your crops and dirty your feet? Now think about what we want. We want that house in which Twining is now living. In order to get into it, we must dirty our feet by walking through the mud of an unfair election. What would you rather do? Keep your feet clean and not get the Twining house, or dirty your feet and get the Twining house?

Nyerere's reason triumphed over the more impulsive passions. He converted the vast majority of the delegates, and amidst immense cheering, it was resolved to contest the elections. Provided that the government allowed fair elections, Nyerere's policy of constitutional, nonviolent, unrelenting pressure toward self-rule was reaffirmed as

TANU's national strategy, and he himself was established as its unassailable *mwalimu,* or teaching leader.

One of the results of the Tabora decision was that a former official, Zuberi Mtemvu, decided to form an opposition party. He accused TANU of being too concerned with non-Africans. While he believed that Tanganyika should become completely African, he denied that he wished to drive non-Africans out of the country; rather, he considered that they should not be accorded any influence. Mtemvu's Tanganyika African Congress was refused registration and never achieved any mass support, but it helped TANU—just as the formation of the UTP had. With the appearance of the Congress in the arena, the TANU lions suddenly seemed very tame to Europeans.

Governor Twining was due to retire in June, 1958. But his last few months were far from peaceful. He tried to use the chiefs in an effort to block TANU's advance, but the party had been shrewd enough to recognize the importance of securing support from some of the elders from the start. During the early months of the year, one of the unions had declared a boycott of beer because the brewery employers were using scab labor to break a strike over wages. TANU backed the boycott, thus cementing the alliance between party and unions.

Finally, and most important of all, Nyerere was prosecuted for criminal libel against two government officials. The case stemmed from friction that had arisen between administrators and TANU officials in certain districts. This was inevitable so long as the Governor and government continued to regard Nyerere and his party as agitators to be harassed. But it is also true, and it was equally inevitable, that some TANU officials and members in the countryside made wild statements and came to regard themselves as above the law. When Nyerere wrote bitter criticisms of the two administrative officials in his party paper in May, 1958, he was charged with criminal libel. The case aroused intense emotions; the government simply could not win: If acquitted, he would be thought to have beaten the government; if condemned, he would become a martyr. In the event, he was fined, with the alternative of six months in

prison. All precedent from colonial Africa and other parts of the empire pointed to the advantage of refusing to pay the fine and going to
prison. He could thereby become one of the British Empire's famous
"prison graduates," that select band of nationalist leaders who had
spent time in colonial jails and emerged to lead their countries to
independence—such as Mahatma Gandhi, Jawaharlal Nehru, Jomo
Kenyatta, and Kwame Nkrumah. Nyerere did not take advantage
of the opportunity the government blindly set before him. He
paid the fine, thus again avoiding the turbulence and violence that
would assuredly have followed his imprisonment. One may wonder
whether he would have taken this conciliatory attitude if Twining
had still been Governor, but Twining's term had expired the month
before the trial took place.

On July 15, two significant public events took place in Dar es
Salaam. In the Court House, Julius Nyerere was on trial; in Government House, Richard Turnbull took the oath as Tanganyika's
new Governor. From the start, Richard Turnbull brought a new
atmosphere to Tanganyika. Not only did he deliver his inaugural
address in Swahili, as well as in English, but he actually invited
Nyerere to visit him at Government House while the nationalist
leader was awaiting judgment in his trial. Turnbull's first words to
Nyerere were prophetic: "I am glad to meet you, Mr. Nyerere. You
and I have a great responsibility in this country." When Turnbull
announced that the second half of the elections, planned for September, 1959, would be brought forward to February, the African
nationalists recognized that there could be different kinds of
governors under the colonial system and that they had been fortunate enough to be allocated one who might become a friend. It
was Nyerere's early recognition of this possibility that moved him
to reject prison and pay his fine. If he had gone to prison, serious
disturbances would certainly have broken out, and the new governor would never have had a chance to prove that he was anxious
to help the country to achieve independence. As it turned out,
Turnbull was to be very useful to Nyerere in guiding him through
the intricacies of British constitutional practice so as to introduce
independence as smoothly as possible.

In September, 1958, the first stage of the elections for the legislative council was held. Despite its dislike of the system, TANU realized that, because one member of each race would be elected in each constituency and each voter would have to cast three votes, it was necessary to take some attitude toward the European and Asian candidates. The Tabora conference had called for responsible government in 1959; the outcome of the elections would largely determine the practicability of this objective. So, for the twelve seats that were actually contested—the other three involving unopposed candidates—TANU not only nominated its own candidates but also indicated which of the Europeans and Asians it regarded as most sympathetic to the African cause. This policy resulted in at least one event symbolic of the interracial cooperation on which Nyerere was relying. At Moshi, the center of a white farmers' community, Nyerere addressed a large meeting—flanked by Solomon Eliufoo, the TANU candidate; Sophia Mustafa, the Asian; and Derek Bryceson, the European. Nothing could so dramatically illustrate Nyerere's objective of raising politics above the racial level.

There were 28,500 voters registered for the five constituencies. TANU received 67 per cent of the 22,769 votes cast, and every TANU-supported candidate was elected. Nyerere himself polled three times as many votes as his opponent in the eastern-province constituency he had chosen. The UTP was unable to secure a single seat, and Mtemvu, the sole Congress candidate, polled only 53 votes. It was now proved beyond a doubt that TANU represented the nation; the UTP quickly disappeared, and the Congress had never really appeared as a party.

In October, Turnbull opened the new legislative council. Some of his words on that occasion are worth recalling, for they reveal why Africans and their European and Asian supporters felt that the new governor was proving himself to be one of their team.

> In terms of population the Africans always will be an overwhelming majority in Tanganyika, and, as the country progresses, it is right and proper, as indeed it is natural and inevitable, that African participation both in the legislature and in the executive should steadily increase. It it not intended, and never has been intended, that parity

should be a permanent feature of the Tanganyika scene. It *is* intended, and always has been intended, that the fact that when self-government is eventually attained both the legislature and the Government are likely to be predominantly African should in no way affect the security of the rights and interests of those minority communities who have made their homes in Tanganyika. I am glad to note that the responsible leaders of major political parties in the Territory are in complete agreement on this important matter.

This was all Nyerere had ever asked of the government. Turnbull had even deliberately changed the term "multiracial" to "nonracial" as a description of his government's policy. It was but three short years since Twining had introduced "parity."

The TANU victory was so overwhelming that in the second half of the elections the following February only three seats were contested, one for Europeans and two for Asians. Again those supported by TANU were elected, giving the party a clean sweep of all elective seats in the legislature.

It seemed as though most of the hurdles had been cleared and TANU would soon be in control of the country. Yet, certain problems remained. The first was the state of discipline within the party itself. In the natural jubilation caused by the resounding electoral success, some party members, believing that self-government had virtually been achieved, began to treat the law with contempt. They defied authority, taunting those who would impose it with the boast that the nationalists would soon be in power. The situation became particularly bad around Mwanza, where party militants defied regulations concerning cattle and land. Nyerere flew to Mwanza and bluntly told a large crowd that membership in TANU did not put them above the law. His speech and its effects on discipline received wide praise, including a special commendation from the Governor.

The second issue was much more important and not so well known publicly. The current British Government was entering its fifth year, which meant that a general election would have to be held not later than May, 1960. As British governments rarely leave an election until the final possible moment, it was likely to be held sometime in 1959 (in fact, it was held in October, 1959). In 1959, disturbances broke out in the two Rhodesias and Nyasaland, and states of emergency were declared in Southern Rhodesia and Nyasaland. The House of Commons was very much disturbed about the Devlin Report on conditions in Nyasaland and also over the scandal of Hola Camp in Kenya, where a number of detainees had been killed.

It seemed as though the very existence of the Central African Federation might be threatened by repression and violence in the Rhodesias and Nyasaland, where Africans were making a determined stand against what they regarded as white domination. It was feared by those who were friends of Tanganyika and also close to the British political scene that democratic progress in Tanganyika might well be sacrificed on the altar of preserving white power in Salisbury and Nairobi.

Since then, these fears have been proved justified. Roy Welensky, then Prime Minister of the Federation, reports in his book that on March 19, 1959, Lord Perth, Minister of State at the Colonial Office, told a meeting of his federal cabinet, "so far as our general colonial policy is concerned, a halt is being called to the rapid advance of colonial territories to independence. For Tanganyika, for example, we are proposing a long-term programme." This was starkly contrary to the expectations Turnbull had been offering to Nyerere and his colleagues. It is now clear that the British Government was prepared to sacrifice progress toward democratic government and independence in Tanganyika lest it inspire the Africans of Central Africa to make similar demands. Perhaps London did not realize how much chaos and bloodshed this would have caused in Tanganyika, though Turnbull can be trusted to have warned them. But it is clear that during 1959 and at the beginning of 1960 British policy was teetering on the brink of disaster.

Fortunately the Conservatives, or at least Prime Minister Harold Macmillan and his intimates, realized that African issues could be disastrous to them in the election and to their new government. The position was held until the election by the appointment of the Monckton Commission for Central Africa; after the Conservatives took office, Alan Lennox-Boyd was replaced by Iain Macleod, who had a much livelier insight into African realities and sensibilities. Macmillan's "wind of change" speech in Cape Town at the beginning of 1960 marked a recognition by the Conservatives that before long Britain would have to leave its African empire to be governed by its African inhabitants.

The third concern was about the outcome of the deliberations of the Ramage committee, which was to make proposals for future constitutional development. The committee was appointed in May, 1959, and the doubts expressed over its possible proposals were linked to fears about Conservative policy. Fortunately, and wisely, the committee did not report until after the British general election. By that time Macmillan had changed his policy and Nyerere and Turnbull had both been to London to discuss the future; when the report was published at the end of the year, TANU had no serious worries over it.

Once the elections were over in February, 1959, and TANU had shown its strength, the Governor appointed a Council of Ministers, which was to include five unofficial members of the legislature. Nyerere, now chairman of the Elected Members Organization in the legislature, decided not to accept one of the posts, but to remain leader of the opposition with five of his colleagues joining the government. Accordingly, Bryceson, Eliufoo, Chief Fundikira, Jamal, and Kahama became ministers; Nyerere was waiting until the elected members were granted a majority in the Council of Ministers. Indeed, Nyerere had experienced some trouble in persuading his TANU colleagues to refrain from bitter opposition to the Governor over the creation of his council. TANU had demanded self-government in 1959; this was then amended to "responsible" government, which would entail a majority of the ministers being appointed from the elected members. Turnbull could not concede this. The danger was that if he did not accede to the demand Nyerere might be overthrown inside his own party. A strike was talked about, and the Governor was ready to declare a state of emergency. A compromise was negotiated, increasing the original four unofficial members to five, with a promise of another statement later in the year; Nyerere's reason again prevailed, and he wisely told his party that he would not be one of the five.

Two other issues arose. The first concerned the position to be accorded non-Africans in the new constitution. TANU had proposed that the new legislature consist of 82 members, 79 of them elected, 21 of the elected seats to be reserved for non-Africans, 13 for Asian, and 8 for Europeans. The object of this reserved-seats system was to pave the way to full democracy by sustaining confidence among non-Africans that they were not being ignored as Africans advanced into power. In its report, the committee accepted almost all of TANU's proposals, though it altered the proposed figures. It suggested 71 seats, 50 elected from a common roll, 11 reserved for Asians, and 10 for Europeans. But this issue was wider than that of representation. Nyerere constantly urged his people to recognize that the way was open to self-government but that self-government entailed an era of extra hard work. Symbolically, the party changed its slogan from *Uhuru,* or "freedom," to *Uhuru na Kazi,* "freedom and work." If this difficult effort was to be efficient, it would be essential to persuade as many skilled Asians and Europeans as possible to remain in the country, especially in the civil service and in economic activities. Yet there were those in the party and outside it who bitterly opposed this policy. To them, self-government must be accompanied by Africanization of all sectors of national life. TANU's policy was described as "localization"—the employment of Tanganyikans, irrespective of race, in place of aliens—as distinct from "Africanization." More was to be heard of this dispute both before and after independence.

The second issue concerned the place to be accorded the chiefs. A suggestion had been made that the chiefs might form a Territorial Council, which would act as a kind of second chamber. Nyerere made his position quite clear when he said, "We tell the Chiefs quite frankly that their authority is traditional only in the tribes, which were the traditional units. Tanganyika is not a traditional unit at all, and if the Chiefs want to have a place in this thing we call Tanganyika, they have got to adapt themselves to this new situation. There is nothing traditional in the Central Government of Tanganyika today." Thus Nyerere sharply distinguished his concept of African national progress from the conception prevalent in, for instance, his neighbor Kenya, where the chiefs retained strong influence. And thus he prepared the way for his later efforts to use self-government as a means to modernization.

Constitutionally, the road to independence was now comparatively smooth. The next election, not due until 1962, was brought forward to August, 1960, only eighteen months after the previous one. Tanganyika was promised that responsible government would follow it. This decision represented not only another triumph for TANU but also confidence in Nyerere personally. The government, which until recently had been condemning him as an agitator, now told the United Nations that "in Mr. Nyerere we have an outstanding political leader—indeed a great African statesman."

In February, 1960, on Nyerere's recommendation, Ernest Vasey, a liberal European who had been finance minister in Kenya, was appointed as an unofficial minister on the Council of Ministers, thus ending the official majority. After spending a month in the United States at the invitation of the State Department, Nyerere stopped off in London to join Turnbull and Vasey in discussions with the Colonial Secretary on the future structure of the council. In April, it was announced that after the elections a majority of elected ministers would be appointed to the council, one of them to be Chief Minister, though the Governor would remain chairman and retain responsibility for the police.

In August, the election was held with an electoral roll open to about 1,500,000 inhabitants. In fact, only slightly over half of those qualified actually registered. This foreshadowed a problem for the near future. It was widely felt that TANU had won the battle and faced no serious opposition, so there seemed little need to register or vote. Popular participation in the tasks ahead was gravely undervalued. Moreover, of the 71 elective seats only 13 were contested, 58 candidates being unopposed. After the elections, every successful candidate but one was a member of TANU or supported the party, and the single exception soon joined the fold. Although he had denied having any intention of creating a single-party state, Nyerere had had one thrust upon him.

The way was thus opened for Nyerere to assume a position of governmental responsibility with power for the first time. Within a few weeks of the election, he was appointed Chief Minister and he formed his own government, though still subject to the over-riding authority of the Governor. In a radio address that evening, he told his fellow countrymen, "It was the character of our people which made inevitable the achievement of responsible government and which again renders inevitable the achievement of our complete independence. It is that same character which ensures our success in the struggle against ignorance, poverty, disease, and fear—a struggle in which I am proud and privileged to lead you."

The following March another constitutional conference took place in Dar es Salaam, attended by Britain's Colonial Secretary, Iain Macleod. Within two days, the conference was completed in entire agreement. At the beginning of May, full internal self-government would be granted. This meant that all official members, including the Governor, would leave the Council of Ministers, which would then become a cabinet. Internal security would be the responsibility of elected ministers, and the Governor's powers would be confined to defense and foreign affairs. In December, Tanganyika would become independent, a fully sovereign state. It would apply to join the Commonwealth and the United Nations, the U.N. Trust Agreement terminating on the day of independence. When the announcement was made, wild cheering broke out among the thousands gathered outside Karimjee Hall. Warm appreciation of the part played by the Governor was expressed by Nyerere, and, as Macleod, Turnbull, and Nyerere emerged, they were garlanded by the crowd, which formed a triumphal procession into the town.

On May 1, Nyerere became Tanganyika's first Prime Minister and his cabinet of twelve was sworn in by the Governor. Its average age was thirty-seven. Most of the TANU stalwarts—Kambona, Kahama, Bomani, Bryceson, Jamal, Fundikira, Kawawa, Swai— were among its members. The Governor was henceforth constitutionally bound to accept its advice on domestic matters. One section of the Prime Minister's office was devoted to working with the Governor on foreign affairs and defense so as to prepare for taking over these responsibilities on independence.

The constitutional path to independence might now be smooth; the preparation of the party and its personnel to assume sovereign responsibilities was not. Early in 1960, Nyerere had revealed his anxiety over the attitude of some party officials when he had spoken at TANU's annual conference: "I have seen some TANU officers getting drunk with power," he told delegates, "and scheming to undermine one another. Some officers are too interested in finding ways of dominating others and in seeking to eliminate their friends from their posts . . . many of our leaders are working for responsible government to provide themselves with high positions."

There was trouble with the trade unions too. Annoyed over Nyerere's insistence that his government sought to replace aliens with local employees regardless of their racial origin, the Federation of Labour took its stand on giving Africans preference. C. K. Tumbo, a railway-union official, declaring that he stood for "revolution," attacked the government's gradualist approach. Nyerere reacted sharply. He reminded the unions that they, being part of TANU, should cooperate with party policy.

Despite this rebuke, anti-government criticism continued to mount in trade-union circles right up to the time of independence. A number of unions threatened the government with strikes in support of their wage demands. Nyerere again reacted strongly. He was always conscious of the great gap that yawned between the few organized workers in the towns and the mass of rural peoples who had no unions to represent them. He told the unions bluntly that the country could not afford to increase wages at that moment, and he threatened to dismiss any government workers who struck. It was clear that, if the government was to represent the interests of the majority after independence and pursue any coherent program of social justice, it would soon have to face the issue of the trade unions, which, though representing only a tiny minority, were the only group with the organizational capability to challenge TANU.

What made it more difficult to resist the workers' wage demands was the fact that the economic division of the country largely coincided with its racial division. Nyerere was very conscious of this. He had publicly warned that, unless the standard of living of the masses could be raised soon after independence, racial harmony might be destroyed by those who would play on economic contrasts to undermine the government's nonracial policy. Amir Jamal, meanwhile, urged the Asian communities to recognize their responsibility to identify themselves with the nation and to cease to regard themselves as the privileged few.

But these efforts did not prevent economic-racial hostility from building up within the country as independence approached. There were disturbances in the countryside, particularly around Mbeya and in the Lake Province, the victims usually being Asian shopkeepers. Most menacing was the hostility shown to the government when it introduced its citizenship regulations. The provision that any citizen of a Commonwealth country who had lived in Tanganyika for five years would be qualified to register as a citizen brought a storm of criticism in the National Assembly. A group of members led by Tumbo bitterly condemned the automatic admission of non-Africans to citizenship. Although Nyerere roundly condemned their attitude as racist, comparable to that of the Nazis, and saw his bill approved by a large majority, another seed of post-independence dissension had been sown.

Neither these differences of opinion nor the fervor with which they were expressed should cause surprise. TANU had been formed as a national movement to liberate the people of Tanganyika from colonial rule. TANU's achievement was to retain such mass nontribal and nonracial confidence during the preparations for independence that the arguments, criticisms, and divisions that arose never threatened the nation as they did in the neighboring Congo during the same period.

Despite this dissent and its portent for the future, independence itself was welcomed with a spirit of national unity and rejoicing. On the sweltering midnight of December 8–9, the lights of the new stadium in Dar es Salaam dimmed over a throng of 75,000 people. The band played "God Save the Queen" as the Union Jack was lowered. A spotlight shone on the green, black, and gold flag (representing land, people, and mineral wealth) of independent Tanganyika at the top of its pole. All broke out into wild cheering, culminated by the singing of the new nation's Swahili national anthem, *"Mungu Ibariki Afrika,"* which can be loosely translated as "God Bless Africa." At the same moment, in the midst of a snowstorm, an African army officer lit a torch on the summit of Kilimanjaro, symbolizing Tanganyika's freedom. Nyerere himself put the moment into words that both gave character to the achievement and took his people over the bridge from colonialism to the responsibilities of independence.

> How have we come by this great event? The answer is that we are free because we spoke with one voice; you have all stood shoulder to shoulder in unity and in a common determination to run our own affairs. . . . Today we rejoice but tomorrow we have our freedom to preserve and strengthen. We Tanganyikans will not seek to do this with armies and navies and air forces. We shall do it by work, work that will increase our riches, so that we do not have to depend on our friends to provide us with our daily bread, and so that we ourselves can lift from our own shoulders the burdens of poverty, ignorance and disease. . . . *Uhuru na furaha!* [joy] *Uhuru na Tanganyika! Uhuru na Afrika!*

The next morning, Prince Philip, Duke of Edinburgh, representing the Queen, handed to Nyerere the instruments of sovereignty; a new nation had been born.

8 The People and Their Life

The family forms the core of African life. The significance of the family to Africans has not been experienced in the Western world for centuries, if ever. Indeed, although family life is universal, it is doubtful whether it is adequate to describe by the same word the vastly different institutions that exist in Africa and in Europe and America. The Western concept of family may be described as nuclear, with a single center; that of the African is essentially cohesive, all-embracing, and infinite.

African family relationships involve less intense but more widely diffused emotions than those typical of the Western. Whereas the Western habit is to try to compress the major domestic feelings into a single husband-wife relationship, extended slightly outward to include mother-child, father-child, and sibling relationships, the African pattern is much broader. Polygyny, which is common but not universal, must embrace multiple husband-wife, wife-wife, mother-child, child–half-mother, and sibling relationships. For, although the children of polygynous families normally live with their own mothers, they are definitely all members of the same family. The traditional African family, therefore, not only is larger than that of the West but also creates a wider community of interest—particularly among the women. Moreover, this form of family provides a high degree of security for its members.

Not only are the children protected from the loneliness of orphanhood, but the women also are shielded from that of widowhood. Family customs vary, but the usual practice is for the rights and responsibilities of a man to be passed at death to a brother or son. Because all children belong to either the father's or the mother's kinship group—according to the variations between patrilineal and matrilineal custom—their status is not reduced by the death of a parent. And, because a mother derives her position from bearing a member of the lineage group, she retains it on the death of her husband, even if her children belong to their father's group. Indeed, the only people whose position in the African family system is insecure are the barren women and, to a lesser extent, the sterile men. Everyone else has their place ensured by their relation to children.

Various myths have arisen in the Western world concerning the character of African family life. Western women find it intolerable to think of sharing a husband (despite the fact that so many of them, knowingly or unknowingly, do so themselves). But the Western woman usually thinks of this as sharing her house with another woman. In Africa, each wife has her own home and usually brings up her children in it. Moreover, it is the practice to refrain from sexual intercourse as long as she is suckling her child, often for two years. She therefore does not usually bear more children than she would in a monogamous union. Men father more children, but because they marry later than the women, there is no shortage of wives; nor is the birth rate higher. Indeed, the birth rate is generally lower in polygynous than in monogamous families.

Nor is it true that polygyny reduces the status of women to that of serfs. African women usually have guaranteed legal rights, participate in religious and political affairs, and attain a high degree of economic independence. Of course, quarrels and jealousies occur in the polygynous family as in the monogamous. It is vital for the husband to treat his wives and children with absolute equality. Even then, co-wives may dislike each other, while such is the focal position of the children that any threat to the interests of a mother's child undermines her own security. One might also add that, if a husband can be henpecked by one wife, the possibilities are multiplied when he has several! As regards the great distaste shown toward the practice of paying a bride price, it should be recognized that this forms part of a social contract rather than being a purchase. The deposit—usually of cattle—is a guarantee that the husband will fulfill his duties, that the children will be acknowledged as his, and that he will be accorded his rights by his wife. If the marriage fails, the deposit must be returned. It acts as much as a protection for the wife as for the husband. It is also an essential element in the relationship of lineages with each other.

In short, the traditional African family is a community in which rights and responsibilities are determined by custom and known to all. It therefore provides a stable and secure structure from which social activities and duties can be undertaken. But it is only the innermost of a number of concentric circles composed of still wider communities. Kinship and lineage take on various forms in different African societies. Descent can be in a variety of directions. But each of them links members of families to larger communities that, in turn, form part of a larger whole—the tribe. At each stage in this progression, custom regulates rights and duties. The most essential portion of a child's life is the period of indoctrination into the mysteries and traditions of clan and tribe, usually taught within the child's age group, which forms yet another close and permanent association. Thus, every African is indissolubly linked to others of his kind and associated with relatives, friends, and colleagues in a variety of communal groups.

This concept of social organization is crucial in relation to land, still the basic element in almost all African societies, and certainly in Tanzania. The Western attitude to land derives from the assumptions of ownership. All land is "real estate," is marketable, can be bought and sold, even if by a corporation or by the state itself. It is, therefore, always envisioned as divided by boundaries, split into lots. A community—city, town, village, parish, homestead—exists as a collection of people living on a specifically defined area of land.

The African traditionally has a totally different conception of land. To him it is an element, like air, not a possession limited by boundaries. It is an essential part of his social organization, tribe, clan, lineage group, village. His land rights are basically derived from his membership of his community. And his community may not have been always attached to a particular area. Its members may have cleared the forest or scrub, planted, and reaped so long as the soil remained fertile, then left it fallow to recover and repeated the process elsewhere. Membership in the social group involved the right to farm a portion of the area being used by the group at a particular time; but the idea of "ownership," or of "buying" or "selling," was inconceivable. The right to use of a plot alongside and in conjunction with fellow members of the group derived from membership; it lapsed once membership ceased. Land usage has thus been one further binding factor in African social organization.

Many Tanzanians, probably most of them, still live this kind of life. Work is organized through the family, kinship, or village group. Women, still important in agricultural activities, and children play their prescribed role along with the men. Community labor, needed for constructing paths or roads, building bridges, clearing land, and similar communal tasks, is arranged through one of the social groups. Often an age group will work together, again cementing social cohesion. Because the social group already has its established structure, leadership and authority do not have to be specially created, and it is universally recognized that contributions to communal efforts are among the obligations of group membership.

Thus, most Tanzanians spend their life as President Nyerere did his boyhood, in a mud-brick thatched hut—though wood and stone are increasingly being used—as part of a family that cultivates a plot of about five acres, on which it grows the corn, millet, sorghum, and beans that supply the family diet. Usually the family will also possess a few sheep and goats, which are grazed along with their neighbors' and provide occasional meat. Some families own a few of the indigenous shorthorn Zebu cattle that are also grazed communally and, partly because they supply milk, are rarely killed for meat unless old or barren. Cattle still provide social status in many African societies and, as mentioned above, are also valuable in fulfilling social obligations. In addition to producing their own needs, members of the family will at times join with others in the community to break a new path, repair the market, or build a bridge. The family may live in a village or settlement, which is more common in the south, but in some parts of the country a homestead may be isolated in deserted countryside.

Many factors have been and are today effecting slow changes in this traditional pattern of life. The introduction of industry in a few centers, the consequent urbanization and need for the young in towns, the growth of cooperatives, efforts to induce permanent settlement, the increase in the number of schools—all impinge on the habits of rural life. Nevertheless, Tanzania remains very largely a rural country. The habits of the agriculturalist are varied on the lakesides and seashores by fishing; certain tribes, the Masai in particular, still remain essentially pastoralists, their diet based on milk and blood, their herds being driven to wherever water and grazing are available at different periods of the year. But these are only variations in the traditional life, which still dominates among most of the inhabitants.

The most important impact on traditionalism has been the introduction and encouragement of cash crops. In many areas, these have been added to traditional occupations rather than replaced them. To the subsistence foods grown by the family, crops such as oil seeds and cotton have been added, to be sold for money as the need for cash increases. But the major impact of cash crops came first from coffee-growing. Despite the early opposition of European growers, Africans soon mastered the art of production and revealed their organizational skills. Thus, on the slopes of the two neighboring mountains in the north, Meru and Kilimanjaro, many Africans live as smallholders and grow coffee.

The Arabica type of coffee flourishes best in a cool climate, in fertile soil, and with a well-spaced rainfall. These conditions are found on those two mountains and in other mountainous areas, for instance, in the vicinity of Songea, Rungwe, Mbeya, and Morogoro. Robusta coffee is favored by the warmth of lower altitudes, which has enabled Bukoba to become the center for its growth. The

Chagga in the north showed the way in coffee production in the period between the wars. They proved that the cooperative method of farming and marketing could provide a natural bridge between traditional African communal life and the demand for cash crops. Now the Tanganyika Coffee Growers Association and the Kilimanjaro Native Co-operative Union, together with the Bukoba cooperative, ensure that methods of production are constantly improved while the government-appointed Coffee Board markets the entire crop.

In the coffee areas, many African families spend their time working on their smallholdings, then send their crops through the local cooperative to the board, receiving cash advances from the cooperative until the board makes its payment. Usually coffee-growing is supplemented by continued production of the subsistence crops for family use, though wealthier growers have begun to buy their food instead of growing it. A handful of workers are also employed by the larger European and Asian coffee plantations—which are also members of the Growers Association. These estates vary from fifty to a thousand acres and grow the Arabica type.

Another crop that has begun to diversify some African farmers' lives is cotton. Tanzania has found that a variety of cotton known as "American upland" can be adapted to its conditions; it has been named "African upland." Almost all the cotton is grown on small family plots of between one and four acres. The most successful area is around the shores of Lake Victoria in Sukumaland. It is now being developed also in the east, in the Kilimanjaro and Arusha areas, near Tabora and Morogoro, and down the coast from Tanga, but in the east pests are much more prevalent than in the lake area. Nine-tenths of the country's crop is still produced beside Lake Victoria.

So, in these areas, many African families spend much of their time around the turn of the year in planting their cotton and some five or six months later in picking the crop. Planting and picking take place earlier in the lake district because of the variation in rainfall periods. After the seed has been picked, it is taken to the local cooperative, where it is weighed and the farmer is paid.

It is the cooperative's responsibility to pack it and transport it to the local ginnery, each one, whether a cooperative or privately owned, holding a monopoly over its own district. Then another government board auctions the bales to buyers in Dar es Salaam.

There are other occupations that vary the rural life of some African families, though none of them involve more than a small minority. The pastoral cattle-herders have been mentioned, though the wide prevalence of the tsetse fly severely limits the area they can use. There is fishing in the lakes and along the coast, though the lack of cold-storage facilities necessitates it being concentrated in high-population districts where a ready market is available. The fish, dried in the sun and smoked before being sent to inland markets, provide the people's only regular source of first-class protein. Cashew nuts, which originated in Brazil and were taken by the Portuguese to India in the sixteenth century and, presumably, from there to East Africa, are grown along the coast. They are sent by the growers to cooperatives and thence to the Agricultural Board, which then sells them to Indian merchants. The chief problem with cashews is that they have to be sent to India for processing, canning, and exporting, mainly to America. For, though two factories have been built, in Dar es Salaam and Mtwara, many more are needed if Tanzania is to gain the employment and export revenues it could expect from exporting directly itself.

Another occupation of some Tanzanians is tea-growing. Most of this crop is confined to the large foreign-owned estates in the highlands of the south and on the mountains near Tanga. The dried leaves are sold in Nairobi, Kenya, or in London. But smallholdings for tea-growing have also been started on a cooperative basis in the same areas and in Bukoba. A few Tanzanians work on these estates and others on their own holdings.

Pyrethrum, another cash crop, is grown in the south and around Kilimanjaro. Tanzanian production is second only to that of Kenya in the world market. Most of the plants are grown in producer cooperatives by Africans; the oil is extracted from the flowers in a factory in Arusha, then exported to Britain or America. This substance is valuable as an insecticide, often used in aerosols, its special advantage being that it is not poisonous to humans and is, therefore, safely used in homes.

In tobacco-growing too, attempts are being made to encourage smallholders to replace estate production. Three types of crops are produced: flue-cured for most cigarettes, fire-cured for pipe tobacco, and aromatic for special Turkish cigarettes. Tobacco is grown in the regions of Ruvumu, Iringa, Tabora, and the northwest. Both the government and the British-American Tobacco Company are helping to develop smallholding participation, and the crop is expected to be particularly suitable for some of the new village settlement schemes. This will mean that people brought together in these villages will be able to diversify their activities by working on smallholdings producing a cash crop in addition to providing the food needed by their families.

Despite these varied agricultural activities in the production of commodities for sale, the bulk of production in Tanzania remains tied to local consumption. It is here, therefore, that effort on expansion is concentrated. The four sugar estates of 1953 had multiplied output sixfold by 1965; another estate has been planned, and it is hoped to raise the production to ten times that of 1953. Almost all this sugar will be needed for the domestic market. Attempts are also being made to increase the production of wheat and rice. Grain for local consumption has been so scarce that it has had to be imported, partly because of difficulty with the strains, plagues of birds, and lack of suitable land. In the effort to increase the output of rice, a staple food of the Asian inhabitants and of many small producers, a state farm was started. The growth of another and more generally staple food, corn, has expanded so successfully as to provide a small export income. Other cereals, sorghum, millet, and the cassava root, help to supplement the diet—though it will be noted that all these staple foods consist mostly of starch. Unless protein consumption can be greatly increased, undernourishment will remain endemic.

Finally, some Tanzanians add to their domestic activities the exploitation of various local products. The ubiquitous palm trees provide wood for building, fronds for thatching, and coconuts, which supply copra, oil, fiber, and fuel. Peanuts also provide oil, and beans, peas, and various seed flowers are grown quite widely, as are many tropical fruits—bananas, pineapples, papaw, mangoes, and citrus fruits. Again, a state farm has been started in the Mtwara area to encourage production.

Some 100,000 Tanzanians work in the country's factories. Industry is expanding in Tanzania, but slowly and in a controlled way that will be explained later. Before independence, the country had to rely heavily on imports from the other East African countries or from outside the continent. Nairobi and Mombasa in Kenya and Kampala and Jinja in Uganda attracted more investment and consequently experienced more rapid industrial growth, while Tanganyika was regarded mainly as a source of raw materials. Even the few industries operating in the country were almost entirely foreign-owned. Since independence, however, many more factories have been built, and there are now about seven thousand of them. This industrial growth has two main objectives: to supply Tanzanians themselves with goods that formerly had to be imported and to increase export revenues so as to enable the country to buy the essential goods it cannot yet produce. Inevitably, this progress has been impeded by the effects of earlier policies in East Africa, with the result that in 1964 and 1967 negotiations had to be conducted with Kenya and Uganda in an effort to adjust the imbalance of trade among the three neighbors. The creation of an East African Common Market for the three was intended to encourage industrial production throughout the region, to rationalize industrial development, and to provide a market large enough to stimulate expansion.

Tanzanian factories produce the kind of goods characteristic of developing economies all over the world. They manufacture consumer products instead of exporting materials and then buying back the processed product at an inflated price. Examples of this effort are to be seen in sisal-spinning, cashew nut–processing, and the production of soap, shoes, beer, tobacco, insecticides, and matches. Then there has been the growth of import-substitute manufactures—industries designed specifically to reduce dependence on imported goods, even if it is necessary in some cases to import the materials for local processing. Such activities as the manufacture of bicycle tires, pharmaceuticals, and aluminum ware, oil-refining, and the assembly of radios, trucks, and tractors come into this category.

The general policy is to concentrate on the use of local materials and local labor, giving priority to products that have a high export or import-substitution potential. New industries are given fiscal protection, and foreign capital is encouraged, provided that the economic structures laid down by the government are accepted. Both capital and profits can be repatriated. As will be explained more fully later, the economy is a mixture of private and state enterprise, with the state often acting in partnership with private firms. But the private and public sectors are clearly defined. However, a National Development Corporation engages in commercial enterprise with powers granted by the government.

The factor in the industrial sector of the Tanzanian economy that is most significant from the point of view of the people is the emphasis on labor-intensive investment. A basic need of the country is to absorb more workers into industry so as to reduce unemployment and encourage people at present confined to subsistence agriculture to leave the land. This is essential for a more rational development of modern farming techniques and for economic diversification. Therefore, it is in the interest of Tanzanians to develop industries that employ a large number of workers, rather than to use the latest methods of automation and capital-intensive machines. This policy also allows for simpler equipment, which is easier to handle, service or replace. The Chinese have recognized this possibility more clearly than anyone else. Consequently, when they built the Friendship Textile Factory outside Dar es Salaam or organized rice-growing or poultry production, they applied methods many Westerners thought laughable; experience has taught that these are precisely what the Tanzanians want and need at the present stage of their social and economic development.

About seven thousand Tanzanians are employed in mining. This is a very tiny proportion of the population, yet their work has considerable significance to the national economy. By far the most important activity is in the diamond mines at Mwadui, in the Shinyanga area of the northwest. Here J. T. Williamson, a Canadian mining geologist, made a major find in 1940. When he died in 1958, the government took a direct financial interest in the mine. Through the National Development Company, the government is now a 50 per cent owner of the mine and entitled to a quota of its sales. This brings in several million pounds to the treasury each year, depending on the amount of sales and the international control, which regulates diamond sales throughout the world. There is also some gold-mining in several areas, which probably can be extended with further exploration, some tin-mining in the northwest, as well as mica production on a small scale and a considerable output of salt near Lake Tanganyika. Coal and iron are known to exist, but high production costs have so far prevented any substantial exploitation. One of the most widely known minerals is meerschaum, found in a deposit near Kilimanjaro, from which are fashioned tobacco pipes famous throughout the world.

Only a small number of Tanzanians find employment in commerce, building, transport, and a variety of public services, but, as the country develops, that number naturally increases. There are railway workers, bus and truck drivers, and workers in the construction industries. Most of these are urban dwellers, and competition for employment is usually strong. Commerce has traditionally been almost entirely in the hands of Asians, both in the towns and among the itinerant salesmen who take their wares deep into the countryside. But efforts are now being made to introduce many more Africans into the commercial world. The national Association of Chambers of Commerce and its constituent bodies in eleven towns are all concerned with pursuing this policy, for the Asians realize that the jealousy caused by their group's relative wealth could be very dangerous to them as a minority community. Yet it is still said that most of the property of the capital, Dar es Salaam, belongs to one small Asian sect, the Ismailis. Paradoxically, this has been the stanchest group of Asian supporters of Nyerere and his nationalist movement.

About half the children of Tanzania spend some of their time in school. The number of schoolchildren and the proportion of children of school age actually attending school have both risen dramatically since independence. Yet education remains one of the thorniest problems of the country, as it is in all developing lands.

The central issue is not so much the number of pupils as the character of their education. As in most colonies, education in Tanganyika was molded by the metropolitan power—Britain—according to its own traditions, so the literary element was stressed as against practical agricultural or technical training. Examinations were conducted under British auspices, Cambridge school and higher school certificates providing the standard qualifications. The requirements of these examinations were necessarily geared to British conditions and inevitably dominated the courses of instruction.

Nor is the content of education the only handicap inherited from colonial administration. The European, and particularly the British, educational structure is essentially elitist. It is based partly on the assumption that knowledge of the humanities is superior to technical knowledge, partly on the ability of wealthy parents to buy advantages for their children, and partly on a loose form of meritocracy. All these obstacles to an egalitarian educational system were transplanted to the colonies. They were compounded by the harsh fact that in a developing society such as that of Tanganyika only a tiny proportion of pupils can hope ever to gain the high-status positions. Yet, unless those few are to be educated separately, which would perpetuate the divisive influence of class education, they have to learn alongside the vast majority, who will spend their lives on the land or in factories. At the same time, the needs of an egalitarian society demand that those in high posts recognize that willingness to serve the community must replace the sense of social superiority that educational attainment has usually accorded in Western society. While it may be legitimate in an industrialized society for education to offer greater cultural and aesthetic opportunities, such advantages simply cannot be afforded in a nation fighting to avert hunger, sickness, and early death from the majority of its people.

These reservations have to be made in any assessment of the progress of education in Tanganyika. In bald figures, this progress has been remarkable. Whereas at the time of independence only some 45 per cent of school-age children were in primary schools, by 1968 the figure had risen to about 50 per cent, despite the constant increase in population. Most primary schools are day schools, attended by children living in the district. As soon as a child has been accepted, its attendance becomes compulsory. Enrollment usually begins at the age of seven or eight in a class termed Standard I. The normal primary period lasts for seven years, from Standard I through Standard VII. At about the age of fourteen, the small minority hoping to continue on to secondary school take an examination; the successful pupils then begin in Form I of the secondary school, usually a boarding school. In Form IV, they take the Cambridge school certificate, and, if they continue for another two years, they take the higher school certificate in Form VI. At this point, entrance to the Dar es Salaam campus of the East African University, or to one of the other campuses in Nairobi and Kampala, becomes a possibility. A few students go overseas to study.

The major emphasis of government policy after independence was on an expansion of secondary education, sometimes at the expense of opportunities for younger children. It was felt that the immediate task was to train young people for middle- and top-grade jobs, in order to reduce the necessity of relying on aliens. So the increase in secondary-school education showed the most remarkable rise: In 1961, about 12,000 pupils attended secondary school; by 1970, the figure was over 30,000. The major emphasis in the primary schools had been on increasing the number of children who continued beyond Standard IV, where previously there had been a large dropout rate. It was hoped that under the second five-year plan the backlog of primary-school opportunities would be overcome.

Meanwhile, since the Arusha Declaration of 1967 defined the socialist aims of Tanzania, deliberate efforts have been made to redirect the trends in education. President Nyerere pointed out that, under the British system that the country had inherited, many students in universities and colleges were accustomed to being waited on by servants; yet the country was now committed to a policy of self-reliance. He, therefore, urged that self-help schemes be introduced into these institutions. In 1966, he clearly demonstrated what he expected from university students. A system of partial national service had been established. Certain young people were called on to undergo training in elementary social and military service and then to spend another period in uniform, doing their normal jobs but being paid only a fraction of their usual wages. The purpose was to inculcate a spirit of service to the nation. When university students objected to being included in the scheme, Nyerere became very angry and told them that they constituted the privileged few who should be showing gratitude for their advantages by setting an example in public service. He sent them back to their villages and told them that they would only be allowed to return to the university when their parents vouched that they had done useful work for their local communities.

Efforts have also been made to introduce agriculture into the schools. At the Standard V level, agricultural science based on school farms has become compulsory so that all pupils learn something of work on the land, which will remain the adult occupation of most of them for many years. With the introduction of Swahili as the medium of instruction into almost all primary schools, the teaching of civics from Standard IV upward, and the encouragement of social service among boys and girls in secondary schools (boys building bridges, painting public buildings, repairing school equipment; girls helping the handicapped, mothers and young children), the school system is gradually being directed toward fitting its pupils for their role in a socialist society.

In order to provide the teachers needed for this new kind of education, their training has had to be reorganized. Teacher-training colleges and the training course in the university are designed for this purpose. Since 1967, all public secondary schools and training colleges for boys have been given headmasters who are citizens of Tanzania, and the girls' schools will follow suit as soon as enough suitable women are available. Yet expatriate teachers still play an important role. They come from the United States, Britain, Canada, Denmark, India, Egypt, and a few other countries. Religious bodies are also still prominent, particularly in providing primary schools. Yet, in the public schools, while religious training may be given to the various religious groups by outside instructors, no one religion is binding on all the pupils of any school.

Tanzania has developed, in addition to the academic educational structure now being diversified to include more practical training, the usual British model of parallel colleges for technical instruction. The government runs three of these establishments at Dar es Salaam, Moshi, and Ifunda. Moshi specializes in metalwork training; Ifunda, in the preparation of students for the engineering courses at the university.

As has been seen, education is organized by an alliance among government, the local authorities, and voluntary organizations, with religious bodies predominating in the last. Soon after independence, it was considered to be too complicated for the government to retain direct responsibility for the five thousand primary schools, scattered across the country's large territory, so the local authorities were entrusted with the task of controlling them, finance being shared equally between the central government and local councils. The government usually contributes part of the money to sustain the schools provided by voluntary agencies, too, although in some cases such organizations do not ask for governmental help.

Despite this duality in educational organization, it is the Tanzanian Government that controls the direction of educational development. As we have seen, its purposes are to train sufficient citizen teachers at all grades so as to be able to dispense with the services of aliens, to provide trained manpower capable of filling all skilled jobs within the next decade, and to prepare the next generation for the tasks of building a socialist society, still largely based on agricultural pursuits but with an increasing industrial sector—all purposes related to the creation of a self-reliant, cooperative national community.

It is well nigh impossible for people in the developed world to imagine the normal physical life of the average person in a developing country like Tanzania. A few stark facts may assist the imagination. Half the population is under fifteen years old, for people do not live long, yet the birth rate continues to rise. About one- third of all infants die before the age of two, and, in the poorer, more remote areas, the infant mortality rate is much higher. Sickness is universal. Anemia and several types of worms affect almost every Tanzanian. Malaria, bilharzia, diarrhoea, eye infections, blindness, scabies, venereal diseases are widespread. Thus every household accepts sickness and death as a normal part of daily life. Most Tanzanians live for a short span, most of their days and nights being spent with the burden of some degree of physical pain.

A systematic attack on disease began only with the arrival of missionary societies in the late nineteenth century. Previously, sickness had been treated by local healers. These village doctors, who were usually expensive to consult, used a combination of psychology, superstition, and a knowledge of herbs. Many of them remain active in the villages of today.

An alliance between missionary and governmental medicine was created under German rule. Scattered clinics and hospitals were supplemented by government doctors. Endemic diseases such as malaria, sleeping sickness, leprosy, and dysentery were attacked; yet the fact that during World War I twice as many British soldiers died of disease as in battle demonstrates the health hazards of the territory.

This combined effort to fight disease has grown steadily under British rule and since independence. Rural dispensaries and health centers, as well as general and specialist hospitals, are run and financed, sometimes jointly, by the government, local authorities, and voluntary agencies. They provide a mixture of curative and preventive medicine, together with hospital beds for general cases, maternity, infectious diseases, and mental illnesses. The accommodation in hospitals is divided into grades. All residents of Tanzania are entitled to free treatment and drugs at government hospitals or dispensaries and to free accommodation at any hospital, but superior accommodation in rooms with only one or two beds is available for those who wish to pay for it.

It is clear that, in the face of tremendous difficulties, an immense effort has been made, especially since independence, to provide a growing health service for the people of Tanzania. Yet the situation is even more complicated than it appears to be on the surface. It is not simply a matter of numbers. It has been estimated that there is one physician for every twenty thousand patients compared with one for about every thousand in Western Europe. But even these proportions are distorted. Many qualified doctors prefer to go into private practice in the towns where they can earn large fees than to devote themselves to the greater needs in the rural areas. Moreover, the emphasis has been on curative medicine, which shows practical results and is therefore popular. Yet the roots of sickness can only be seriously attacked through preventive methods.

It is common in developing countries that economic progress actually brings a deterioration in certain vital aspects of health. Unfortunately, a reduction in mortality, particularly in infant mortality, results in increased population. This usually adds to the unemployment problem and increases the proportion of children in the community. Both consequences increase the burden of social demands on the economy just when resources are most needed for economic development. And, because birth control is a delicate subject in countries where children have always been prized as well as being an economic asset in terms of peasant production, population explosions are rarely checked. In any case, birth-control training takes time to be organized and even more time to produce results. Thus, in many developing countries, modern medical techniques result in an increased number of people seeking food supplies that are growing at a slower rate than population.

Equally dangerous are conditions during the early stages of a money economy. In traditional village life, food was always scarce and often low in protein; it was also traditional for the men to consume most of the more nutritious foods, leaving the women and children with little except carbohydrates. As a money economy appeared, foodstuffs previously grown for home use began to fetch tempting prices. Eggs and fruit, for instance, which provide protein and precious vitamins, began to be sold instead of eaten. Corn and wheat were sent to refineries and the less nutritious refined varieties bought in the village store. Sugar became popular, while brewers and tobacco manufacturers advertised effectively. In short, eating and spending habits have tended to follow the pattern of developed countries, where taste, habit, and commercial persuasion take precedence over balanced diets.

The remedy for these trends lies essentially in education. One advantage that developing countries have over industrialized communities is that their habits are not so ingrained that recent practice has to fight against centuries of custom. In health progress, particularly in preventive medicine, in hygiene, in food production, and in eating habits, a massive educational program is crucial if the expansion of public health services is to become effective. Fortunately, this is perhaps better realized among influential Tanzanians than in many older nations. The road to the creation of a healthy society will be long, arduous, and tough, but a start has been made in the right direction.

Traditionally, African communities have spent their leisure hours in dancing, miming, conversation, and the relating and hearing of folk stories. These activities remain the commonest forms of entertainment throughout the rural areas. Yet interest in less localized amusements is spreading. As in much of the world, association football, or soccer, leads the way. It is becoming more and more common to see pairs of rickety wooden goalposts at the approaches to villages. In Dar es Salaam and other large towns, the growth of interest in soccer has been rapid. The fame of noted African players such as Eusebio from neighboring Mozambique, one of the greatest soccer players in the world, inevitably excites the ambitions of young Tanzanians. With other sports as well, enthusiasm is encouraged by the exploits of fellow Africans, particularly those who have impressed themselves on the international scene, such as the Kenyans and Ethiopians in athletics. Boxing also attracts increasing interest, but tennis and cricket, both popular in Kenya and West Africa, remain largely confined to Asian and European sportsmen.

The most productive craft form is wood-carving, of which Tanzania is a rich source. It is concentrated in two communities, the Zaramo on the outskirts of Dar es Salaam and the Makonde near Mtwara in the south. The wood most used is ebony obtained from the belt of ebony trees that extends from Tanga down the coast into Mozambique. The work of the two communities is fundamentally different. The relatively conventional Zaramo produce figures of various local stereotypes. Masai warriors are popular, as are old men and nude women. Carved walking sticks and figures of animals or birds are also part of the Zaramo repertoire. Their figures are shaped entirely by hand with very simple tools, and each piece is different.

The Makonde are much more imaginative and unconventional. They display in their carvings an emotional individuality that reflects the artist's mood at the time of their creation. The pieces have a grotesque, gross, bawdy, or even manic character. Often very humorous, they are invariably unique creations.

There is also some art work done in animal skins, jewels, and ivory, though it never approaches the originality of the wood-carvings. But, with the abundance of big game, Tanzanians naturally find opportunities to make attractive souvenirs for tourists. The skins of crocodiles, lions, leopards, elephants, zebras, and snakes provide material for a variety of objects, varying from handbags to hats, wallets to poufs. Local gems also abound: Rubies, sapphires, moonstones, garnets, and amethysts are plentiful. They are fashioned with gold or silver settings in rings, bracelets, brooches, or necklaces. Local cloth, especially the bright colored *khanga* (cotton square) worn by African women, is another item popular with tourists, while the zebra-skin drum, also made by the Zaramo, is an attraction in Tanzania as in the rest of East Africa.

Perhaps the closest approach to the craftsmanship of wood-carving is the work done in ivory. Simple tribal designs in a combination of ivory and ebony are characteristic of this art, some of which is exquisite.

Such artistic creation is, of course, the work of only a few, even in the tribes that specialize in it. In discussing the leisure activities of Tanzanians, their hobbies, sports, and other personal interests, we are considering a part of life still in its infancy, for it should be realized that the African family living by subsistence agriculture has very little leisure and even less energy to employ it actively. The demands of providing food, carrying water, building and mending huts, tending herds, caring for children, and treating the sick occupy most Tanzanians throughout the daylight hours. But, as will be described later, new activities have been added to the traditional ones: there are party meetings to attend, new villages to build, co-operative organizations to form, and information on new crops, methods of husbandry, education, and collective responsibility to absorb. Customary communal endeavors have been supplemented by new activities in building a nation from village roots upward. Clinics, schools, roads, and markets are all being built by the people themselves in their own localities. It is scant wonder that little leisure time remains.

9 The Political Story Since Independence

On attaining independence in December, 1961, Tanganyika inherited the British-style constitution that had been developed under colonial rule. A governor-general represented the Queen, from whom legal authority flowed. Political authority resided in the government, headed by Julius Nyerere as Prime Minister. He and his ministers consisted of members elected from local constituencies. The ministers were in charge of departments dealing with various aspects of national affairs and staffed by civil servants. The system also retained the British multiparty tradition, any organized registered group being entitled to put up candidates for election.

By the time of independence, this structure had begun to reveal inadequacies in meeting the urgent needs of a new African country —a totally different environment from that of stable, industrialized, conservative Britain. TANU had so monopolized the political imagination of Tanganyikans that elections had become a farce. No other party or its candidate could attract serious support. Consequently, in elections most seats were filled by unopposed TANU candidates, and, where there were contests, the TANU candidates won by huge margins. Because candidates were chosen by internal party decision —there being no provision for primary elections in the British model—the electorate itself was deprived of the chance to choose its representatives.

TANU had been formed and mobilized for a single objective—to lead Tanganyika to independence, and, when it became obvious during 1961 that this aim was about to be achieved, the *raison d'être* of the party disappeared. Members became apathetic over party matters and the *élan* of the organization vanished.

Moreover, it had become increasingly clear during the month preceding independence that the leadership of the party and government had been so preoccupied with constitutional negotiations and executive duties that it had lost contact with important sections of the movement. Nyerere and his intimates were shocked to find that in the party and trade unions loud voices were demanding what was virtually a racialist approach to questions of citizenship and Africanization. To Nyerere the only qualifications for citizenship should be identification with the new nation, irrespective of skin color or racial origin, and promotion into skilled and managerial posts should follow the concept of localization rather than that of Africanization. In other words, he considered it essential to fill high-ranking posts with Tanganyikans, irrespective of race, as quickly as possible; his critics, on the other hand, insisted that Africans be given preference in promotion. He had to concede this to his critics as a temporary measure.

To general amazement and consternation, Nyerere resigned as Prime Minister in January, 1962, just a few weeks after independence. No doubt it was a relief to him not to have to be responsible for putting into effect the policy of Africanization in which he did not believe and not to be forced into a confrontation with the aggressive trade-union leaders. Yet his decision was made for quite different reasons. He realized that the only body capable of mobilizing the country for its major task of national rehabilitation was TANU. But the party's local leadership had little idea of its function now that independence had been won, and there was a danger that the only national unifying force would disintegrate into localized groups intent on nothing more than pursuing immediate factional interests. At the same time Nyerere, in carrying out the responsibilities of state office and negotiating for independence, had lost contact with the masses throughout the country. He needed to renew it, refresh himself by listening to their ideas, and reassure them that independence would be used to advance their interests.

So Rashidi Kawawa was left in charge of the government while Nyerere returned to his people, examined the party machine and pondered his future strategy. Kawawa's government took one action designed to strengthen the identification of party and government early in 1962 when it appointed regional commissioners drawn from party activists. As the regional commissioner, and the area commissioners appointed a few months later, replaced the colonial district and provincial commissioners, became secretaries of local party organizations and were given civil-service staffs, the inhabitants of the locality were impressed with the fact that it was TANU, not the old colonial regime or the civil service, that now governed the country.

Nyerere felt the need to inject a more positive element into the party. In April, 1962, he read a paper, *"Ujamaa:* The Basis of African Socialism," to a party study conference. Although he still maintained that socialism and democracy were attitudes, rather than specific programs, this paper marked the beginning of his attempt to marry African tradition with the modern techniques necessary to expand the economic life of the nation. He recalled the traditional egalitarianism of African life, the focal significance of the extended family and its implication of brotherhood, the custom of communal land-holding, the respect for age and service to the community, the universal obligation to work. These traditions, he believed, could become the foundation of the nation's strategy in facing the challenge of independence, provided that where necessary they were adjusted to take account of current needs. Colonial capitalism, with its emphasis on individualism, must be discarded. Equality must become genuine and must include women as well as men, which had not always been the custom in traditional society. Trade unions must not try to secure for their members a larger share of national wealth than their numbers warranted. Although the paper tended to set forth ideals that could be variously interpreted, rather than programs of action, it did open the way to what is essential in a developing country: a continuity of traditional values during a period of necessary change.

Nyerere's lead was followed by the government shortly afterward in the introduction of self-help as a practical application of the *Ujamaa* principle. People were urged to cooperate in building their own roads, schools, clinics. The enthusiasm tapped demonstrated the degree of involvement that still existed once leadership was offered in a practical way. So great was this enthusiasm, however, that schemes proliferated to the extent of creating giant bottlenecks inevitable in the absence of resource-planning; lack of control became so widespread that a new method of management had to be introduced within a few months.

In June, 1962, the National Assembly decided that Tanganyika should become a republic with an executive President, elected, on the first occasion, by popular vote through universal adult suffrage with a lower age limit of twenty-one. The election took place in October of that year. Nyerere was the obvious TANU candidate, but the validity of the election was established when he was opposed by his regular critic Zuberi Mtemvu, who still claimed to represent the almost defunct Congress Party. In the election, Nyerere received 1,127,978 votes, and his rival 21,276.

These figures reveal certain significant facts. The supremacy of TANU was unquestioned and hardly needed to be established. The same was even more true of Nyerere's popularity. What was more important was that Mtemvu and C. K. Tumbo, a former railway workers' union leader who tried to form an opposition party in 1962, were challenging Nyerere and TANU on the basis of racial policy. They both believed that the new nation's African inhabitants had been the most handicapped and that they should be given priority in every situation; they therefore openly opposed the color-blind principle of the party. Because there were certainly members of TANU who sympathized with this outlook, and it might be expected to appeal to the narrow self-interest of many voters, the challenge might have reflected disapproval of Nyerere's idealism. His resounding victory thus greatly strengthened not only his personal position but his party's policy principle as well.

On the other hand, the electoral figures demonstrated also that Nyerere's concern about party organization was well founded. The total of votes cast formed probably less than a quarter of the electorate and certainly less than the number of members claimed by TANU. It was thus clear that a great deal needed to be done before a majority of the population would become involved in the party and its nation-building.

Tanganyika became a republic on the first anniversary of independence, December 9, 1962. The governor-general withdrew, leaving the President as holder of all executive power. Legislative power was vested in the parliament, consisting of the President and the National Assembly, but no bill could be placed in the statute book and so become law without the President's assent. The President also had a modified power of veto, could nominate ten members to the Assembly, address that body at will, and dissolve it whenever he saw fit, though when he did so he had to submit himself to an election. He was not a member of the Assembly. The cabinet consisted of the vice-president and ministers, and it was their responsibility to advise the President, though he did not have to accept their advice. Because he was Head of State and commander in chief of the armed forces and controlled the civil service, his power was considerable.

Shortly after Nyerere returned to office as President of the new republic, he took the second step in transforming his country's constitution from its colonial shape. In January, 1963, he offered to the annual conference of TANU a proposal that Tanganyika should become a *de jure* one-party state. For several years, Nyerere had shown himself critical of the British system, which insisted on a multiparty structure. Tanganyika had been a *de facto* one-party state since TANU had received a vast national response to its appeals during the years immediately preceding independence. But members of the Assembly had to act as though a genuine opposition were in existence by voting solidly for every government bill and suppressing most of their criticisms. Nyerere wanted an Assembly that would seriously debate government measures, free from the dictates of the party caucus.

The new President was also deeply aware of the divisive effects of the multiparty system. He had seen the British model working at close quarters and had also watched the operations of parties in the

United States. He was convinced that the multiplication of parties was inextricably bound up with factionalism, and that the parties in the Euro-American context arose from representation of conflicting group interests, whether they be class interests or those of other groups. But, where no such conflicting interests existed, artificial divisions were provoked when formation of parties was encouraged. Comparing this form of democracy with a "football match," he asserted that African politics must be taken more seriously than this, and then he summed up his argument by declaring, "The politics of a country governed by the two-party system are not, and cannot be, national politics; they are the politics of groups."

The national aims and principles of TANU had been accepted by the vast majority of the population. It would be stupid and destructive to preserve a system that could only encourage division at a time when unity was essential to the interests of all. Yet Nyerere remained a convinced democrat. He believed that the African tradition was democratic, but in a unifying rather than schismatic manner. All the people were involved in decision-making (this might be modified to "all the male adults"), with the objective of reaching collective agreement. His problem was how to preserve such general participation, essentially based on free discussion, without inviting the divisive effects of an organized clash of opinion. His philosophical answer was somewhat indefinite: "There should be no conflict between our commitment to freedom for the individual and the need for the national effort," he wrote, "In fact, these can work together harmoniously as long as the emphasis is on the national interest as implying the interests of the individuals who comprise the nation."

Yet, although Nyerere showed greater insight into the weaknesses of the two-party system than clarity as to how democracy could operate within a one-party state, he stoutly maintained his deeply rooted belief in the right of the people to make their own choice of representatives. He therefore proposed a unique form of elections: Rival candidates from the single party would be selected to contest each constituency, and the voters would be invited to choose between them. In this way the unifying influence of the party would be preserved, based on national acceptance of its aims and general policy, but voters could discuss and debate policy details and support the candidate who seemed most likely to represent their views. By this means, Nyerere hoped to ensure that policy stemmed from the people as a whole but that national reconstruction could proceed without the delays and divisions of an artificially induced opposition.

Nyerere's proposals did not meet with anything like universal acceptance. Some local and national leaders in the party felt that their positions would be threatened under such an electoral system. They were certainly correct, for one of Nyerere's objectives was to prevent the party leadership from becoming a self-perpetuating elite. However, for another twelve months, no further steps were taken to put the proposals into effect. The delay was not solely due to criticism within the party; this was also the period in which Nyerere hoped an East African federation would be created, as the last of the East African territories, Kenya, moved toward independence. As early as January, 1961, Nyerere had announced that he was prepared to postpone Tanganyika's independence in order to join with Kenya and Uganda in an independent East African federation. Only when it became clear that federation would have to be negotiated over a number of years and when Kenya had gained its independence in the same manner as Tanganyika and Uganda, as a sovereign unit, did Nyerere turn back to his own state's structure. In January, 1964, a presidential commission was appointed under the chairmanship of the vice-president, Rashidi Kawawa, to consider how a democratic one-party system should be introduced and what constitutional changes were needed in the nation and party.

The commission was appointed in the midst of Tanganyika's most traumatic experience: On the night of Sunday, January 19, troops from the Colito barracks just outside Dar es Salaam mutinied and moved into the capital. There they occupied key installations— the radio station, the airport, police stations, and the State House, where the President lived and had his office. President Nyerere went into hiding; Vice-President Kawawa also disappeared. The atmosphere of the city was tense; no one, including the soldiers, knew just what was happening or what the next moves were likely to be. For the mutiny followed a week after a revolution on the island of Zanzibar, visible across the sea from Dar. There the majority Africans had overthrown the Sultan's government, which was considered to be dominated by Arabs and Arab interests. This government had been duly elected six months earlier, but, although it had secured a majority of parliamentary seats, the opposition African Afro-Shirazi party had gained more votes. The revolution thus took on the appearance of a popular African uprising against a minority Arab government. At this stage little was known even in Dar of the nature of events in Zanzibar, though it was clear that certain Communist countries were supporting the revolutionary regime. Minds naturally turned to the possibility that the Tanganyikan mutiny had been instigated from Zanzibar and might be directed to the overthrow of Nyerere's regime and its replacement by an alien-controlled faction.

There was some civilian looting in Dar, with certain racial overtones, for it was mainly Asian stores that suffered (though this was almost bound to be the case, because most stores were owned by Asians). There was also some roughing up in the streets—government ministers and Europeans suffering indiscriminately. Meanwhile, Oscar Kambona, the Minister for Defense, negotiated with the mutineers, displaying considerable personal courage in doing so. During that week, a chain reaction seemed to be sweeping East Africa as army mutinies broke out in Uganda and Kenya, while the second battalion of the Tanganyikan Army, stationed in Tabora, joined its Dar comrades in revolt.

As the week wore on without any settlement, with the troops remaining in the city and even the President, on his return after two days, unable to persuade them to return to barracks, Nyerere decided to take a desperate step, profoundly distasteful to him: On January 25, he asked the British Government for help; commandos landed from a naval vessel that was lying off the coast and chased the mutineers out of the city. The latter were then disarmed, a few being killed while resisting, the ringleaders arrested, and the battalion in Tabora also brought under control. The same methods were used with the company that had joined the revolt at Nachingwea in the south.

These events were, of course, a terrible shock to Nyerere's pride. For an African leader to have to use the troops of an ex-colonial master against his own people was for Nyerere a matter of deep shame. He apologized to his people for having had to do so and called a special meeting of the Organization of African Unity to explain his action. At this meeting, he asked for African troops to replace those of Britain, and shortly afterward Nigerian forces were sent to reorganize and train a new Tanganyikan Army. Yet the truth was less shocking than it appeared at the time.

Before independence, Nyerere had hoped that independent African governments would be able to demonstrate to the world that it was possible to live in peace without armed forces. One of his first actions after independence was to end Tanganyikan participation in the tiny East African Navy, and one of his big problems was what to do with his army.

But Tanganyika was surrounded by international pressures that necessitated the retention of armed forces. The anticolonial war across the border in Mozambique might lead to reprisals against Tanganyika; the troubles in the Congo and Rwanda brought thousands of refugees and sometimes even armed forces across the borders; the Zanzibar revolution might lead to difficulties on the mainland; South Africa and Rhodesia were constantly hostile and shortly were to be joined in their hostility by Malawi; even the Zambian border became unstable during the Lumpa uprising. So Nyerere was forced against his will to retain a small army—a mere two thousand strong—in order to protect his own people. The focal issues were how the force was to be organized and what place it should have in the nation.

In January, 1964, more than two years after independence, all army officers above the rank of captain were still British. Moreover, the British tradition of insulating the army from politics had been retained. The army was thus subject to the same discontent over the absence of Africanization as communities in other parts of the country, but it had no political philosophy or leadership to explain the government's policy. One of the first acts of the mutineers, therefore, had been to depose their British officers. The second was simply to demand higher wages. They told the President bluntly that they had no desire to overthrow the government but wanted pay increases such as a raise for privates from $15 to $37 a month.

In short, the army acted like a trade union—though with guns instead of picket signs. The soldiers felt the same resentments as many of their fellow workers, those same discontents that had already caused Nyerere so much trouble. And no one had explained why what they saw as simple justice would undermine the national effort.

It was probably no coincidence that the mutiny occurred a few days after the President had announced that the period in which Africans had been given preferential treatment in employment, recruitment, and promotion must now come to an end, with efficiency and ability replacing the racial criterion. For over two years, the government had compromised with those who placed racial solidarity before the rights of citizenship or the need for efficiency. Nyerere realized that he could no longer afford to do so if economic development was to be effective and non-Africans, many of them well trained, were to be persuaded to remain as citizens. But reaction among some African workers was inevitable.

Nor was it a coincidence that the Presidential commission on the constitution was announced immediately after the mutiny had been suppressed. But this was not sufficient to meet the new challenge to the stability of the state. It is true—and significant—that, with minimal exceptions, no one in the country had taken advantage of the breach in legitimate authority to try to overthrow the regime. The remoteness of other concentrated populations from the capital, which made centralized administration difficult, had provided protection for the government. The mutiny was not and could not become a national uprising, but simply a revolt of two thousand men. Ministers and party officials had remained loyal, thereby demonstrating the success that had been achieved in party organization since the confused days around the time of independence. Oscar Kambona, whom some had considered a rival to Nyerere, had proved his loyalty and was publicly praised by the President for the part he had played. Above all, despite the open invitation to subversion, the country stood solidly behind Nyerere, the masses obviously relieved to know that he remained their leader, with declarations of loyalty coming from all parts of the country.

Still, there remained the problem of how to avoid any recurrence of the threat to governmental authority. The Preventive Detention Act, which had been law since 1962, but scarcely used, was now activated to detain more than five hundred people, many of them tradeunionists—all subsequently released. But this was a negative reaction. What was needed was a new army. At first, the President thought that it should be built around the TANU Youth League, but this was quickly seen to be impractical. So a form of national service was introduced to combine communal nation-building work such as road construction with preparation for service in the armed forces. To set an example several members of the cabinet, including Vice-President Kawawa, joined the national service. Recruitment soon expanded widely, but it had to be restricted for financial reasons.

Meanwhile, after the Nigerians had completed the immediate task of retraining the army, Israel, West Germany, Canada, and China all gave assistance in building up the security forces—army, police, national service, Youth League, and even a small air force.

Perhaps the most significant new departure was the introduction of politics into the armed services and police. One of the regional commissioners was actually appointed political commissar of the defense forces, each company commander headed the TANU committee in his company, and officers were expected to give their troops political education. Large numbers of the forces and police soon flocked into the party, membership of which became a prerequisite for recruitment.

Nevertheless, it was shrewdly recognized that the mutiny was not only an army concern. It reflected a wider opposition to the government's policy, especially in the two crucial fields of Africanization and wage demands. A bill had already been drafted to bring the trade unions under government control. It was quickly brought forward and passed through all its stages during one day in February, 1964. In place of the several existing unions, one central union was created, with a number of industrial sections. The general secretary and his deputy were henceforth to be appointed by the nation's President to avoid the many personality conflicts that had factionalized the labor movement in the past. Later, the general secretary became an ex officio member of the party executive. The unions were thus effectively integrated with party and government. It was hoped to halt in this way their tendency to develop into pressure groups aiming at securing for their workers conditions that militated against the development of social justice throughout the nation— and to keep them from making trouble for the government if they did not get their way.

It is a remarkable sign of the speed with which Nyerere recovered his confidence after the nerve-racking experience of the mutiny that within three months he took the hazardous step of uniting Tanganyika and Zanzibar. He seems to have made this move after very little consultation with his ministers—an indication, perhaps, that he was still very conscious of the uncertain security situation consequent upon the mutiny. But the measure itself certainly reveals that his self-confidence had returned, for by it he accepted responsibility for a revolutionary situation on the islands of Zanzibar and Pemba and, at the same time, greatly aggravated his economic problems.

When Britain declared an official protectorate over Zanzibar and Pemba in 1890, its main intent was to prevent the islands' being used as a base from which Germany could threaten the vital British position in the Indian Ocean. But, as elsewhere in the British Empire, the later years of the nineteenth century and the earlier years of the twentieth saw a more positive imperial policy develop. In Zanzibar, two major influences increased the momentum of imperial intervention. Zanzibar and Pemba were notorious for their slavery and slave trade, and the appalling conditions in some parts of Zanzibar town, together with the corruption of officials and extravagance of the Sultan's court, affronted British officials.

It was not long, therefore, before the British were appointing their own sultans. In 1893, for instance, the new Sultan was proclaimed "by the decision of the Protecting Power." By various methods of coercion, slavery and the slave trade were reduced, though their importance to the economy constantly retarded reform. When the Sultan tried to resist British authority, military force was either threatened or used. Naval forces were landed on the island in 1895, and, in the following year, the palace was actually bombarded by the British Navy, causing about five hundred casualties.

Yet, despite this coercion of the sultans, British officials on the islands tended to protect the interest of the plantation-owners, almost all of whom were Arabs. The Indians were considered to be essentially moneylenders or traders, and the Africans were stereotyped as manual laborers. Because the administration depended on clove exports for almost all of its revenues, it was natural that British officials should be tender toward Arab susceptibilities. The concept of "indirect rule," later to be applied by Governor Cameron to Tanganyika, was interpreted in Zanzibar as a partnership between the British and the Arab elite.

In the early 1900's, British colonial concern for cleanliness and order was seen in Zanzibar. A public health department did much to make the town into the cleanest in East Africa, new roads were built, radio and telephone introduced, and government schools opened.

During and after World War I, the ascendancy of the Arab community appeared to be still more firmly established. Although the sultanate was now firmly under British control and the worst excesses of the court had been restrained, British rule had consolidated the hierarchical structure of Zanzibar's society. Conflict over succession on the death of each Sultan no longer took place; a British protégé was automatically chosen. So, despite the resentment sometimes felt by members of the royal family and court over British interference in Arab dynastic affairs, the institution of the sultanate was actually strengthened. Nor had the British any intention of changing the social pattern. The steep rise in clove and copra prices caused by the war and postwar shortages brought increased profits to the Arab landowners. The government helped them by controlling labor and recruiting workers from the mainland. Meanwhile, the British administration maintained a policy of educational segregation, with schools teaching in the vernacular according to race—a sure way to perpetuate racial division. According to one education commission, the objective of education should be "for the Arab agriculture, for the Indian commerce, and for the African industries."

Yet, below the surface, some change could have been observed if anyone had been looking beneath superficialities. Many Arab landowners were living beyond their means, thus becoming still more deeply indebted to the Indian moneylenders. This led slowly but increasingly to African purchase of land, particularly in Pemba. The process was hastened as Arab children began to leave mortgaged family land at the conclusion of their education and seek employment in offices in the towns.

In 1925, Zanzibar was administratively separated from Kenya, and, in the next year, executive and legislative councils were created on the island, in conformity with British policy in the rest of Africa. The influence of the Sultan was preserved by appointing an executive composed of himself and a number of officials. The members of the legislature were all appointed—a number of officials and a few laymen. It was significant that the latter represented communities but were confined to members of European, Indian, and Arab groups, the Africans being omitted.

The last ten years before World War II saw Zanzibar, like the rest of the world, suffering from the effects of economic slump. Clove prices fell catastrophically, greatly increasing the indebtedness of growers. One of the economy measures, however, had a progressive effect. In an effort to reduce the level of government expenditure, it was suggested that more local people should be used in the administration and that local councils should be created. This policy would allow Africans into administrative functions and local government. The government also tried to improve the conditions of the clove-growers by encouraging them to cooperate in a single growers' association, which was eventually granted a monopoly. Because this association excluded Indians and the government was also protecting the growers against the moneylenders, the Indians in both Zanzibar and India declared a boycott of the clove trade in protest against it. Their economic power was sufficient to break the grower's barrier against them and induce the government to arrange a debt settlement.

World War II provided Zanzibar with its first significant modern boom. The major turning point was the entry of Japan into the hostilities. By invading Southeast Asia, the Japanese severed the allied nations from their main source of spices. The cloves and copra of Zanzibar immediately became tremendously important, with prices rising accordingly. The age-old burden of debt was wiped out, and the government was provided with revenues sufficient to allow it to take positive social action. An income tax was introduced for the first time, medical and educational services were expanded, and slum clearance began. Although bad harvests curtailed this economic expansion soon after the war, from 1950 onward boom conditions gained a new momentum with massive harvests and high prices.

In the meantime, in accord with its general colonial policy, Britain had begun to widen the representative system. An African was appointed to the legislature for the first time in 1945. Pressure started to mount for elections to the legislative council. But communal rivalry was still maintained. The demand for elections came almost entirely from the Arab community, which insisted that Africans were not yet ready for them. To some Africans, it already began to appear as though the Arabs were trying to usurp political power before the Africans could organize their superior numbers.

In the mid-1950's politics and race began to intermingle in constantly changing patterns. The Africans were divided between those who were indigenous to the islands, calling themselves Shirazis, and those from the mainland East African countries. In rough proportions, the total African population formed three-quarters of the islands' people, the Arabs and Indians making up almost all of the rest. Within the African population, three out of four were Shirazis.

When elections were planned for 1957, the African and Shirazi leaders opposed them, fearing that they would lead to domination by Arabs because of their superior organization. But they then united to form the Afro-Shirazi Party (ASP) and, dropping their boycott policy, won five of the six elective seats in the legislative council. Yet the Shirazis in Pemba were under the influence of the Arabs to a much greater extent than those in Zanzibar. It was not long before they broke from the ASP to form their own party. The Arab party, the Zanzibar Nationalist Party (ZNP), now contended with the ASP for Pemba support. Politico-racial tempers were rising; the African-Shirazi alliance boycotted Arab trade, and Arab landowners evicted Africans and Shirazis from Arab estates. Elections on a wider basis in 1961 brought complete deadlock, both parties with their allies securing eleven out of twenty-two seats. Another election had to be held in the same year, amid growing communal violence and accusations of British gerrymandering in favor of the Arabs. This time the ZNP, now in alliance with the Pemba party, won a majority of seats, but with a minority of votes. Two years later, immediately before independence, this result was repeated. The Afro-Shirazis were convinced that the British had connived with the Arabs to ensure that an Arab-dominated government would be in power at the time of independence, despite the fact that it would represent only a minority of the population. In December, 1963, the islands became independent under a government composed of the ZNP and its allies. To many Afro-Shirazis, this was not independence but the substitution of Arab for British rule. The leader of the ASP, Sheikh Abeid Karume, had already warned of the consequences. In the previous year he had declared:

> We therefore now clearly state that no government will be acceptable to the majority of the people unless that government is predominantly African in character. If there is anyone who imagines that when the British leave these islands they will hand over power to the immigrant element who total a mere 42,000 out of a population of 300,000 let that person or persons forget it.

In January, 1964, a group of Africans overthrew the police force, the only security force, and placed in power a Revolutionary Council composed of the revolutionaries and ASP leaders, with Karume as its head. A massacre of Arabs began on the islands, and many fled to the mainland. The resentment of centuries, dating back to the days of slavery and aggravated by the plantation-owner–worker conflict, spilled over; Zanzibar was torn out of the Arab world and returned to Africa. Where constitutional means had failed to secure majority government and social justice, force was used as the only alternative. Before long, estates were being taken from Arab land-owners and distributed to African peasants. Communist states, led by East Germany and China, quickly recognized the new regime. Other Communist countries came to help—and compete for influence with the earlier arrivals. The Western states hesitated so long that Communist influence, though those who brought it often were divided, was firmly established before they made up their minds. The Sultan fled to Britain to live with a handful of retainers in a remote seaside boarding house. The rough, often brutal, measures of a revolutionary regime began to reshape the history of Zanzibar and the lives of its people.

The Afro-Shirazi Party of Zanzibar, which had taken office from the Sultan's government, had close links with TANU on the mainland. Immediately after the January revolution, it was reported that the Zanzibar leader, Sheikh Abeid Karume, went to visit Nyerere. Whatever was said in the yet undescribed negotiations conducted between the two leaders over this three-month period, Nyerere himself was certainly not unaware of the risks he was taking in deciding on a union. The revolution itself, conducted in a mysterious fashion, had involved some peculiar characters, notably, John Okello, self-styled field marshal, who seems to have led the first part of the coup. Not only were cold war Communist-capitalist conflicts introduced into the area but also Sino-Soviet tensions. And the dangerous growth of unemployment, which was still one of Tanganyika's major problems, was certain to be aggravated by the high incidence of unemployment and underemployment on the islands.

So, in proposing union, Nyerere was deliberately grasping a set of very painful nettles. Yet he believed that, if he did not do so, the dangers to his own state and to East Africa as a whole would become incalculably greater. Uncertainty and insecurity have a habit of spreading, offering opportunities for subversive elements to take advantage of an unstable situation and undermine the kind of ordered progress that was his objective in Tanganyika. A union of the two states might mitigate these dangers and provide a moderating influence in Zanzibar; it certainly would be consistent with Nyerere's belief in African unity. He realized that he was unlikely to be able to exercise unquestioned control over the islanders until they had time to settle down and plot the direction of their future; he therefore did not try to define too exactly the form union would take or to insist on immediate rigid integration. Legal definition was left to future negotiations. But the nomination of Karume as first vice-president in the united state, with Kawawa as second vice-president, the inclusion of Zanzibaris as ministers and parliamentary secretaries of the union government and others as members of the Assembly, brought the political systems of the two units as close together as was practical in the uncertain situation. Indeed, far from opening the way to Zanzibar subversion in East Africa, as had been widely suggested in Africa and in the Western world, Nyerere could legitimately complain that his courageous gamble for stability never received the support he could have expected from others in East Africa who stood to benefit most from the risks he was accepting for himself.

The union with Zanzibar increased the domestic political difficulties of Tanganyika by introducing an element calculated to strengthen the orthodox Communist criticism of Nyerere's brand of socialism. Mohammed Babu and A. K. Hanga, who both became ministers in the union government, were particularly likely to reinforce those elements that supported the orthodox policy of widespread nationalization, large-scale collective farming, and quick industrialization.

In foreign policy too, the influence of Zanzibar could be expected to challenge some aspects of TANU policy. Nyerere's government had, from the start, based itself on nonalignment in the cold war and complete commitment to the struggle against the white supremacists in southern Africa. But nonalignment meant that every international issue must be decided on its merits; it did not imply an automatic anti-Western posture. Those who saw friendship with Communist countries as synonymous with entering the Communist bloc were simply adopting a subjective view from within the Western camp. Under colonial rule, Tanganyika had been made a part of the anti-Communist alliance without any consultation with the Tanganyikan people. To reach a genuine position of nonalignment, it was necessary after independence to make greater efforts to establish relations with Communist countries in order to move from the colonial position. Yet Nyerere was always a fervent supporter of the Commonwealth, a longstanding friend of Britain and the United States, and a passionate devotee of the United Nations. He recognized the dangers of domination by the Communists as equal to those arising from membership in the Western bloc. He even insisted on maintaining the uncomfortable role of friendship with the Egyptians and other Arab countries, together with continued amity toward Israel.

Zanzibar's position was different. It had been offered its first helping hands by the Communist countries at a time when the Western states were still hesitating about whether to recognize the revolutionary regime. Its nonalignment, therefore, implied a commitment to socialism that often identified that philosophy with the Communist world. Nyerere had to try to persuade Zanzibar that the dangers of Communist imperialism were as great as those from the West, that nonalignment required neutrality from both power blocs.

The effects of the Zanzibari influence, together with the impact of cold war maneuvers in the new situation and the insecurity induced by the mutiny, affected Tanzania's international relations for some time. In addition to a quarrel with West Germany over recognition of East Germany, tensions grew between the new union and the United States. The Communist influence in Zanzibar raised suspicions in Washington, even though Nyerere pointed out that there were more American Peace Corps teachers in Tanganyika than all the Chinese technicians. Some Tanzanian leaders reacted by becoming supersensitive about American antagonisms. In November, 1964, Oscar Kambona, then Foreign Minister, announced that he had discovered an American conspiracy based in the Congo. While never entirely accepting Kambona's evidence, Nyerere told the Americans that the onus of proving innocence rested with them. The documents produced were almost certainly forgeries, and there is reason to suppose that Nyerere accepted the American assurance, but he did not repudiate Kambona. To have publicly admonished his Foreign Minister and party secretary-general would have broken the party's unity.

Diplomatic tension between the two countries did not disappear after the close of this incident. A few weeks later, early in 1965, two American diplomats were expelled from Tanzania on allegations of subversive activities. The U.S. Government reacted by expelling a Tanzanian official from the embassy in Washington. Both countries then temporarily recalled their ambassadors. Despite the efforts of the African desk in the State Department, the U.S. Government put its *amour propre* before sympathetic understanding of a young country's difficulties. The Tanzanians, for their part, had become so security-conscious that they were ready to believe the worst interpretation of the slightest aberration.

The breach with Britain at the end of 1965 was of a different character. It stemmed from Harold Wilson's refusal to pledge himself to majority rule in Rhodesia during the Commonwealth conference the previous July. It seems probable that Kambona overstepped his brief when the Organization of African Unity (OAU) foreign ministers met early in December and resolved that all members should break off diplomatic relations with Britain if Ian Smith's rebellious white regime had not been defeated by December 15. But, whether he agreed with the OAU tactic or not, Nyerere believed that OAU resolutions must be honored. He was also very angry with Britain's pusillanimous attitude toward a white rebellion, which he and other Africans found in sharp contrast to its actions toward rebellious colored colonial subjects. In particular, inertia in Rhodesia, where 4 million Africans were left to the mercy of 200,000 whites, was seen as an antithesis to the airlift in the Congo, where the Belgian, British, and U.S. governments combined to rescue whites held as hostages in Stanleyville.

So the break in diplomatic relations with Britain, which cost his country a $18 million loan, would certainly have happened even if the union with Zanzibar had never been contemplated. Yet, in conjunction with the coolness of the Americans and Germans and threats from South Africa, Portugal, and Rhodesia, it added to the sense of tension, almost approaching an atmosphere of siege, which developed during this period. Moreover, after the freedom fight against Rhodesia, Portugal, and South Africa began in earnest during 1967, it became ever clearer that only Communist countries were prepared to train, arm, and support the freedom fighters. The central issue of southern Africa, the conflict between democracy and white racism, had begun to polarize those who could be relied on as Africa's friends and those who would passively or actively support the white supremacists.

Early in 1965, the presidential commission on the constitution reported. With minor exceptions—for instance, to avoid the election of a member by minority vote, the proposed three-member constituencies were reduced to two members—the report was accepted, and it provided the framework for the elections held in September that year. Tanzania was now to become *de jure* a one-party state. The powers of the President were scarcely changed. He was still not to be a member of the Assembly, and he could not pass bills without the Assembly, but he had limited power of veto over its legislation. If a bill was rejected by the President but passed again by a two-thirds majority within six months, the President had either to assent to it or dissolve the parliament; this would entail his submitting himself for re-election. The cabinet remained in an advisory capacity to the President.

Elections to the Assembly were to be held in 107 constituencies with two candidates in each. Any TANU member over the age of twenty-one who could secure nomination by twenty-five local voters could apply to be accepted as a candidate. If more than two were nominated, a secret ballot would be taken, with the national executive as the final arbiter. The two candidates finally selected would then go to the polls, where there would be universal adult suffrage. In the interests of nation-building, certain restrictions were placed on electoral conduct. The national language, Swahili, was to be the only one used at meetings of candidates during elections, and appeals to tribal, religious, or racial considerations were forbidden.

The President retained the right to appoint ten extra members, in addition to the elected members, while regional commissioners and representatives of national organizations were also to be members. In the interim period, until the final constitution of the union with Zanzibar was drafted, members from the islands were also to be appointed.

In the event, 803 candidates were nominated at the primary stage. In only six constituencies was only one candidate nominated; therefore, there were contests for 101 seats. The total registered electorate numbered 3,174,471 for the Assembly elections (confined to the mainland) and 3,392,509 for the presidential election (which included the islands). Each candidate was allocated a symbol, either a hoe or a house, to assist the voters—many illiterate—in identifying them. Because only Nyerere was nominated a candidate for President, the electorate had to vote either "yes" or "no" on whether he was to serve for another five-year term.

Although registration was not as high as expected, probably because in some rural areas it was equated with taxation as it was used to identify tax-evaders, the percentage polled was considerable—76.1 per cent in the Assembly vote, 77.8 in the presidential. Nyerere received 2,519,866 affirmative votes and 92,359 opposed him.

Perhaps the most remarkable feature of the election was the defeat of two ministers and six junior ministers. Indeed, only 21 former members of the Assembly were returned, though 10 former members were not chosen by the party and 27 did not stand for re-election. So, of the 107 elected members, 86 were new to the Assembly.

The rejection by the electorate of so many former members of the Assembly and government showed that, although the country as a whole retained its faith in TANU, it was critical of many of its officials and representatives. It also established that the elections were genuine and not just a rubber-stamp process for either party or government. It was not long before the new blood in the Assembly was making itself felt. The elected members in particular brought a new questioning spirit into the body and were clearly determined to show appointed members that it was those who had been elected that represented the will of the people. Another significant aspect of the election was that neither racial nor sex discrimination was shown by the voters. Among the successful candidates were one European and three Asians—all Tanzanian citizens, of course—and four of the eight women candidates were successful.

The next year, local-government elections were held in accordance with the same system. There were 58 district councils, 13 town councils, 1 municipal council, and the city council of Dar es Salaam. These bodies have the power to decide on tax rates and to supervise licensing, primary education, agriculture, marketing, forestry, street-lighting, public health, roads, water supplies, veterinary services, and so forth, in their areas.

As with the elections to the National Assembly, the local-government elections brought new men and women into positions of responsibility. The period in which those who had distinguished themselves in the struggle for independence were rewarded by office in the independence regime had ended. Ability, commitment to national ideals, understanding of the people's needs and ambitions, now became the qualifications for public life. Fresh attitudes appeared in national and local affairs—attitudes characterized by greater irreverence, nonconformity, imagination. These were precisely the attitudes Nyerere wished to see expressed when he insisted that elections were essential to avoid the growth of a self-perpetuating oligarchy in party and state. They rapidly created an atmosphere in which new and radical initiatives could be taken to halt the growth of antisocial features in national life. The doors were open to bold, imaginative measures designed to direct the country toward a more clearly defined social order than had previously been attempted.

10 Economics Since Independence

When Tanganyika gained its independence in 1961, it was a country of some 10 million inhabitants, scattered in enclaves across a territory of 362,688 square miles (including 19,980 square miles of inland water). The clusters of populated areas were generally remote from each other and from the capital, Dar es Salaam. Communications were meager for the size of the country and often disrupted by rains. Most of the people were subsistence farmers or semi-nomadic cattle-grazers. Only 2.7 per cent of the population lived in towns of over 5,000 inhabitants. The per capita income was estimated to be about $59 per annum, but this figure had little real meaning. The average cash income of Africans in Tanganyika has been calculated at about $20 a year. Yet it is impossible to estimate the value of subsistence agriculture, except to say that it represented over one-third of the gross domestic product—and also that it could not be taxed by the government. Moreover, subsistence food production, and cash crops as well, was continually threatened by droughts, while the fertile enclaves were already overpopulated. Only about half a million Africans were in paid employment, most of them in agriculture. Of these, 97 per cent were paid less than $100 a month. There were 5,365 factories, about a quarter of them without electric power. Most of them were concerned with processing agricultural products and were owned by Asians or Europeans. The Africans, comprising more than 98 per cent of the population, received only about 70 per cent of the domestic product.

The economic life of the people of the newly independent country was heavily dependent on agriculture, and their prospects seemed inextricably bound to this sector of the economy. Forty per cent of cash income came from exports, and 80 per cent of export earnings was derived from agriculture and livestock. Sisal, cotton, and coffee dominated these exports, with sisal alone earning nearly 25 per cent of the total revenue. Minerals accounted for no more than 13 per cent of export earnings. Of the total national product, agriculture provided 45 per cent and manufactures only 7 per cent.

Moreover, most of the export crops were produced on plantations owned by Asians or Europeans. Even the Chagga, who had pioneered the African production of coffee through their cooperative, regarded this cash crop as secondary to the cultivation of their own food supplies. Most Tanganyikans at the time of independence were using primitive methods to fight the elements, prevented from achieving substantial improvement by the inadequacy of their equipment, their lack of capital, and their meager marketing facilities. They, therefore, usually produced only sufficient cash crops to provide for their tax liabilities and basic purchases.

To change this pattern would clearly require the conversion of these conservative, tradition-minded farmers to modern methods of production, land conservation, cooperative organization, and marketing. Capital would have to be found for training, investment in expansion and equipment, and new marketing methods. The examples set by the Victorian Federation of Cooperative Unions, which marketed all the cotton grown in the Lake Province, and the Bukoba and Kilimanjaro Cooperatives, which marketed coffee, would have to be adapted to less-fertile areas. The ministeries of agriculture, cooperatives, lands, water, and local government would have to combine in a mighty effort of coordinated development. Only through government initiative and financing would this effort be feasible; yet the government itself would have to search for the essential funds—and would certainly have to seek help from abroad —besides having to establish some order of priorities.

There were pressures on the new government to concentrate on each of various sectors of economic life, much of the pressure applied by voices more strident than those of the humble farmers. There was obviously a case for spending resources on improving communications so that the expanding economy could avoid disastrous bottlenecks. It was not that the roads were crowded, for only 35,000 vehicles were registered, but in this vast country there were no more than 27,000 miles of roads, many of them in very poor condition and only 8,000 miles of them classed as main roads. It is true that the railways and ports were adequately operated and could probably handle increased traffic; Dar es Salaam, Tanga, Lindi, and Mtwara all possessed deepwater berths. The postal and telegraph systems, organized on an East African regional basis, were also reasonably comprehensive—though it was not only weather but also elephants and giraffes that sometimes fouled the lines. East African Airways, another regional service, was handicapped by the primitive state of many of its airstrips and by the uneconomic character of domestic service, which was, nevertheless, socially and economically essential. But roads were obviously of first priority for improved communications; yet road-building and maintenance are expensive and tedious tasks in tropical climates.

Claims could be made, too, for an improved tourist industry, because of the valuable foreign currency it would provide. Yet, again, more and better roads would have to be built, together with many new hotels, before the potential attractions of the game reserves, excellent beaches, and magnificent scenery could be realized. The government and private investors would have to find means of cooperating if the opportunities were to be made the most of—but where was this need to be placed in the order of national priorities?

By far the loudest claim on government resources was that made for increased industrialization. At the time of independence, only about twenty-thousand Africans were employed in manufacturing industries, approximately a third of them in the processing of agricultural produce. Other small industries included carpentry, furniture manufacture, sawmilling, automobile repairs, clothing, brickmaking, and general engineering. This last category included work in the repair shops of the East African railways and harbors—the largest employers in the country. To increase this tiny industrial sector would require investment on a scale no Tanganyikan government could expect from the savings of its own impoverished inhabitants or from the kind of national revenues it could anticipate raising itself. Moreover, any serious industrial expansion would depend on the services of skilled and semiskilled workers who were not to be found in Tanganyika and who could not be trained in sufficient numbers for many years. The stark conclusion, therefore, was that increased industrial activity depended substantially on external aid, foreign investment, and alien personnel. The pressure for rapid industrialization, therefore, had inescapable political implications.

The need for trained personnel was directly linked to another pressure on the government—the demand to expand social services. The provision of increased health facilities in the form of new hospitals and clinics was clearly calculated to increase efficiency as well as to satisfy humane claims. But this would necessitate acquiring more doctors and nurses. Similarly, the need for increased house-building raised a demand for trained builders, and agricultural modernization required more agronomists and skilled demonstrators. But it was the pressure for greatly expanded educational facilities that bore most heavily on the government.

By the time of independence, places in primary school had been provided for nearly 50 per cent of African children, but only one in eight pupils received more than four years' education. In the last full year before independence, only 480 candidates sat for the school-certificate examination. These figures showed considerable improvement on those of a decade earlier. The number in primary schools had doubled, and in 1948 only 28 pupils had applied for the school-certificate examination. In the year of independence, too, a university college was opened in Dar es Salaam, becoming part of the federal East African university; yet, at the same time, only about 400 Tanganyikan students were studying at foreign universities, a woefully inadequate number to manage the life of a new state. Yet this meager advance in educational facilities had necessitated a rise in government expenditure from $1,701,600 in 1950 to over $7,200,000 in 1958–59 on current account, and from $700,000 to over $2,400,000 over the same period in capital expenditure. The problem of finding the money and teaching personnel to meet the new educational demands of independence loomed dauntingly. What place in the order of priorities should such a massive expenditure of resources be given?

Further complicating the issue of expanding the social services was the menace of a rapidly increasing population. Some gave the superficial answer that Tanganyika was underpopulated and could, therefore, comfortably cope with increased numbers. This argument ignored the simple fact that a rapid increase in population would inevitably bear heavily on the social services just when any expansion in the economy was bound to be restrained by the need for diverting resources to social provisions. As death rates fell, the population growth rate passed the 2 per cent mark. Not only did this exceed the rate increase in food production, but it inflated the proportion of young people in the community, the section that most needed those social services that could not produce short-term economic dividends. During the early 1960's the under-sixteen section of the population grew to nearly 45 per cent. It aggravated the problem of unemployment, strengthened the trend toward perpetuating subsistence agriculture, and swelled the flow into the towns. Dar es Salaam, in particular, found its streets filling with unemployed or underemployed youths waiting for odd jobs, besieging party offices and hampering efficient administration, living off relatives or friends and thus preventing those with jobs from raising the standard of living of their own families. Inevitably, this led to a growth in crime and lawlessness.

Some of these pressures had been applied to Nyerere and his TANU colleagues before the actual moment of independence. Once colonial rule had finally disappeared, however, the government was naked before the importunings of pressure groups. No longer was it possible to plead the imperial fiat as a reason for inability to comply. As I have shown, during most of the first year of independence, the government was also deprived of the man most capable of diplomatically assuaging discontent—Nyerere himself, who resigned early in 1962 and spent until December of that year tending to TANU party problems.

Nor was the government entirely free to make its own choices.

It had inherited a 1961–64 three-year development plan, based on the World Bank's report "The Economic Development of Tanganyika," published in 1960. This plan was mainly concerned with a program for capital expenditure, involving a number of projects. There was no conception in it of making basic changes in the economic structure, nor did it aim at a rate of growth higher than the current 5 per cent a year. The plan was based on the premise that, although industrialization was desirable, it would only become practical when agricultural expansion had created a sufficiently sophisticated domestic market. This was to be achieved by strengthening the infrastructure—by improving roads and railways, irrigation, and water supplies, and building more schools. In short, British colonial policy toward economic development was to be continued and extended, increasing agricultural exports would enable more goods to be imported, with the gradual growth of a market economy making possible some introduction of light industry, privately owned, financed, and managed by foreigners. No radical change in the structure, organization or objectives of economic life was contemplated.

Yet the TANU government could not just abandon the three-year plan until it had a substitute. And it would take time to gather advisers capable of drawing up a new plan for development. The party and government had still to determine their priorities and decide on their strategy. Nevertheless, they did try to supplement the three-year plan with greater popular involvement in economic efforts. In early 1962, they launched a "Peoples' Plan," which aimed at reorganizing in the villages development committees designed to give a lead in "self-help" projects. To some degree, these were forerunners of later and more coherent schemes for village participation in national development. But, in 1962, there was little they could do except to begin to involve people in improving their local environment.

It was sometime before TANU leaders had thrashed out their order of priorities in a clear enough manner to determine a coherent strategy. But, in the meantime, they tacitly accepted the received doctrine of development by assuming that emphasis must be placed on industrialization. It was not enough to wait until increased monetary incomes obtained from agricultural expansion had created a demand for industrial products. Independence itself necessitated an industrial effort, initiated by the government if private enterprise was not forthcoming. The absence of such attitudes in the three-year plan represented a major cause of its unacceptability.

Yet, very early in the life of the independent government, warnings were sounded indicating what the consequences of such a policy would be. The efforts of trade unions were sufficiently successful to force upward many wage rates among organized workers. Between 1962 and 1963, wages rose by 9 per cent and cash earnings by 35 per cent. In the ownership and employment conditions of Tanganyika at that time, this was inevitably accompanied by a decrease in employment, to save costs. Over the five-year period from 1958 to 1963, the number of employed fell from 397,000 to 342,000, a decrease of 15 per cent. The government was consequently beset by demands from the unions for increased employment, higher wages, and Africanization of managerial and executive posts. To have accepted such demands would have been to reduce output and organization by introducing inexperienced, unskilled workers into key positions. Even more important, because the vast majority of inhabitants were not organized workers but rural, subsistence farmers, to have accepted the unions' demands would have been to widen the dangerous gulf between urban industrial workers and the mass of the population. Premature industrialization, initiated without integration into a coordinated strategy for a rural renaissance, would have created a class society in which a tiny elite achieved standards that would be the envy of the masses who were denied similar opportunities.

The Tanganyikan leaders might be skeptical about the value of the three-year plan they had inherited from the colonial government, but they did not question the importance of economic planning itself. In this, they accepted the general assumption of virtually every developing country, and certainly of all those in Africa, that planning was essential for any form of development, and particularly for the achievement of defined objectives. Because Tanganyika, like its fellow African countries, had only a minute private sector in its economy (and this was almost entirely in foreign hands), there could be little doubt that, unless the government took the economic initiative, no serious economic expansion was likely to take place. The real question was not whether the government was to play an economic role but what part it would arrogate to itself. Was it to provide facilities calculated to encourage private initiatives, or would it direct and control a substantial sector of the national economy?

In December, 1962, on the first anniversary of independence, Tanganyika became a republic. Nyerere returned to executive office as the elected President. In March of the next year, a Ministry of Development and Planning was created, with Nsilo Swai, the party treasurer, as its first minister. The chief responsibility of the new ministry was to draw up a new five-year economic plan to succeed the three-year plan due to expire in 1964. A French engineer named Faudon was appointed Director of Planning. The French had not been involved in colonial rule in East Africa, and it was deemed important to break completely with the colonial past. At the same time, the choice was a little surprising, for the French had been a major colonial power in Africa; there were certainly as many British as French economists who had shed colonial preconceptions, and if all imperial connections were to be avoided, one would have expected someone like an Indian or a Yugoslav to be chosen. It was, indeed, hoped that personnel for the planning unit would be recruited from Communist as well as capitalist countries, but the hope was never realized. The United Nations, Britain, the United States, Israel, and West Germany all contributed technical experts, so the unit from the start was composed of people generally opposed to the concept of a centrally directed economy. The attitude of the French toward planning arose from their vision of a mixed economy in which the government could and should do no more than indicate priorities on the lines of development and provide for their pursuit. Their own domestic experience was of state planning with an accepted market economy. The other members of the unit also accepted this basic premise.

It was not simply the particular ideologies and personalities of this small group of experts that determined the character of the five-year plan. These men were selected, and their work was examined, by representative Tanganyikans before it was published or accepted. The more fundamental fact was that at this stage TANU and its government had hardly developed any ideology of their own. They were in office because they had taken a leading role in the anti-colonial movement. This had been based on *Uhuru*. But the purposes for which such self-government were to be used had been left in the vaguest terms. The party itself was deliberately representative of all shades of interest in Tanganyika. It included large estate-owners, wealthy merchants, rich lawyers, trade-union officials and privileged members, cooperative leaders and their followers, politicians with financial prospects, as well as members from the mass of subsistence peasants. To have enunciated a specific ideology would inevitably have resulted in antagonizing one or more of these groups. So, to maintain the consensus that had been essential for gaining political independence, ideological definitions were eschewed. Vague aims such as "nation-building," hard work—as reflected in the slogan *"Uhuru na kazi"*—self-help, and economic development took the place of commitment to a strategy based on an order of priorities that would have risked opposition from those who saw their interests threatened. Nyerere himself had come closest to ideological definition in his paper *"Ujamaa: The Basis of African Socialism,"* which he wrote in 1962 while out of the government. In it, he rejected capitalism and a system based on exploitation of man by man, as well as doctrinaire socialism because of its assumption of conflict between man and man. African socialism, he believed, arose out of the African traditions of the extended family, of universal participation in communal work, and of egalitarianism—though he recognized that the principle of equality had never been perfectly applied, particularly toward women. Yet even Nyerere's analysis of his concept of African socialism at this time provided a philosophy rather than a program. He could urge people to follow its principles, but he had not yet reached the stage of telling them how to do so. It may be that further education and practical experience were necessary before he could move into the practical phase without disrupting his nation; Nyerere has always been essentially a *mwalimu,* a teacher-leader.

The five-year plan had to be composed within one year. By January, 1964, a draft outline was presented to the Economic Development Commission, a body that consisted of the cabinet sitting as a committee on economic policy. There does not seem to have been any substantial amendment of this draft, which was submitted to the party executive the next month. It should be recognized that this was the time of the revolution in Zanzibar and the mutiny in Tanganyika, so it is not surprising that economic planning was not as thoroughly examined as it might otherwise have been. Yet there seems no evidence that the leaders of the party or the government were critical of the plan's main provisions.

President Nyerere presented the plan to the Assembly in May, 1964. It was to run from July of that year until June, 1969. But its objectives were for a longer term: It was to initiate a period of development that would take fifteen years to complete. Thus, the three main objectives were not to be achieved until 1980. They were to raise annual per capita income from $55 to $126, to substitute trained Tanganyikans for expatriates in all skilled professional and managerial posts, and to raise life-expectancy from between thirty-five and forty years to fifty years. The vision glimpsed was of a Tanzania in 1980 inhabited by about 18 million people, receiving more than twice their current personal income, with sufficient educational opportunities to fill all the skilled positions and with a life-expectancy of fifty years.

In order to lay the foundations for this long-term achievement, the 1964–69 plan provided its own shorter-term targets. Average income was to be increased by 50 per cent. This would necessitate, given a continuation of population increase at the current rate, an annual growth rate of 6.7 per cent in both the subsistence and cash sectors. The plan was to cost $688.8 million in public and private investment, of which over half was to be provided by the public sector. Of this, it was estimated that 78 per cent would come from foreign loans and grants, the rest from domestic borrowing and taxation. Because most of the private sector would also have to depend on foreign finance, it can be seen that very heavy revenues from foreign sources would be crucial to success.

The weakness of the plan mirrored the indecisiveness of the party and its leaders. The long-term objectives reflected the basic assumption that "more" means "better." More money, greater skills, longer life were the aims, but no attempt was made to break Tanzanian society down into its components, to choose which sections should be given priority in development help, which should be held back for future assistance. For this would have required an imaginative picture of the future character of Tanzanian society and a deliberately chosen set of priorities. Neither party nor leaders had yet reached this stage of political imagination. The only approach toward it evidenced at this time was the emphasis placed on secondary and higher education at the expense of postponed primary expansion. Yet, even here, though the choice of expansion in education was made, the content and form of the education given were not yet questioned. The assumption of colonial rule that educational "standards" are universal and based on European experience remained unchallenged.

This quantitative attitude extended to foreign assistance. It was assumed at this stage that foreign aid and investment automatically assisted development, no matter what was being produced, whatever the terms and whoever the owners. Although freehold was abolished and the land nationalized in 1962, Asian and European estates remained under foreign ownership, South Africans continued to grow coffee and wheat in the north, absentee landowners increased after independence, and industry and commerce remained largely in alien hands. Now foreign investment and aid was actually being encouraged by the government. This policy soon found its critics in the National Assembly, demands being made for more state-owned industries, more collective and cooperative farms.

Another, and even louder, criticism heard in the Assembly was aimed at the alleged discrimination in favor of the wealthier regions. This is one of Tanzania's profoundest problems. Again it relates to the issue of priorities. Although general national averages may indicate the total economic picture, they are grossly misleading about the standard of living of many inhabitants. There are comparatively wealthy areas where cash crops have been firmly established and well organized; there are others that drought, the tsetse, poor soil, and lack of organization condemn to endemic poverty. Obviously, investment in the wealthier areas would bring greater and quicker returns. But this could only widen the gap in living standards. It is significant that Chief Fundikira, in defending the government against the criticisms of members representing the poorer regions, claimed it to be an economic fact, rather than the government's intention, that industries must be established where there was the greatest wealth and, therefore, the highest buying potential. Nothing could better illustrate the conventionally passive economic attitude of the leadership at this point—an outlook adopted, no doubt unconsciously, from colonial teachings.

A further illustration of the influence of colonial economists is provided by the employment objectives. The aim was to have about 4 million workers in agricultural and non-agricultural paid employment by 1980. It was hoped that, in the subsistence sector, half the incomes would be provided by cash crops. Average incomes in paid employment would be more than twice the average.

As a corollary to this conventional approach, the plan placed heavy emphasis on industrialization. This was in line not only with conventional colonial economic theory but also with the general postwar attitude of the developing countries themselves. Once underdevelopment had been diagnosed as primarily due to monoculture and economic diversification had been accepted as the remedy, industrialization became a panacea for economic development. This attitude also fed the natural appetites of developing countries for dignity and prestige; for they could not avoid being conscious of the contrast in technical achievement between themselves and the industrialized world. Industry was to receive 14.3 per cent of the central government's development funds, aimed at increasing the industrial share of the gross domestic product from 13 to 19.4 per cent by 1970. It was expected that the industrial sector would grow at more than twice the rate of agricultural expansion.

One final critical comment on the plan remains to be made. Most of the critical analysis made above would be accepted now by Nyerere and his fellow leaders. They would probably say, with a great deal of justification, that at the time the plan was produced the inhabitants of the country were not prepared for a more radical policy and that only the lessons of experience could educate them into this awareness. But on one issue the leadership has never been convinced that they were digging dangerous pitfalls for themselves. This is the question of tourism. The plan actually underestimated the attractions of the country to outside visitors—or their potential affluence. It was anticipated that ten thousand tourists would visit the country each year. In fact, twice this number arrived in 1964 and the figure increased in succeeding years.

It is true that the twenty thousand tourists of 1964 provided Tanzania with $4.8 million in precious foreign exchange and that this amount has been progressively increased ever since. But there are two significant dangers in the tourist industry: First, it diverts resources and people from the primary task of building the foundations of a healthy society for Tanzanian citizens themselves. Second, and even more dangerous, it creates a society within a society, a community of visitors with vastly different standards and philosophies of life, a parasitical community. It is not sufficient answer to suggest that the tourist community can be isolated from Tanzanians themselves, simply providing extra income that can be applied to constructive ends. Tourists—and especially the wealthy tourists provided for in the expensive hotels being built in Dar es Salaam and other centers—create their own hangers-on, obsequious servants, and imitators. Their life and its demands tend to dominate at least one important section of urban activities and to be inimical to the attitude toward life that the leadership is trying to instill. Chalets, rest houses, and modest motels would be more suitable than luxury hotels. Otherwise tourism, apparently so harmless and lucrative, can become a cancer within the new character of Tanzanian society.

Difficulties in securing foreign aid and the delays often typical of aid negotiations soon made it obvious that the expectations about funding the plan had been seriously overestimated. During the first half of the plan period, only 41 per cent, instead of the anticipated 78 per cent, of development expenditure was financed from abroad. Despite a development levy of 5 per cent imposed on salaries and export crops in 1965, sufficient domestic savings could not be accumulated to bridge the shortfall. By midterm, the ministries had been able to spend only 65 per cent of their target figure in monetary terms. Because of the rise in costs of between 10 and 15 per cent, the real performance of the ministries fell to about 50–55 per cent of the planned achievement.

It was not only lack of money that caused the failure to reach targets. Two of the most restrictive factors were lack of skilled technicians in all branches of development and an almost total absence of preparation for projects. Both caused low utilization of those resources that could be made available. The speed with which the plan had been prepared and then was to be implemented made such confusion inevitable.

Not surprisingly it was the government's sector that suffered most, thus allowing the private sector to expand faster and reducing the ratio of public to private investment. The tax system of Tanzania was simply not geared to massive public investment. Most people paid taxes only to local councils, which levied an income tax of between 1 and 3 per cent on adult males. But, owing to chaotic local rate structures, registration loopholes, and acute difficulties in collection, much time was wasted and tax returns were small. They accounted for only about a quarter of national revenues. The rest had to come from central taxation, income tax, personal tax, and excise duties. These applied to only a tiny proportion of the population and accounted for a mere 14 per cent of the domestic product. To have increased taxation would clearly have been both costly and unpopular; yet, without doing so, there would have been little prospect of the government's keeping to its own development target, still less of making good the deficiency caused by the lack of foreign support.

The effects of this confusion were felt throughout the countryside. Regional and area commissioners were constantly exhorted to organize their people and to stimulate greater production, but were never told which projects were to be encouraged and which discouraged. Little lead was given as to what crops should be selected, which methods of farming should be adopted in different areas, or how land should be divided. Consequently, individual decisions were often made according to subjective opinions, or there was no decision at all.

The failure in the countryside was the most wounding to Nyerere's concept of African socialism. A Village Settlement Agency had been established in 1963, and five highly capitalized schemes were begun in the same year. The Agency was run by expatriates. Control was weak and management inefficient, so that by 1966 it was found necessary to halt the expansion of the programs. It was found that overcapitalization had saddled the farmers with heavy long-term debts and that they had shown little enthusiasm for accepting their new responsibilities. It was therefore decided that no new schemes would be initiated, the existing ones would be consolidated and made viable or closed down. In the meantime, spontaneous, voluntary village schemes had been starved of funds, but had still shown local enthusiasm far greater than those that had been financed. In the future such schemes and the modernization of existing villages were to receive more encouragement.

Perhaps the most promising success story of the plan was in the field of education. The emphasis on postprimary education allowed the schools to achieve and sometimes surpass their goals. This was perhaps because a manpower survey had measured both the requirements and resources by the end of 1964, and thus indicated the scale of investment needed. (It incidentally showed that in 1957 only 23 per cent of the men and 7.5 per cent of the women of Tanganyika had ever attended school.) The plan required that 25,000 pupils should have passed out of Form IV during the five years; in fact, more than half this number passed by 1967. The same success had been achieved with the 3,720 students to have completed Form VI by 1970, and the number of students predicted to enter the university, 898 by 1966, had also been exceeded. The content of the education they received is another matter, but there was an encouraging increase in enrollment in such practical subjects as engineering, medicine, agronomy, veterinary science, and teaching.

When the successes achieved in postsecondary institutions, such as the civil service center, and the large enrollment in adult-education classes are added to this story, the educational effort can be judged to have been commensurate with the plan's expectations. As the government began to confine entry permits for foreign workers to those hired by employers with an adequate training scheme for local workers, educated young Tanzanians could feel that genuine efforts were being made to find them employment. And the government also took precautions to ensure that those children whose education they were financing did not find lucrative posts in other countries, as has been common in many African states. Those who received government grants were required to accept government employment for a fixed number of years after completing their education.

Nevertheless, these few years of educational success could not solve the major problem of acquiring sufficient skilled technicians to service the needs of the plan itself, of training local personnel, and of maintaining momentum once development was under way. The five-year plan called for 444 new expatriates in high-grade jobs in the government sector—and this excluded teachers, police, and nurses. In the secondary schools and teacher-training colleges in 1968, only 20 per cent of the teachers were Tanzanian citizens, and a mere 20 of these possessed degrees. It was estimated that another 1,200 graduate teachers were required to fulfill the plan's requirements. Yet recruitment of expatriates had become increasingly difficult. Experts of all kinds were in short supply throughout the world.

One feature of Tanzanian life that the planners could not predict was the effect of the government's foreign policy on foreign aid and investment. No one could have foreseen the international frictions that were to provoke from the Tanzanian Government reactions inimical to meeting its expectations of foreign financial and technical assistance. The breach with the West German Government in 1965 over allowing the East Germans to open a consulate in Dar es Salaam, the suspension of diplomatic relations with Britain later in the same year over British policy toward Rhodesia, the suspicions aroused in the United States by Tanzanian friend-

ship with China—all led to a reduction in foreign economic assistance. The Rhodesian crisis also necessitated crucial changes in
development strategy to help the besieged Zambians. An oil pipe-
line had to be built between the two countries to allow Zambia an
alternative oil supply to the severed Rhodesia line. Immediate
priority had to be given to the trunk road linking the two countries so that Zambian imports and exports could be diverted from
the south. And strenuous efforts had to be made to survey the
route for a railway between the two countries so that Zambia could
rely on a permanent, all-weather connection to and from the coast
without having to depend on Rhodesia, South Africa, or Portugal.
When Western countries refused to assist in this scheme, the
Chinese stepped in with a generous offer of help. Each of these
projects was to the long-term advantage of the Tanzanian economy,
which will certainly benefit from securing a large proportion of
Zambia's rich copper trade, but the sudden necessity for regarding
them as of top priority inevitably distorted the Tanzanian development strategy and caused the postponement of other projects which
had already been prepared.

In the meantime, political policies toward the southern African
white-supremacist regimes also had an impact on the economy.
Not only had the government severed all relations with Rhodesia,
Portugal, and South Africa because of their denial of human rights
to their majority African inhabitants, and thus sacrificed any potential economic assistance from their governments, but it was also
in the forefront of African efforts to undermine their minority white
regimes. The Coordinating Committee for the Liberation of Africa,
a section of the Organization of African Unity involved in mobilizing and guiding the nationalist struggle in southern Africa, had
its headquarters in Dar es Salaam. This certainly laid Tanzania
open to attack by any or all of the white regimes. It also necessitated part of southern Tanzania being turned over to the task
of military provision for the guerrilla freedom fighters engaged
in neighboring Mozambique. The wars in southern Africa also
uprooted many people from their homes, and Tanzania opened its
doors to them. Despite its own poverty, it accepted thousands of

people fleeing from white oppression in southern Africa or from the chaos of the Congo and Rwanda. In 1967 alone, 36,000 refugees from the south entered the country.

All these were serious and weighty factors that profoundly affected the economic development of Tanzania. Yet the dislocation they caused should not be allowed to hide the significant consequences of the five-year plan. Bald figures amply illustrate the impact of these factors on the Tanzanian people. During the first half of the plan period, the domestic product grew at a rate of about 5 per cent, instead of the 6.7 per cent planned. Drought and catastrophic drops in world prices for certain primary products, especially sisal, certainly restricted growth, but this only emphasizes the unpredictability of the variables on which the plan rested. More important, however, were the direct results that could have been predicted from the nature of the plan itself. Industrial production expanded to reasonably near its target, reaching 11 per cent a year, compared with the 14.8 per cent expected. This led to increases in average wages within the private sector of 16.7 per cent in 1965 and 15 per cent in 1966 and in the public sector of 8.6 per cent in 1965 and 13.5 per cent in 1966. Meanwhile, the cost of living increased by 10 per cent in 1965 and 5 per cent in the next year. Because employment in agriculture fell during this period while it rose in industry and public services (total employment fell by about 5.4 per cent in 1965 and about 4 per cent in the next year), the result was unavoidable. The yawning chasm between the standards of living among urban, industrial, and service workers, on the one hand, and the mass of small farmers in the rural areas, on the other, rapidly widened and deepened. Social equality was fast receding under an independent government whose declared *raison d'être* was to provide the social justice denied by colonial rule.

These circumstances dominated the Tanzanian social and political stage during 1965 and 1966. They may be seen as the prologue to 1967, when the curtain rose on the first act of the true national drama. To understand and interpret this first act, which may be entitled "The Arusha Declaration," one needs to place it in the context of this prologue.

11 Arusha: Beacon for the Future

The year 1967 saw the economic, social, and political paths of Tanzania beginning to merge into a single road leading toward a new form of society. It is still too early to judge whether the efforts to build this road as a tarred, macadamized highway taking Tanzanians into their utopia will succeed or whether, as with so many roads in Africa, it will peter out into the bush or end in a series of dirt paths leading in different directions, culminating in a *cul de sac*. But whatever the nation's destiny, the fresh initiative taken by Tanzanian leaders in that year has made an indelible mark on African history; for it represents a unique and revolutionary attempt to direct a people's progress along ways never previously trodden.

The simplest interpretation of the dramatic policy announced by President Nyerere in February, 1967, is that he was setting his people the task of leaping from a precapitalist structure straight into a socialist society without going through the conventional stage of capitalism. He was thus defying all historical precedent, as well as the entire body of received historical theory.

Nyerere has always had a particularly sensitive ear for the voice of his people, no matter how faint the murmurings. He was, therefore, well aware of the fears that there was growing in his country a privileged class composed of such people as ministers, party officials, members of the Assembly, civil servants, as well as people in the professions, merchants, and property-owners. Even though members of the Assembly received a salary of only $1,680 a year, plus a constituency allowance where appropriate of up to $720, this represented great wealth compared with the poverty of the vast majority of his people. It also gave them opportunities to earn other forms of income. The President's salary was fixed at the ridiculously low figure of $7,200 a year, but Nyerere symbolically reduced even this in times of national need. Nevertheless, life in this sector of the nation was quite different from that of the masses in the countryside and from that of the unemployed, under-employed, or unskilled in the towns. When, at the end of 1966, the President heard the storm of parliamentary censure that greeted an announcement that twenty Mercedes-Benz cars were to be bought for the use of government officials, he immediately recognized its significance; it was being said that a new tribe called the *Wa-Benzi* had arisen in Tanzania—those who drove around in large, luxurious cars, remote from, and superior to, the common people. An edict soon went out limiting the size and usage of cars for everyone on government business.

Nyerere had also observed events in Ghana, Algeria, Nigeria, Sierra Leone, and various other African states where regimes had been overthrown. Although the circumstances had been peculiar to each case, one thread had run through all of them. This common feature had been the rise of an elite, both in the party and in business, the two often combined. Nyerere had been particularly affected by the fall of Ben Bella in Algeria, and the deposition of Nkrumah was especially relevant, for he had been trying to frame general policy in Ghana along somewhat similar lines to those attempted in Tanzania. Nyerere, therefore, recognized that the appearance of an elite, even if it was a vanguard leading national reconstruction, would not be permanently tolerated by the African masses.

The presidential commission on the constitution had rejected the concept of an elitist party, preferring to keep TANU open to all citizens. Yet there were distinct signs of class formation in Tanzania during the years following independence. As was said earlier, wage rates had risen and employment fallen during the first half of the five-year plan. Industrial workers, along with public servants, businessmen, traders, and those in the rural areas enjoying the benefits of land concentration, new techniques, and cooperative organization, were gaining economic advantages far greater than the average. When Nyerere toured the country at the beginning of 1967, he heard the same sounds of resentment as had been voiced in the Assembly. It had also become clear to him that the five-year plan was not bridging the gap between urban and rural conditions nor producing the rural renaissance an agricultural country like Tanzania needed; rather, it was tending to concentrate economic power in a few hands. In other words, it was one of the factors encouraging class division in the country.

Nyerere's suspicions of the direction in which Tanzanian society was moving were catalyzed when he read the English translation of a book written by René Dumont, the famous French agronomist, entitled *False Start in Africa*. Dumont, who had spent most of his life helping developing peoples throughout the world, addressed severe, but sympathetic, admonitions to his friends in Africa, pointing out to them the dangers of elitism, prestige projects, neglect of rural peoples, thoughtless mechanization and industrialization, imitative education and social values, corruption, and indiscipline. By 1966, the book had been made required reading for all ministers and leading public figures in Tanzania.

This was the context in which Nyerere expressed himself early in 1967, first to the regional commissioners in Arusha, then to the party's executive, and finally to a mass meeting in Dar es Salaam. His addresses were divided into two parts. The first enunciated philosophical principles, some of them new or more specific than before; the second announced a distinct new direction for party and government policies, together with certain required actions. Although, since these speeches were made, it has been commonly claimed that "The Arusha Declaration and TANU's Policy on Socialism and Self-Reliance" expressed the unanimous view of the party and was universally acclaimed, this was not actually the case. On first hearing Nyerere's proposals, many commissioners and party

officials were aghast. For some hours, there was considerable consternation in Arusha as some of those who had been enjoying membership in the privileged class faced the prospect of losing their
advantages. Surface unanimity had been established by the time
the Arusha meetings concluded, but undoubtedly many left the
town with grave misgivings about their future. These doubts spread
to other privileged groups when word of the new policies was made
public. Evidence of opposition to the new principles was shown
when Oscar Kambona went into self-imposed exile rather than
conform to them, and later when the women's leader, Bibi Titi
Mohammed and the trade-union leader Michael Kamaliza openly
defied the Arusha Declaration.

In his declaration at Arusha, Nyerere firmly committed his party
and government to building a socialist society in Tanzania. This
would be founded on a classless national community in which
Tanzanian citizens would be discouraged from becoming capitalists
or *rentiers,* and those engaged in these pursuits would be entirely
excluded from political power. The foundations of Tanzanian
society would be largely formed of cooperative farming communities, organized in the *Ujamaa* structure he had outlined in
1962. The industrial and commercial sectors of the economy, together with the infrastructure of construction, social services, and
administration, would be developed so as to assist in the development of these villages. They would, therefore, have to be subject to
popular control and staffed by officials who shared the concept of
rural socialism.

In his speeches, and later in supplementary statements expanding
the Arusha policy, Nyerere laid down the strategy to be followed
in pursuing these objectives. First, to use Aneurin Bevan's phrase,
the "commanding heights of the economy" were to be owned and
controlled by the nation through its government. This was put
into effect immediately. All commercial banks and insurance companies, together with most large firms engaged in importing and
exporting, were nationalized. The government then acquired a
majority interest in a number of local companies: Tanzania Brew-
eries, Tanganyika Extract, Metal Box, British and American To-

bacco, Bata Shoe, Portland Cement. The government already had its own agency, the National Development Corporation, to handle nationalization and control. But the Arusha policy only provided for national control of this sector of the economy for the purpose of directing it toward supporting the declared lines of socialist development. The detailed strategy of how its financial and commercial policies were to be ordered so as to provide such support had still to be worked out.

Second, it was laid down that those leading the party, government, and civil service were to be forbidden to engage in private business, own property, employ workers, or possess more than one income source and many salaries were to be reduced. The leaders were to be given one year in which to decide whether to continue in public life or remain in business. TANU was explicitly declared to be a party of "workers and peasants"—no longer an organization open to all—and every leader was to be required to accept membership in this class and to set an example of austere living.

In order to ensure that those who were leading or would in the future lead the country were aware of, and committed to, these socialist principles, new efforts would be made to use the education system in a positive way. Political education would be given to the party leaders, and higher education would embrace the social values of the nation and the spirit of service to the community, while primary education would be turned toward the needs of the rural communities in which most pupils would spend their lives.

Finally, the spirit of *Ujamaa* was revived and given more practical direction. The village was to become the core of rural life, but the grandiose schemes of 1963–64 were rejected in favor of more voluntary association and persuasion. It was hoped in this way to transform the wasteful, customary scattered individual homesteads, or shambas, into collective, cooperative villages where agricultural production could be combined with communal social provisions.

Above all, the whole philosophy of this program was based on the principle of self-reliance. Nyerere had become convinced that one of the greatest weaknesses of development in Tanzania had been the acceptance of the colonial approach to economic growth, with its assumption of dependence on money. This had been seen particularly in the failure of the early villagization schemes and in the attitude toward foreign aid and investment. The President now urged his people to work together in their localities to produce a rural renaissance around the core of cooperative villages, supported by light industries geared to their needs. Nationally, he rejected the earlier dependence on foreign resources for planned growth. He did not reject either foreign aid or foreign investment, but, in the future, Tanzanian planning would not depend on receiving either. They would be welcome where offered, but always provided that the donors and investors accepted the national strategy he was enunciating, which meant that they must recognize that the public sector of the economy was closed to private activity and that private enterprise must operate within the guidelines drawn for national development.

The President always insisted that these were "guidelines." He deliberately disclaimed any intention of laying down a complete, detailed program, which he knew would have to be devised through trial and error. But, for the first time, the President, the government, and the party had declared a definite political philosophy, painted an idealistic picture of the ultimate society they envisioned, and drawn up a set of priorities to be observed as the milestones along the road to its achievement. In making this bold bid to convert the nation to utopianism, Nyerere was not only risking the opposition of those who would lose the privileges they assumed to be a legitimate reward for public service; he was also gambling on the acceptance by townsfolk of the rural priorities he was laying down for both the near and the distant future. And this hazardous transformation was to be accomplished by persuasion, by relying on the people themselves to perceive and pursue their interests within the guidelines laid down for them. Force was ruled out; education and leadership were to be the only spurs to action. As Nyerere was later to insist, after explanation and leadership the people "must decide for themselves what their future is to be by following the principles of democracy." National decisions would be made by the party's executive or annual conference or through parliament, with the debate conducted throughout the party. Local decisions would be made by the district committees.

With leadership and persuasion so crucial to the whole program, the part to be played by the party was clearly vital. Yet the party was still a mass organization mainly composed of those who were loyal to it because of its achievement in gaining independence. Moreover, its officials, the administrators, and the educationists had been reared without any ideological guidance or commitment, most of them conditioned to the legacy left them by their former colonial rulers. Could they be transformed into a set of pioneers who would adopt the philosophical outlook enunciated by their President and practice the self-discipline demanded by a nonviolent, nonauthoritarian revolution?

Two major tactics were employed to promote this critical transformation. The first was already in existence but was to be strengthened in order to become the key to party transformation. Although Nyerere had turned away from his original concept of the party as a closely organized body and still disliked the idea of "cadres"—which René Dumont had insisted were essential for national leadership—the Arusha Declaration for the first time suggested some qualifications for party membership. It was now to be based on commitment to the party's ideals and restricted to peasants and workers. Moreover, whether one uses the word "cadre" or not, the organization of party cells, which was begun at the end of 1964, provided for the local leadership the structure essential to persuasion and made possible grassroots influence on the party. Every town and village was divided into cells of ten houses each, with all the party members living in them forming a unit. A group of cells made up the local branch, and the branches were linked to the district, regional, and national structures. The cell leaders constituted the membership of village development committees, crucial to the plans for rural reconstruction. If the cell leaders could be educated in the political philosophy declared at Arusha, the spearhead of leadership throughout the nation would have been forged.

The second vital element was the civil service. The British tradition of insisting that civil servants remain apolitical, although clearly inappropriate in a one-party developing nation, had never been completely broken. If for no other reason than the acute shortage of manpower, Tanzania could not afford to provide parallel bureaucracies for government and party. Yet, despite the policy of having personnel interchangeable between civil service and party, which was adopted soon after independence, a separation of responsibilities remained. The civil servants tended to play for safety in order to escape criticism, whereas in a revolutionary situation such as that in Tanzania the best brains and trained experts of the country needed to demonstrate boldness and imagination. It was obvious after the Arusha policy had been announced that many civil servants still regarded certain subjects as "political" and therefore not their concern. Even the creation of *Ujamaa* villages was often held to be in this category and to be irrelevant to economic development in the rural areas—which is exactly what it was intended to promote.

It was obvious, therefore, that, if a powerful drive was to be mounted to use human and material resources in the application of the Arusha policy, closer integration would be needed between the party and the civil service. As a corollary, the party itself would need to recruit a larger staff of experts in order to hold its own when economic and social planning issues were under discussion. For the party was the engine of Tanzanian policy-making, leading and driving the government. It must therefore be capable not only of calling on civil-service experts to argue on behalf of projects in pursuit of Arusha objectives, but also of having on its own staff people capable of discussing these issues on equal terms with the civil-service expert. A start was made in this direction when, in 1968, an *Ujamaa* section was added to the party-headquarters staff, its task being to train leaders who would promote the cooperative village concept in the rural areas. This was essential, but still left the party staff very weak in economic planning expertise when faced with any negative attitudes on the part of civil servants. Much would depend on the success of political education—which was to include the civil service. Certainly, with its extremely small resources of trained personnel, it was essential for Tanzania to mobilize all its "intellectual" talents behind the implementation of policy directives and to avoid alienating this group from the ideals of party and President.

The most serious weakness of the new nation was the fantastic reliance placed on the slim shoulders of Nyerere. He personally initiated most ideology while simultaneously being responsible for carrying on all the affairs of state. No human being is capable of bearing both these burdens very long. The success of the Arusha principles therefore depended on the emergence of men and women capable of accepting responsibility for coherent implementation of policy.

At first, there were inevitable misunderstandings and large gaps in the application of the Arusha principles. The President's anger over cattle-thievery, which he considered to be cheating his hard-working people, resulted in suspects being rounded up under the Preventive Detention Act, though he had to back down quickly and release the suspected persons. In 1968, local officials in Mwanza became so overzealous in arresting tax defaulters that thirteen prisoners died in an overcrowded cell. The officials were tried and sentenced to prison on charges of manslaughter, but the incident revealed the danger of stimulating local officials to increased zeal where administrative supervision could not be maintained because of a shortage of personnel. Yet these cases were exceptional. It became more common for Nyerere to be accused by some of his colleagues of too great a concern for personal liberty in a society experiencing a revolution. It was the knowledge that some officials were bound to abuse their power that led him in 1966 to establish an ombudsman to hear grievances from individual citizens about official actions. It took the form of a Permanent Commission of Enquiry, composed of a chairman and two other members. Because the judiciary, including local and resident magistrates and a High Court with a Chief Justice and eight judges, was independent, concern for protection of individual liberty against arbitrary victimization had been well established. The courts also took traditional tribal law into account by providing for two members of an accused's tribe to sit as assessors with a judge.

A more serious weakness of the post-Arusha period was the absence of direction of economic policies. The essential purpose of nationalizing sections of the economy was to guide their activities into promoting those objectives laid down in the Declaration. Yet there was little evidence that the nationalized concerns were working out a strategy that, through investment, price, profit, and employment policies, would enable them to play an effective part in stimulating the other projects necessary to the new policy. Nor was the endemic problem of regional inequalities attacked. If the Arusha principles were to survive in the public mind as more than pious ideals, the people themselves would have to see specific changes in their way of life and in the opportunities offered to their children. The danger of cynicism arising from frustrated hopes was increased by a recurrent vagueness in the responsibility for promoting *Ujamaa* villages. The President actually told the TANU conference in 1967 that the initiative for creating these villages "can be taken by anyone." He added, "it does not have to be a TANU leader or government official." Such indecisiveness can often lead to "anyone" becoming "no one." Again, the lack of sufficient trained personnel and organized agencies for action could result in fine ideas remaining paper plans never translated into action.

In 1969, in the presence of Presidents Obote of Uganda, Kaunda of Zambia, and Mobutu of the Congo, Nyerere introduced the second five-year plan to the party conference. The new plan showed some attempt to learn from the first plan and to fill gaps that had become apparent in the machinery for implementing the Arusha Declaration. It recognized that the highly mechanized and overcapitalized settlement schemes had been failures, and it replaced that approach with the *Ujamaa* village policy. The President also drew attention to inaccurate predictions in the first plan. The hope of expanding the sisal industry, for example, had been dashed. Whereas in 1964 sisal was selling at about $204 a ton, by 1968 the price was only $91.80; employment in the industry had dropped from 96,400 to 41,668, and foreign exchange earned fell from $52.8 million to under $22.44 million. Nothing could so dramatically demonstrate the hazards of planning in a developing country. Another inaccurate estimate had been that of population increase. It had been thought that the increase would be about 2.2 per cent, but it had turned out to be 2.7 per cent, or some 350,000 people a year. This was one cause—the accent on postprimary education was another—for the proportion of primary-school entrants at the start of the five years (about half those of school age) remaining the same at the end of the period, though the total number had increased.

The second plan differed in important respects from the first. Because of the government's greater control over the economy, it was possible to budget for the public sector to take a much greater share of development expenditure. Thus, in a total investment plan involving $960.2 million, $366.4 million was to come from government expenditure, $276 million from the parastate bodies and cooperatives, and $69.6 million from the East African Community. Also the reliance on foreign financing had been drastically reduced compared with 1964. It was planned to find 60 per cent of government expenditure and between 60 and 65 per cent of parastate funds inside the country. Moreover, though an over-all target of a 6.5 per cent growth rate, allowing for price changes, was set for the five-year period, this plan allowed for greater flexibility than the first. Provision was made for regular review, and emphasis was laid on organizing projects over the first two years.

Yet the central change in the character of the second plan was the recognition of the need for priorities. First, as was categorically stated, "rural development receives top priority, as most of our latent wealth lies in our under-utilized land and the energies of the rural people." Second, priorities were laid down within the planning sector itself. The plan concentrated on increasing the production of certain crops—meat, dairy products, fish, rice, wheat, tea, flue-cured tobacco, cotton, pulses, oil seeds, vegetables, and fruits—and expressly indicated that other crops would not be increased. This list also provided for more important foods and a better balanced diet provision than previously. Third, the plan deliberately set out to reverse the growth of a class system in the rural areas and to base its development on the *Ujamaa* principle. Although the need for *Ujamaa* villages to be run by the people themselves was reiterated, it was now recognized that the assignment of more specific responsibility for initiation was needed. So the plan pledged government help for groups committed to *Ujamaa* growth and also made provision for TANU, the youth league, and government departments to undertake the training of volunteer cadres and the education and demonstration needed.

In the industrial sector, the new strength of government control was significant for future development. The bulk of investment was concentrated in the parastate bodies, though some small projects could be undertaken by workers' and cooperative organizations and by private enterprise. The total capital expected to be available for industrial expansion was only $156 million, clearly considered subordinate to rural investment. It was nevertheless hoped that more local goods would be available for sale, that exports to the East African Common Market, expected to reach $7.2 million by the turn of the century, would increase, and that a foundation could be laid for the development of a capital-goods industry under the next plan. It was hoped that this growth would increase industrial employment from 40,000 in 1969 to 60,000 in 1974. One other feature of industrial planning was the acceptance of some degree of regional balance. Thus, a concentrated effort, led by government allocations, was made to decentralize urban growth away from Dar es Salaam. An attempt was to be made to develop Tanga, Arusha, Moshi, Mwanza, Tabora, Dodoma, Morogoro, Mbeya, and Mtwara, by locating new industries and housing projects in these centers. This might go some way to redress regional imbalance. Yet, though the problem was recognized in the plan's strategy, there was still little sign of its being seriously tackled in the schemes for rural development.

The second five-year plan, following on the Arusha statements, created a new spirit of forward thinking in all sections of the party and among many Tanzanian citizens, especially the younger generation. It inevitably led to a ferment of discussion, argument, and criticism. Tanzanians began to think of themselves as in the vanguard of the African revolution, leading the march away from the colonial heritage, forging new methods for gaining economic independence. Nyerere's political style of speaking moderately but acting radically and his emphasis on honesty, austerity, personal liberty, and self-reliance, appeal to his people. Above all, his insistence on the interests of the common man, his faith in policy stemming from the masses, his ideals rooted in the village—all offer the opportunity for Tanzania to achieve a peaceful revolution to a society based on self-help, where, without exploitation, everyone works but the old, infirm, and children, where equality and cooperation are first principles, and where respect without awe characterizes human relations. Nyerere is trying to preserve the best of African traditional values while guiding his people to standards of life that will exorcise the traditional scourges of poverty, disease, hunger, and early death. His success will depend on the degree to which he gains the willing support of his people—including those with knowledge and training, who stand to sacrifice most in the short term—and the extent to which he is able to insulate his revolutionary experiment against interference by hostile influences from outside his country.

Bibliography

BENNETT, N. R. *Studies in East African History.* Boston, 1963.

BIENEN, H. *Tanzania.* 2d ed. Princeton, 1970.

CHIDZERO, B. T. G. *Tanganyika and International Trusteeship.* London, 1961.

CLIFFE, L., ed. *One Party Democracy.* Nairobi, 1967.

COLE, SONIA. *The Prehistory of East Africa.* London and Baltimore, 1954.

COUPLAND, R. *The Exploitation of East Africa, 1856–1890.* Oxford, 1939.

DAVIDSON, B. *East and Central Africa to the Late 19th Century.* London, 1967.

DE BLIJ, H. J. *A Geography of Subsaharan Africa.* Chicago, 1964.

DUMONT, RENÉ. *False Start in Africa.* rev. ed., London and New York, 1969.

DUNDAS, SIR C. *African Crossroads.* London and New York, 1955.

FORDHAM, P. *The Geography of African Affairs.* London and Baltimore, 1965.

FREEMAN-GRENVILLE, G. S. P. *The East African Coast: Select Documents.* Oxford, 1962.

———. *Medieval History of the Tanganyika Coast.* London, 1962.

GREENBERG, J. H. *Studies in African Linguistic Classification.* New Haven, 1955.

HARLOW, V., and E. M. CHILVER, eds. *History of East Africa,* vol. 2. Oxford, 1965.

HATCH, JOHN. *The History of Britain in Africa.* London and New York, 1969.

HUGHES, A. J. *East Africa: The Search for Unity.* London and Baltimore, 1963.

KAYAMBA, M. *The Story of Martin Kayamba Mdumi, Ten Africans.* London, 1936.

KIMAMBO, I. N., and A. J. TEMU, eds. *A History of Tanzania.* Nairobi, 1969.

LISTOWEL, JUDITH. *The Making of Tanganyika.* London, 1965.

LOFCHIE, M. F. *Zanzibar: Background to Revolution.* Princeton, 1965.

LONSDALE, J. M. *The Emergence of African Nations.* Nairobi, 1968.

MAGUIRE, G. A. *Toward Uhuru in Tanzania.* London, 1970.

MAZRUI, A. A. *On Heroes and Uhuru-Worship.* London, 1967.

MURDOCK, G. P. *Africa: Its Peoples and Their Cultural History.* New York, 1959.

NYERERE, J. K. *Education for Self-Reliance.* Dar es Salaam, 1967.

———. *Freedom and Socialism.* London, 1969.

———. *Freedom and Unity.* London, 1966.

———. *Nyerere and Socialism.* London, 1970.

———. *Socialism and Rural Development.* Dar es Salaam, 1967.

OGOT, B. A., and J. A. KIERAN. *Zamani.* Nairobi and London, 1968.

OLIVER, R., and G. MATHEW, eds. *History of East Africa,* vol. 1. Oxford, 1963.

POSNANSKY, M., ed. *Prelude to East African History.* London, 1966.

RANGER, T. O. *African Reaction and Resistance to the Imposition of Colonial Rule in East and Central Africa.* Stanford, 1968.

RICHARDS, A. I., ed. *East African Chiefs.* London, 1960.

———. *The Multicultural States of East Africa.* London, 1970.

STAHL, K. M. *History of the Chagga People of Kilimanjaro.* London, 1964.

———. *Tanganyika: Sail in the Wilderness.* The Hague, 1961.

STEPHENS, H. W. *The Political Transformation of Tanganyika, 1920–67.* New York, 1968.

SVENDSEN, K. E. and M. TEISEN, eds. *Self-Reliant Tanzania.* Dar es Salaam, 1969.

TANZANIAN GOVERNMENT. *The Arusha Declaration.* Dar es Salaam, 1967.

———. *Tanzania Today.* Dar es Salaam and Nairobi, University Press of Africa, 1968.

TAYLOR, J. C. *The Political Development of Tanganyika.* Stanford and London, 1963.

TORDOFF, W. *Government and Politics in Tanzania.* Nairobi, 1967.

Index